Bloomsbury CPD Library: Mentoring and Coaching

By Marcella McCarthy

B L O O M S B U R Y

LONDON • OXFORD • NEW YORK • NEW DELHI • SYDNEY

Bloomsbury Education
An imprint of Bloomsbury Publishing Plc

50 Bedford Square	1385 Broadway
London	New York
WC1B 3DP	NY 10018
UK	USA

www.bloomsbury.com

Bloomsbury is a registered trademark of Bloomsbury Publishing Plc

First published 2017

British Library Cataloguing-in-Publication Data
A catalogue record for this book is available from the British Library.

ISBN:
PB: 978-1-4729-3710-0
ePub: 978-1-4729-3712-4
ePDF: 978-1-4729-3711-7

Library of Congress Cataloging-in-Publication Data
A catalog record for this book is available from the Library of Congress.

10 9 8 7 6 5 4 3 2 1

Typeset by Integra Software Services Pvt. Ltd.
Printed CPI Group (UK) Ltd, Croydon, CR0 4YY

This book is produced using paper that is made from wood grown in
managed, sustainable forests. It is natural, renewable and recyclable.
The logging and manufacturing processes conform to the
environmental regulations of the country of origin.

To view more of our titles please visit www.bloomsbury.com

Contents

With thanks to Carmel McNamara and Mal Dolan, my wise mentors and friends, and to Stefan Hawlin, who still coaches me daily in everything that matters.

How to use this book

The Bloomsbury CPD Library provides primary and secondary teachers with affordable, comprehensive and accessible 'do-it-yourself' continuing professional development. This book focuses on mentoring and coaching.

The book is split into two halves: Part 1 **Teach yourself** and Part 2 **Train others**.

Teach yourself

This part of the book includes everything you need to develop your own practice in coaching and mentoring. It is split into four stages:

STAGE 1: ASSESS

This section explains the difference between coaching and mentoring, and allows you to assess which practice is most suitable for different situations. It includes a self-assessment questionnaire so that you can readily discover where your strengths and areas for improvement lie.

STAGE 2: IMPROVE

This section goes through some of the main styles of coaching and mentoring, and gives you some context for the ideas explored later. It explains how research ideas feed through into practice, and gives examples of how you can script conversations and respond to challenging situations, with practical tips.

STAGE 3: EVALUATE

This section offers the opportunity to evaluate and reflect on where you have already improved or changed your practice, and consider which areas still need some work.

STAGE 4: EXCEL

This section considers how you can consolidate your practice and start to expand it throughout the rest of your school, thinking strategically about ways in which coaching and mentoring can help towards whole-school improvement.
This first section of the book includes many ideas to help you along the way. Coaching and mentoring can be a lonely process if you are not careful, and so this guide gives you recommendations about how you can share your work with others both inside and outside school, as well as suggestions for further reading online and off.

Train others

This section of the book looks at how you can develop coaching and mentoring more widely across your school, for staff and students. As external training becomes more costly and difficult to arrange and personalise, controlling the CPD process through well-planned internal training sessions which link back to specific whole-school projects is becoming a more popular way of using teachers' valuable time. Whether you would like to start things off with one whole-school session, or would like to run a series of coaching sessions for a specific group of staff, this section gives you the plans and resources to set up in-house training with the minimum of fuss.

The section includes:

- Advice on how to run effective CPD
- Training plans for whole-school and small group sessions aimed at different audiences
- A complete set of PowerPoints to match the training plans, ready-to-go for use in your own school.

Online resources

For templates, questionnaires and PowerPoints from the book please visit www.bloomsbury.com/CPD-library-mentoring-and-coaching.

Part 1

Teach yourself

1

What's it all about?

Becoming a coach or a mentor is an interesting process, and one that reminds me of a lecture that I attended while training to be a teacher. The lecturer was explaining that there was no such thing as a 'natural' teacher; that it was a misconception to believe that it was, and that everyone, no matter what their natural inclinations, could become an excellent teacher.

Though the lecturer was well intentioned, and trying to make a wider point about growth mindsets, I suspect, nonetheless his audience eyed each other with a clear sense of rebellion. We all knew people who seemed to find the role of teacher a natural one, who didn't struggle with behaviour management or lesson planning, and were confident standing up in front of a class. Among my peers there was a consensus that yes, there were some people who just seemed cut out for teaching from the outset.

Over my years in secondary teaching I have come to agree with this idea – but in a slightly different way. Rather, I would say that there are some people who have a personality type that suits teaching. Such people tend to find the kind of stress that defeats others energising. Give them an unruly class and they see an exciting challenge; give them a change of curriculum and they see a chance to refresh their own expertise. That's not to say that they don't have their own weak spots – far from it – but simply that their existing mindset fits comfortably with the demands of the job.

Such a mindset certainly makes it easier to start life as a practitioner, but it is not something that by itself will make you an outstanding teacher, and those who relied only upon this 'natural' talent, I found, often became unsympathetic colleagues in the longer term. In contrast, as time went on, those who found something like behaviour management hard often found it became their strength simply because they spent more time trying to master the skill.

In coaching and mentoring, my experience is that the same holds true. It is likely that some people will find the role of coach or mentor more appealing than others, and they may resist the idea that anybody can learn these skills and teach them to others. However, you should beware of the idea that some people are 'natural' coaches and mentors; it is dangerously limiting.

The purpose of this book, then, is twofold. In the first place, it is designed to help consolidate your existing coaching and/or mentoring skills, and help you to develop and apply them more systematically and helpfully. Simply by picking up this book, it is likely that you identify strongly with the idea of coaching and mentoring as a powerful tool for change, and also likely that you already have some experience with the strategies involved. In the second place, the book is designed to help you pass those skills on to other teachers who may initially find the ideas challenging. In the process you may find, as with PGCE students, that there seem to be some people who are 'naturals' in coaching and mentoring roles. However, you will also find that just as people who don't start off as 'natural' teachers can develop into strong and expert practitioners, so those who are not naturally drawn to coaching and mentoring can find the skillset hugely enabling. Developing coaching and mentoring skills can help with all aspects of teaching and professional development, and – more than anything else – can facilitate the everyday work of being a teacher.

The origins of mentoring and coaching and the difference between them

Some people use the terms 'mentor' and 'coach' almost synonymously. But having a coach when what you need is a mentor and vice versa can cause some real problems. There is a great deal of crossover between the two disciplines, but it is worth clarifying the distinction as a first step. Looking at where each word comes from is a good way of remembering the distinction.

Mentor comes from the Greek; the original Mentor was a friend of Odysseus who advised his son, Telemachus, while his father was off getting lost following the Trojan War. Embedded in the origin of the word is the way in which a mentor is generally considered to be someone older than you, someone with more life experience, who is able to help you get through times of difficulty or personal growth. Like the original Mentor, a mentor may be seen as a replacement for a parent; a figure of authority who is always on your side.

By contrast, the idea of 'coaching' originally suggested a very different kind of relationship. In Oxford University slang of the 1830s, a student who was 'coached' or used a 'coach' to help him with his studies was essentially allowing someone else to do the work for him, like someone carried by coach rather than walking. It quickly came to be used of sport, and for a long time this was the primary meaning.

In the 1960s, the term started to be brought again into non-sporting contexts. *The Inner Game of Tennis* (1975) by W. T. Gallwey is often cited as an influential book from this time of crossover. The sporting metaphor (the author was a tennis coach at Harvard) readily transferred into the business sphere, and Gallwey became a popular inspirational speaker for business conferences. From there the idea of coaching as a way of achieving wider goals flourished, bouncing back and forth from sport to business, until now, when a brief search on Amazon will find you over 45,000 books on coaching ranging from *Coaching and Mentoring for Dummies* to *Coaching Behind Bars*.

Mentoring and coaching in schools

The idea of mentoring and coaching can sometimes be perceived as a little intimidating by teachers, as they may think of these activities as tied primarily to a business context. The coaching process can appear full of jargon and enthusiastic psychobabble about motivation, with a schedule that seems ever so slightly like signing up for a complete lifestyle change. Similarly, mentoring can be perceived as something that is focused entirely on achieving externally-validated professional success. Both perceptions can sometimes discourage teachers from trying out coaching and mentoring. They feel that they are simply looking for professional development and encouragement, and have neither the time nor the energy to totally revise their whole patterns of working.

However, effective mentoring and coaching in school should be quite different to this kind of expectation, and will fit naturally in to existing working practice. Perhaps the easiest way to convince staff of this is to compare it to the ways in which they already work with students. Staff may well already be familiar, for instance, with the idea of 'peer mentoring', where students help each other to work through both academic and social difficulties, and of course in many subjects, especially physical education and performance art, working closely with a coach is a traditional way of moving practice forward. Not surprisingly, similar strategies readily work with teachers to help them move forward their professional practice, and to support them in the process. Indeed, setting in place a variety of systems that involve coaching and mentoring in a school context is one of the fastest and most effective means towards school improvement.

Where mentoring and coaching is applied to professional development, it's then a natural move forward in many ways – taking on board what we know works well with students, and using it for ourselves. Indeed, so natural may it be, that often teachers don't realise that what they are experiencing, or doing themselves, is actually mentoring and coaching. That encouraging Head of Department who talked you through how to run a meeting effectively in their absence; the line manager who discussed with you where you would like your career to be in three years' time; the colleague who came up when a student was being rude to you and somehow managed to defuse the situation; the teacher a year ahead of you who sat down one evening and did marking with you; all these people may have been subtly working with you as coaches and mentors. Perhaps without even realising it themselves, they were using strategies of coaching and mentoring to help you and support your professional development.

Helpful as these experiences are, systematising coaching and mentoring in school is a more serious and deliberate school improvement strategy. It is worth taking the time to work out if coaching or mentoring is more important for the situation you wish to help with, and also working out who is available to help with the work, and where their talents lie. As the origins of the terms suggest, they are different in scope, despite some overlap.

In the same way as therapists are encouraged themselves to undergo the therapeutic process, it can be especially helpful if you have had the experience of being coached or mentored yourself before you try to pass the skills forward. Not only does this make you more sensitive to potential problems and obstacles, but it may also allow you to gauge more effectively whether coaching or mentoring would work best in a given context.

Developing mentoring and coaching in a school context

How can you develop mentoring and coaching effectively in schools? Both are very goal-focused or solution-focused activities, and for many of those who work in education, there are quite enough external goals imposed upon them without creating more ways to fail. You can feel that, as one colleague told me, coaching is something 'best left on the sports field' rather than brought into the classroom.

However, the current popularity of mentoring and coaching in education – not only for teachers, but also for those in school leadership and for students – argues that they are practical and useful activities. In recent years, the language of coaching and mentoring has become a popular way of talking about developing in professional terms in many different spheres, and coaching and mentoring strategies have become important in professional development for teachers, with some of the most successful initiatives for school improvement working with a coaching or mentoring model. Extensive research suggests the efficacy of both strategies, and the language and imagery used seems to appeal particularly to teachers, involving, as it does, a sense that professional development is associated with increased expertise.

One reason that these strategies are useful is because of the increasing professionalisation of teachers. There was a time when teachers were very much independent beings, and what they did in their classrooms was not subject to very much external inspection. Now the opposite is true, with teachers being over-observed and anxiety creeping into the profession as a result. Having a coach or a mentor provides you with a friendly external eye on your practice to balance those occasions when you may feel pressured by external observation.

Differences between mentoring and coaching		
Feature	Found in mentoring?	Found in coaching?
Personalised programme of improvement	Yes, but generally focused on longer-term goals, sometimes broken down into smaller areas of development.	Yes, generally focused on very specific and short-term goals.
One-to-one sessions	Yes; mentoring is generally more personalised and individualised than coaching.	Yes, though small group work is also extremely effective. You may need a different coach to guide you through different areas of development.
More senior person to work with	Yes, mentors will often be people senior to you, or with more experience of a certain area.	Not necessarily. Coaches are often people at a similar level to you.
Working with a colleague on the same level	Rarely. To be an effective mentor, the mentor will need to have more experience or seniority so as to help take the long view with your career.	Yes. Coaching encourages those at the same level to work with one another.
Focus on specific skills	Mentoring is more likely to focus on a range of skills that will help career development in a specific direction.	Coaching generally focuses on specifics, though these may be part of wider goals.
Focus on career development	Mentoring is designed to make the mentee think of their future aspirations and opportunities, and focuses on ways to develop their career path as a part of this.	Coaching rarely focuses on strategies for career development, though of course improvements in performance may lead to this.
Time commitment	You will need a regular time with your mentor, but this can be quite infrequent. You may keep in touch through e-mail or other means between sessions.	Typically, you will need coaching time and rehearsal/practice time. The latter will be part of what you are doing in any case; the coaching time may intersect with this, but you will need short, regular sessions for reflection and discussion.

Fig. 1 Differences between mentoring and coaching

Schools are in many respects the ideal environment for coaching and mentoring to flourish. Both practices demand a high level of engagement from participants, and a high level of commitment to the ultimate goals identified. Close interpersonal relationships are important, as is a reflective professional sensibility that is unafraid to self-examine and set targets. Often, those who work in schools are used to working with mentoring and coaching models with their students (though they may not explicitly identify these models as such) and so will tend to be more comfortable with them in performance management terms.

Finding a mentor

A mentor in terms of professional development should be a person who is expert, but also senior to the mentee; they might be someone who currently holds a job or role to which the mentee aspires, or someone who has experienced a similar career trajectory to them but moved further forward. A mentor will typically share their own experiences with you, and help you to avoid the pitfalls that they may have experienced on their way to their current position. They may also help you when you are at a time of transition in your career, trying to make tough decisions about your direction forward.

Mentors are often spoken of as inspirational and as role models. They may help you by demonstrating how they have overcome problems, or by showing what is possible. Typically, people will think of mentors as exemplars in some respect, perhaps asking themselves 'What would my mentor do?' or 'How did my mentor manage this situation?' when encountering a problem. Your mentor may very well be someone outside your organisation, with a sharp perspective on it as a result.

Example 1

I am a first year English teacher. I am ambitious and interested in my subject, and keen to know how to develop further in my future career.

Suitable mentor: someone in their second or subsequent year of teaching, holding a departmental responsibility, will be able to talk you through time management, and how best to self-assess your skills.

Example 2

I am a science teacher, working part-time after returning to the classroom following a career break for personal reasons. I would like to know how to get my career back on track, but I'm wary of taking on more than I can manage.

Suitable mentor: colleague from another department who has made the transition from part-time to full-time working, and taken on responsibility in the process.

Example 3

I am a middle leader, uncertain about my next move. I have a whole-school responsibility with a small teaching and learning responsibility (TLR), but am not a department leader.

Suitable mentor: You will need to choose! Have discussions with a department leader of a core department and a member of the senior leadership team (SLT) about their different paths to decide whether you want to move into departmental leadership to prepare yourself for senior leadership, or if there are other whole-school areas in which you could develop.

> ## What happens if...
>
> ### I can't find a suitable mentor?
>
> Look in unexpected places. Don't dismiss those who have retired or who have left the profession – not only may they have more time for you, but they will also have a different and potentially helpful perspective. A mentor does not have to have had the same career route as you!

Finding a coach

Coaching is generally less formal than mentoring, and you may be coached by a variety of people in the same project. It requires someone who may well be more expert than you, but does not have to be, and someone who also does not need to be senior to you or markedly further on in their career. A coach, most importantly, is someone who observes you and knows how to talk to you about what you are doing.

Professional tennis stars do sometimes have coaches who are former star players themselves, but more often they have coaches who are merely good players, but players especially skilled in coaching. The same distinction holds in terms of CPD in education. A coach might be a colleague at the same level of experience as you, a critical friend, or even someone who has a different area of expertise. The main qualification for being a coach is that you are able and willing to take the time to look carefully at what the person you are coaching is doing, and that you are happy to engage in dialogue with them about the direction in which you are developing their skills.

Example 1

I am a maths teacher who has passed my NQT year, but needed it extended due to some issues with lesson planning and record keeping.

Suitable coach: second or third year teacher in your department who is an effective planner and data manager.

Example 2

I am a music teacher, working part-time after returning to the classroom following maternity leave. Since my return, I am concerned that I have two observations that suggest my teaching requires improvement.

Suitable coach: subject or key stage leader with expertise in teaching and learning; or an observation triad with two teachers from different departments.

Example 3

I am a year group leader, and have had some significant absence due to illness. Since my return to work I feel overwhelmed by the volume of work involved with my year group, and I'm worried that they have got 'out of hand'.

Suitable coach: another year group leader or key stage leader who will be able to take you through routines and systems that will help you to prioritise and manage your workload.

What happens if...

I can't find a suitable coach?

The essence of coaching is that it is collaborative. Make sure that you have considered people at the same level as you, or with less experience than you, and don't assume that they have nothing to teach you. Try considering people in different fields with different perspectives. Look in unexpected places.

It's worth remembering the distinction between mentoring and coaching when choosing either one as a route towards professional development. Each technique is valuable in various contexts, but different methods will suit different people at each stage of their career or emotional journey.

Rather than creating artificial distinctions between mentoring and coaching, or combining the two in a confused way, choose carefully which will be most effective for your needs. Coaching is something often most effective when it is peer-to-peer, as an ongoing professional development activity, whilst mentoring may be something used specifically to help someone through a particular stage in their career, especially when making a transition between different roles. Use the quiz below to clarify your ideas. The answers are given at the start of Chapter 3 (p. 46).

Quiz: mentoring or coaching?

Consider the following six cases and decide for each whether you feel mentoring or coaching would be most appropriate:

1. A young teacher has been promoted to Head of Department, but has not previously held a responsibility post. She will need support in terms of how to manage the department, which consists of staff who are more experienced than her.

2. A recently appointed Assistant Headteacher has applied for the post of Deputy Headteacher and not got it in the face of a number of more experienced candidates. He is a key member of the SLT, but feels demoralised and is talking about leaving the school altogether.
3. A teacher has had considerable time off as a result of a stress-related illness. On his return, the teacher demonstrates extreme anxiety about performance management, observations, and learning walks. Parental concerns about the quality of teaching in his lessons have been raised.
4. A new teacher to the school is not attending all her break duty slots, and this has been noted by SLT. On enquiry, the teacher reveals that she feels awkward about confronting students who misbehave, and that she is stressed by the requirement to do break duty. In her defence, she points out that other teachers feel this way, and that she is not the only person who is avoiding break duty.
5. A teacher has been appointed as literacy coordinator, but in terms of performance management concerns have been raised about how effectively this member of staff is able to deal with a whole-school role. The numeracy coordinator is cited, by contrast, as an example of an effective appointment.
6. A member of staff who has always done well under the 'old' OFSTED observation system, and who thinks of themselves as a consistently good or outstanding teacher, is not evaluated as such under the new criteria. Not all students are making good progress in this teacher's lessons, although most of them do make progress.

Chapter 1 takeaway

Reflection

Think about occasions in your life when you feel that someone else has helped you develop professionally. You might reflect on when you first became a teacher, or when you gained a promotion. The person concerned does not have to be a colleague – it could be a family member or friend. What did this person do that helped you? Were they acting in a way that was more like a mentor or a coach?

Pass it on

Sharing your ideas – within your school

Try asking colleagues in a department meeting how they have used others to facilitate their own professional development, and what they have found most productive in helping them to improve their own practice. Did they find 'out of school' INSET most helpful, or in-school training, or something less formal? To help start the learning conversation, share with them the quiz above and ask them if they think that a coach or a mentor would best help the person concerned in each example.

Share and tweet
Who was your best coach or mentor? Share and celebrate them, using: #BloomsCPD

CPD book club recommendation

Coaching and Mentoring: Practical Conversations to Improve Learning
by Eric Parsloe
(see Bibliography and further reading)

Bloggers' corner

Executive coaches have some great tips that teachers can easily learn from. Reading some of their blogs can give you wonderful insights. Try, for instance, the blog at www.coachmentoring.co.uk.

TO DO LIST:

- ☐ Reflect on your own experiences of coaching or mentoring. Who has helped you the most to develop your skills? Can you describe them as a coach or a mentor?
- ☐ Talk to colleagues in your department meeting about their professional development and INSET experiences
- ☐ Discuss the quiz at the end of chapter 1 with colleagues and get their opinions on your choices
- ☐ Reflect on who has been your best coach and/or mentor and tweet your thanks to them as a celebration using #BloomsCPD
- ☐ Look at Eric Parsloe's book *Coaching and Mentoring: Practical Conversations to Improve Learning* and see if you recognise the learning conversations he describes
- ☐ Check out the CoachMentoring blog to see which posts chime with your own perceptions and which challenge you

2 Self-assessment

As T.S. Eliot so wisely said, sometimes 'the end of all our exploring will be to arrive where we started and know the place for the first time'. Self-assessment is a way of knowing where you are setting out from, so that you can explore more effectively.

All trained teachers have experience of being mentored and coached through the process of their training, but often when this is going on, we are focused on our short-term goals rather than on the process itself. Similarly, you may have been supporting staff formally or informally, but not really thought of this as mentoring and coaching. This section is designed to help you reflect on the process and work out what stage you are at yourself as a mentor or as a coach.

It is really important to be honest with yourself in self-assessment. You may find it easiest to go with your 'gut instinct' – the first response – and then reflect on it later. You may prefer to give a more considered response first, or you may wish to combine both strategies. There is no 'best way' here – it's all about what is most helpful to you in finding out your own position.

How to complete the self-assessment questionnaire

On pages 24–41 there is a self-assessment questionnaire. You may feel that you need to try it quickly once, then reflect on your answers, and go through it again. That's fine. Writing down what you think and making a record of it will help you later on to see how you have progressed.

Quick response approach

Simply fill in the quick response section after each question with the first thing that comes into your mind when you ask yourself the question. Do not mull over the question too long, but read carefully and answer quickly. This approach will give you an overview of your current understanding of mentoring and coaching and will take relatively little time. Make sure you are uninterrupted, in a quiet place and able to complete the questionnaire in one sitting with no distractions so that you get focused and honest answers.

What happens if...

I can't decide which number to give for an answer?

Remember that the questionnaire is a self-assessment, designed to help you, and not a test. If you are uncertain about what grade to give, that is worth noting down so that you can explore the reasons for it at the end.

Considered response approach

If you choose to take a more reflective and detailed approach, then you can leave the quick response section blank and go straight onto reading the further guidance section under each question. This guidance provides prompt questions and ideas to get you thinking in detail about the question being asked and is designed to open up a wider scope in your answer. It will also enable you to look at your experience and pull examples into your answer to back up your statements. You may want to complete it a few questions at a time and take breaks, or you may be prepared to simply sit and work through the questions all in one sitting to ensure you remain focused. This approach does take longer, but it can lead to a more in-depth understanding of your current mentoring and coaching knowledge, and you will gain much more from the process than the quick response alone.

Combined approach

A thorough approach, and one I recommend, would be to use both techniques together regardless of personal preference. There is clear value in both approaches being used together. This would involve you firstly answering the self-evaluation quick response questions by briefly noting down your instinctual answers for all questions. The next step would be to return to the start of the self-evaluation, read the further guidance and then answer the questions once more, slowly and in detail forming more of a narrative around each question and pulling in examples from your own experience. Following this you would need to read over both responses and form a comprehensive and honest summary in your mind of your answers and a final view of where you feel you stand right now in your mentoring and coaching.

- I have done this self-assessment before.
- I only want a surface level overview of my current understanding and practice.
- I work better when I work at speed.
- I don't have much time.

Quick

- I have never done this self-assessment before.
- I want a deeper understanding of my current understanding and practice.
- I work better when I take my time and really think things over.
- I have some time to do this self-assessment.

Considered

- I have never done this self-assessment before.
- I have done this self-assessment before.
- I want a comprehensive and full understanding of my current understanding and practice and want to compare that to what I thought before taking the self-assessment.
- I have a decent amount of time to dedicate to completing this self-assessment.

Combined

Fig. 2 How should I approach the self-evaluation questionnaire?

This is the longest of the three approaches to this questionnaire but will give you a comprehensive and full understanding of your current practice, thoughts and feelings in relation to mentoring and coaching. You will be surprised at the difference you see between the quick response and the considered response answers to the same questions. It can be very illuminating.

Rate yourself

The final part of the self-evaluation is to rate yourself. This section will ask you to rate your confidence and happiness in each area that has been covered in the questionnaire with a view to working on these areas for improvement throughout the course of the book. The table below shows how the scale works: the higher the number you allocate yourself, the better you feel you are performing in that area.

Rating	Definition
1	Not at all. I don't. None at all. Not happy. Not confident at all.
2	Rarely. Barely. Very little. Very unconfident.
3	Not often at all. Not much. Quite unconfident.
4	Not particularly. Not really. Not a lot. Mildly unconfident.
5	Neutral. Unsure. Don't know. Indifferent.
6	Sometimes. At times. Moderately. A little bit. Mildly confident.
7	Quite often. A fair bit. Some. A little confident.
8	Most of the time. More often than not. Quite a lot. Quite confident.
9	The majority of the time. A lot. Very confident.
10	Completely. Very much so. A huge amount. Extremely happy. Extremely confident.

Fig. 3 Rate yourself definitions

Top tip

Self-assessment is a vital skill for self-reflection and progression in your professional life, and one which is especially important in coaching and mentoring. It is important that we are honest, kind and constructive when it comes to assessing ourselves, if we want to be able to show the same qualities when assisting others to reflect on their own professional journey. It can be easy to be too harsh on yourself and allow your insecurities to cloud your judgment when you appraise your own practice. Indeed, some people feel that this is more 'honest'. But being too harsh is no better than being too easy on yourself. Being objective and honest about yourself and your practice is a hard thing to do and it takes practice. Before you begin self-assessing, it is important to carefully consider the criteria you are using to assess yourself and focus on that at first without thinking about yourself. Feeling comfortable with what you are assessing will lead to a more accurate assessment. If you jump in before you have fully considered the assessment criteria, you may well be unable to learn as much from the process. Don't rush it – it is too important.

Mentoring and coaching self-assessment questionnaire

QUESTION 1: What is your own experience of being coached or mentored?

Quick response:

_____

_____

_____

_____

Questions for consideration:

- Were you mentored as a trainee teacher or NQT? How close were you to your mentor?
- Did you find the experience helpful? Was it generally positive or negative?
- What could have made this experience better than it was?
- Have you worked with others since you qualified as part of a CPD programme?
- Have you been part of a coaching pair or trio?
- Is there a particular colleague that you look to for advice or support?

Considered response:

_____

_____

_____

_____

_____

_____

Rate yourself

QUESTION 1: How positive do you feel about your own experience of being coached or mentored?

1	2	3	4	5	6	7	8	9	10

QUESTION 2: In what ways have you worked with or supported other teachers in the past?

Quick response:

_____

_____

_____

_____

Questions for consideration

- Have you worked with trainee teachers or NQTs as a mentor?
- Have you ever led or devised INSET training?
- Do you work informally with colleagues to support them?
- Have you ever suggested that a colleague of yours help another colleague?
- Have you helped to support a colleague having temporary difficulty?
- Do colleagues often ask you for advice or support?
- Have senior leaders ever suggested that you informally or formally support another member of staff?
- What support have you had with this work?

Considered response:

_____

_____

_____

_____

_____

_____

_____

Rate yourself

QUESTION 2: How happy are you with the range of experience you have in working with or supporting other teachers?

1   2   3   4   5   6   7   8   9   10

QUESTION 3: How much do you enjoy working with other teachers?

Quick response:

_____

_____

_____

_____

Questions for consideration

- When have you worked closely with other teachers?
- Does it make a difference if you're already friendly with the teacher concerned? Does this make it easier or harder to work with them?
- Were the circumstances formal or informal?
- What circumstances made the experience enjoyable or less enjoyable?
- Do you find it easier when you are offering help and support or when you are being offered help and support?
- Has there been a time when you have faced a challenge when working with colleagues and worked through it to a positive outcome?

Considered response:

_____

_____

_____

_____

_____

_____

_____

_____

Rate yourself

QUESTION 3: How much do you think that you have benefited from working with other teachers?

| 1 | 2 | 3 | 4 | 5 | 6 | 7 | 8 | 9 | 10 |

QUESTION 4: Do you feel that your work with other teachers has had a measurable impact on student attainment and achievement?

Quick response:

_____

_____

_____

_____

Questions for consideration

- When have you had the opportunity to see the impact of your work with other teachers?
- Have you had the opportunity to analyse specific data?
- What student or teacher feedback has helped you see the impact of what you have done?
- What factors do you think contributed to the impact?
- Has there been a time when the impact has not been what you had hoped? If so, what did you learn from the experience?
- How do you think you could evaluate the impact of your work more sharply?
- How do you think you could develop your work to focus more closely on student attainment and achievement?

Considered response:

_____

_____

_____

_____

_____

Rate yourself

QUESTION 4: How much impact on student attainment and achievement do you feel your work with other teachers has at the moment?

1   2   3   4   5   6   7   8   9   10

QUESTION 5: What educational research, theories or case studies on mentoring and coaching do you know about, and how does this inform or influence your practice?

Quick response:

_____

_____

_____

_____

Questions for consideration

- Do you value educational research into other areas of practice?
- What do you already know about research or case studies into mentoring or coaching?
- What barriers are there to looking into research on mentoring and coaching? Is it something you don't have time for, or something you don't feel is important?
- Do you feel that looking at educational research is a part of your job? If not, whom in school do you think should be responsible?
- Have you had discussions with colleagues about research on mentoring or coaching?
- Have you done any active research yourself on mentoring or coaching, alone or with others? What support did you have, and what were the outcomes?

Considered response:

_____

_____

_____

_____

_____

Rate yourself

QUESTION 5: How confident do you feel about your knowledge of educational research into coaching and mentoring?

1	2	3	4	5	6	7	8	9	10

QUESTION 6: Do you feel that your views on mentoring and coaching match those of the school that you work in?

Quick response:

_____

_____

_____

_____

Questions for consideration

- Does your school have a formal system of support for staff that involves mentoring or coaching?
- Does your school involve students in mentoring or coaching activities?
- Do you feel that you have previously had more or less support in terms of mentoring and coaching than you currently have? Why?
- Does your school encourage staff to work informally to support each other?
- Do you feel that your school puts barriers in the way of your working with other members of staff, or does it encourage this?
- Does your school's performance management system encourage mentoring and coaching as ways to move forward professional development?
- If you were able to make one change in the way that the school currently supports staff, what would it be?

Considered response:

_____

_____

_____

_____

_____

Rate yourself

QUESTION 6: How closely do you feel your views on the importance of mentoring and coaching align with your school's views?

| 1 | 2 | 3 | 4 | 5 | 6 | 7 | 8 | 9 | 10 |

QUESTION 7: Do you feel that your views on mentoring and coaching match those of the department that you work in?

Quick response:

_____

_____

_____

_____

Questions for consideration

- What opportunities are available in your department for the mentoring or coaching of staff?
- Are there currently people in your department who you find particularly supportive? Why is this?
- Does your department have any initiatives that involve students in mentoring or coaching activities?
- Does your department encourage staff to work informally to support each other with everyday tasks?
- Do you feel that your department puts barriers in the way of your working with other members of staff, or does it encourage working together?
- Are there any systems or initiatives in place that use mentoring or coaching practices within them?
- Are there any systems and processes that you think your department could improve in terms of how staff are supported?

Considered response:

_____

_____

_____

_____

Rate yourself

QUESTION 7: How closely do you feel your views on the importance of mentoring and coaching align with your department's views?

1	2	3	4	5	6	7	8	9	10

QUESTION 8: Where do you feel your strengths lie when it comes to mentoring and coaching?

Quick response:

_____

_____

_____

_____

Questions for consideration

- What skills do you think are important for mentoring?
- What skills do you think are important for coaching?
- What principles do you think are most important when starting a mentoring or coaching relationship?
- What do you think you have done well in terms of offering support to colleagues?
- What strengths have other people commented on?
- Do you think that you have developed these strengths over time, or have you always been strong in these areas?
- What new skills do you think that you have developed through working with others?
- What opportunities have you already taken for the mentoring or coaching of staff?

Considered response:

_____

_____

_____

_____

_____

Rate yourself

QUESTION 8: How confident do you feel about your existing ability to support colleagues through mentoring and coaching strategies?

1   2   3   4   5   6   7   8   9   10

QUESTION 9: Where do you feel your weaknesses are when it comes to mentoring and coaching?

Quick response:

_____

_____

_____

_____

Questions for consideration

- What areas have you found most challenging when it comes to supporting other staff?
- Have colleagues ever mentioned that there are areas where they feel your skills could be strengthened? How did you feel about this?
- Are there areas in which you yourself think have become less strong over time? Why do you think this is?
- What support have you sought to develop in these areas?
- Have you been offered training in these areas?
- Have you read or researched in these areas in your own time?

Considered response:

_____

_____

_____

_____

_____

_____

_____

_____

Rate yourself

QUESTION 9: How serious do you think the barriers are to developing your mentoring and coaching practice?

| 1 | 2 | 3 | 4 | 5 | 6 | 7 | 8 | 9 | 10 |

QUESTION 10: How would you like to develop your mentoring and coaching skills?

Quick response:

_____
_____
_____
_____

Questions for consideration

- Are there colleagues whose style of coaching and mentoring you particularly admire?
- Do you feel that their skills complement or contrast with your own skills?
- How do you believe your colleagues have developed these skills?
- Do you feel that there are areas where you have managed to develop specific skills?
- How did you develop these skills? Was it a deliberative process, and how did you decide to undertake it?
- What kind of support do you find most helpful when it comes to developing skills?

Considered response:

_____
_____
_____
_____
_____
_____
_____

Rate yourself

QUESTION 10: How confident do you feel about developing your mentoring and coaching skills?

1   2   3   4   5   6   7   8   9   10

QUESTION 11: What might be holding you back in developing your mentoring and coaching skills?

Quick response:

_____

_____

_____

_____

Questions for consideration

- What areas have you found most challenging when it comes to supporting other staff?
- What do you worry about when you are working with other staff?
- What stands in the way of working with other staff?
- What limits you in developing your mentoring and coaching skills?
- What kind of training do you think you would find helpful in developing your skills?
- How have you tried to overcome the limitations?

Considered response:

_____

_____

_____

_____

_____

_____

_____

_____

Rate yourself

QUESTION 11: How much do you think the factors you have identified are holding you back in your mentoring and coaching work?

1   2   3   4   5   6   7   8   9   10

QUESTION 12: Is there an aspect of mentoring or coaching that you have seen work well for other people and which does not work for you?

Quick response:

_____

_____

_____

_____

Questions for consideration

- What approaches have you tried that you have heard worked for others (through a book, a blog, or personal observation) that have not worked when you have tried them yourself?
- What evidence did you have that they worked well for others?
- What did you have to do to adapt your practice?
- What difficulties did you face?
- For how long did you try the strategy before deciding it didn't work?
- Why did you decide that it had not worked for you?
- What do you think was different for the people who did find this strategy worked? Are they factors that you can change?
- Would you be prepared to try a similar strategy again?

Considered response:

_____

_____

_____

_____

_____

Rate yourself

QUESTION 12: How confident with your own ability to mentor or coach do you feel when you compare yourself to other people you know?

| 1 | 2 | 3 | 4 | 5 | 6 | 7 | 8 | 9 | 10 |

QUESTION 13: How effectively do you think the people you mentor or coach find your strategies working for them?

Quick response:

_____

_____

_____

_____

Questions for consideration

- What approaches have you tried to get feedback from the people you mentor or coach?
- How do they respond when you ask for feedback?
- Do you and those you mentor or coach share the same view of effectiveness?
- Do the people you are working with share in your planning for supporting them?
- Have you ever changed your strategies in response to their feedback?
- How do you deal with negative feedback?

Considered response:

_____

_____

_____

_____

_____

_____

_____

_____

Rate yourself

QUESTION 13: How confident are you that you really know what the people you mentor or coach feel about your practice?

1	2	3	4	5	6	7	8	9	10

QUESTION 14: What do you think the people you mentor or coach most enjoy in your work with them?

Quick response:

_____

_____

_____

_____

Questions for consideration

- How can you tell when a mentoring or coaching session has gone well?
- What do you consider a positive response to your support?
- Have other people given you feedback about your work with the people you mentor or coach?
- How often do you talk to the people you support about their own needs and feelings?
- Do you decide on how to organise the support programme, or do you involve them in the planning?
- How far would you go to accommodate their preferences?

Considered response:

_____

_____

_____

_____

_____

_____

_____

Rate yourself

QUESTION 14: How confident are you that you really understand what the people you mentor or coach like or dislike about your practice?

1   2   3   4   5   6   7   8   9   10

QUESTION 15: What do the people you mentor or coach most need so as to make progress, in your opinion?

Quick response:

_____

_____

_____

_____

Questions for consideration

- How do you decide if progress has been made in a session?
- Do you think it is your responsibility or the responsibility of those you mentor or coach to ensure progress takes place?
- Do you and the people you mentor or coach share and establish goals initially?
- What records do you keep about your coaching or mentoring?
- How do you follow up and track progress once specific organised support has stopped?
- Do you compare the different people who you mentor or coach? What is the impact of this?

Considered response:

_____

_____

_____

_____

_____

_____

_____

Rate yourself

QUESTION 15: How confident are you that you really understand what the people you mentor or coach need to make progress?

1	2	3	4	5	6	7	8	9	10

QUESTION 16: Do you have a wide range of coaching and mentoring strategies to use?

Quick response:

_____

_____

_____

_____

Questions for consideration

- Were you taught specific skills for mentoring and coaching (e.g. for PGCE mentoring) or have you picked them up informally?
- How do you decide when to use a new strategy?
- How do you evaluate each strategy that you use?
- If progress stalls, what do you do to change this?

Considered response:

_____

_____

_____

_____

_____

_____

_____

_____

_____

_____

Rate yourself

QUESTION 16: How confident are you that you have a good range of coaching and mentoring strategies to use?

1   2   3   4   5   6   7   8   9   10

QUESTION 17: Do you know if senior leaders in the school value your skills in formal or informal support of staff?

Quick response:

_____

_____

_____

_____

Questions for consideration

- Do senior leaders know about the different ways in which you support other staff?
- Have senior leaders ever spoken to you directly about what you are doing or someone you have helped?
- Who do you talk to about the progress of your work?
- Is there a forum where you could share the impact of your work with senior leaders?
- Does your work, or an aspect of it, feature in the school development plan or the school self-evaluation form (SEF)?
- What support would you like from senior leaders?

Considered response:

_____

_____

_____

_____

_____

_____

Rate yourself

QUESTION 17: How confident are you that your formal or informal support of staff is valued by senior leaders in your school?

1	2	3	4	5	6	7	8	9	10

QUESTION 18: Do you know what other staff in the school think about your formal or informal support of their colleagues?

Quick response:

_____

_____

_____

_____

Questions for consideration

- Are your discussions with staff completely confidential?
- Are there other members of staff working in a similar way to you? Do you exchange ideas with them on a regular basis?
- Has your work ever been a part of INSET training or other form of CPD?
- Has your work been set up as a form of formal support or is it more informal?
- Who else, apart from you and those you mentor or coach, is involved in your work?
- Does the work you do put any strain on other members of staff to support it (e.g. through cover)?

Considered response:

_____

_____

_____

_____

_____

_____

_____

Rate yourself

QUESTION 18: How confident are you that other staff are positive about your support of those you mentor or coach?

1   2   3   4   5   6   7   8   9   10

The results

Congratulations for an honest and thoughtful self-assessment. You have reflected on your own journey in terms of being mentored and coached, and considered how your mentoring and coaching has developed. You have considered the impact of what you do, and how you appraise it, as well as reflecting on how your colleagues view your work, and what expertise you may need to acquire. Take some time to think over what you have written and considered.

Take a look at how you rated your answers for each question in the questionnaire and compare your ratings with the chart below which will give you a sense of where you need to move onto next. You will find that your marks fall into low, medium or high ratings. For each question, reflect on what this means that you need to do, and then consider your overall score.

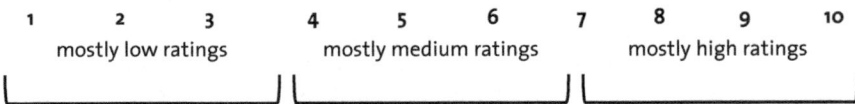

| 1 | 2 | 3 | | 4 | 5 | 6 | | 7 | 8 | 9 | | 10 |
| mostly low ratings | | | | mostly medium ratings | | | | | mostly high ratings | | | |

Fig. 4 How did you rate yourself?

Mostly low ratings

You are probably already well-aware that you are not yet expert in mentoring or coaching, but the honesty of your score shows great promise for your ability to develop in this area. Knowing where you are starting from is an essential first step in the mentoring and coaching process, and if you are able to assess yourself at this level, the chances are you will be able to help others more effectively. Look carefully at the areas where your score is lowest, and start there. A good first step is to read more widely about different strategies, and consider whether the style that you have used up to now is the right one for you. The next chapter should immediately help with this (p. 46).

> # What happens if...
>
> ### my ratings are a real mixture?
>
> Mixed results can be helpful, but you might want to analyse them in more detail. Try grouping together answers where you have similar scores, and reflecting on what those questions have in common with each other.

Mostly medium ratings

You have clearly had some experience in mentoring and coaching, and have a grasp of the basic strategies. You may already have had some success with individuals and in particular situations, and you can build on this to help you to progress further. The good news is that you clearly have aptitude for mentoring and coaching and are well on the way to understanding how to become expert. Look carefully at the areas of the questionnaire that dealt with the barriers to your progress. What do you need to help you develop as a mentor or a coach? Is it more knowledge, more practice, more recognition? Each will demand a different strategy to move forward.

Mostly high ratings

Your confidence in your mentoring and coaching abilities argues that you have already done considerable research into how to develop your skills. You are now at the stage where you will be able to consider how to pass on your knowledge to others, perhaps through working in coaching trios or more formally mentoring someone else. Remember that it is important to ensure that you have backup form senior leaders to help you develop further. Make sure that they are aware of what you do, appreciate its effectiveness, and are factoring your work into their future planning for the school. One word of warning – don't get complacent about what you are doing; it is always possible to improve, especially as new research and new strategies come online. Keeping your eyes open for new learning is an important part of developing as a mentor or coach.

Now what?

Your self-assessment should be the foundation of your action plan. Take the time to go through each of your answers, so as to prioritise the areas that you want to improve, and set a timescale for your planning. Look carefully to see whether there are areas where you can develop your work with others, or if there are 'easy wins' that link together. This document will be something that you can use again and again to reflect on your progress.

Chapter 2 takeaway

Reflection

When reflecting on the questionnaire, consider the areas where you feel strongest, and what they have in common with each other. What support has made you feel more confident in these areas? Can you source similar support to help you with the areas that are more challenging?

Pass it on

Sharing your ideas – within your school

Try and find other colleagues in school who have mentoring or coaching experience, and ask them to reflect on one of the questions with you. For instance, what was the last useful tweet that they saw or the last useful article they read when it comes to working with others?

Share and tweet

Following the discussion with colleagues above, either tweet a reference to an article or retweet a tweet that you have discovered and found useful, using: #BloomsCPD

CPD book club recommendation

The Perfect Teacher Coach by Jackie Beere and Terri Broughton (see Bibliography and further reading)

Bloggers' corner

To sharpen up and challenge your own ideas about coaching and mentoring, try reading a blog like David Didau's Learning Spy which challenged accepted orthodoxies: www.learningspy.co.uk/

TO DO LIST:

- ❑ Reflect on the areas where you feel strongest, and consider what support has helped you develop these
- ❑ Discuss one of the questions from the self-assessment questionnaire with colleagues
- ❑ Ask colleagues which tweets or blog posts they themselves have found helpful
- ❑ Read *The Perfect Teacher Coach*
- ❑ Look at the *Learning Spy* Blog. Try searching 'Coaching' to find some provocative posts

3

Types of mentoring and coaching

Before you start this chapter, look at the answers you gave to the 'mentoring or coaching?' quiz at the end of chapter 1 (p. 16). These are suggested answers – debate how far you agree with them with a colleague!

1. A young teacher has been promoted to Head of Department (HOD) but has not previously held a responsibility post. She will need support in terms of how to manage the department, which consists of staff who are more experienced than her.
   ANSWER: Here, a mentor is clearly needed. Ideally, pair the new HOD with an experienced HOD in a related subject. The experienced HOD as a mentor will be able to advise the new appointee on how they started off, mistakes they made, and advise them on change management – that is, the process through which you plan, as a leader, to bring about effective change in your area. It's all about becoming more strategic and less operational.

2. A recently appointed Assistant Headteacher has applied for the post of Deputy Headteacher and not got it in the face of a number of more experienced candidates. He is a key member of the SLT, but feels demoralised and is talking about leaving the school altogether.
   ANSWER: A mentor is needed in this situation. Ideally a deputy from another school should be used as a mentor to work with the Assistant Head. The successful candidate for Deputy is unlikely to be acceptable as a mentor. The application and interview process should be discussed as a first step, focusing on the reasons for applying for a promotion so soon after a previous one, so as to understand the reasoning behind the decision. The mentor should work with the Assistant Head to talk about how realistic their career ambitions are, strategies for gaining more experience outside school (this is where a mentor from another school can be especially helpful) and the timeframe for possible fulfillment.

3. A teacher has had considerable time off as a result of a stress-related illness. On his return, the teacher demonstrates extreme anxiety about performance management, observations, and learning walks. Parental concerns about the quality of teaching in his lessons have been raised.
   ANSWER: Here, a coach is likely to be most useful. Ideally, someone who the teacher works with already, and someone he trusts. The coach will be able to help the teacher explore why they still feel anxious, and if there is further action that they could take about this, for instance a conversation with HR about wellbeing or work-related stress. Beyond this, building up a series of paired observations and planning together may help the teacher feel more prepared for external observation.

4. A new teacher to the school is not attending all her break duty slots, and this has been noted by SLT. On enquiry, the teacher reveals that she feels awkward about confronting students who misbehave, and that she is stressed by the requirement to do break duty. In her defence, she points out that other teachers feel this way, and that she is not the only person who is avoiding break duty.

ANSWER: There would be two possible ways of dealing with this. One is to use a mentor for each teacher – a more experienced member of staff to work with the teacher and talk them through strategies to support behaviour management. However, this is intensive in terms of time and staffing. A more effective route is likely to be a 'buddy' system, where the teacher is paired with another young colleague, and both teachers are trained explicitly in behaviour management techniques. They would then operate as 'co-coaches', helping each other to work on specific scenarios and problems throughout the year.

5. A teacher has been appointed as literacy coordinator, but in terms of performance management concerns have been raised about how effectively this member of staff is able to deal with a whole-school role. The numeracy coordinator is cited, by contrast, as an example of an effective appointment. ANSWER: A mentor here is readily available; use the numeracy coordinator. As the roles are similar in terms of whole-school scope, but different in terms of detail, this will allow the new literacy coordinator freedom to develop their own role while accessing the expertise of their colleague. Often pairing up whole-school roles like this creates added effectiveness.

6. A member of staff who has always done well under the 'old' OFSTED observation system, and who thinks of themselves as a consistently good or outstanding teacher, is not evaluated as such under the new criteria. Not all students are making good progress in this teacher's lessons, although most of them do make progress. ANSWER: Here a coach is going to be most useful. Ideally choose someone in a similar situation from another department, so as to give most impetus to both parties. OFSTED can be a bugbear, so you should remind both parties that the criteria are there to help teachers rather than to judge them. Training will need to take place (this may be whole-school) to discuss why using progress as a measure can be more focused on students than the previous criteria. Space will need to be given to both parties to discuss the coaching targets and priorities. Focusing on a particular subset of students in a given group (such as pupil premium (PP) students), based on class data on progress, will be an important first step.

What happens if...

I didn't get the 'right' answers?

Read through the section of Chapter 1 again which explains the difference between mentoring and coaching (p. 10). What do you think is the real difference between the two? Why do you disagree with the quiz answers?

Different mentoring and coaching styles

When becoming a mentor or coach, it is important that you work to your strengths; it is also important that you work out what your inherent style of mentoring or coaching might be already. Considering how you deal with stressful situations at work and at home is one way in which to evaluate this.

It is generally acknowledged that different styles suit different people and situations, and one thing that you need to do is to make sure that your style matches up to that of the person you wish to support.

In sports coaching, three styles of coaching are often identified: autocratic, democratic and *laissez-faire*. Business mentoring and coaching has engendered many more styles. People also sometimes talk about mentoring and coaching in terms of 'telling', 'showing' or 'constructing', for instance, or 'zen' or 'mindfulness' coaching. It is easy to get a little lost in the different styles. In educational mentoring and coaching, I have found it helpful to talk about no more than the following ten identifying types. Each style may be useful in different situations, but there is considerable overlap between them:

1. Assertive
2. Democratic
3. Casual
4. Solution-focused
5. Holistic
6. Challenging
7. Reflective
8. Problem-solving
9. Non-directive
10. Supportive.

1. Assertive

This kind of mentoring or coaching – sometimes in sports terms called 'autocratic', 'bossy', or 'authoritarian'– is characterised by the lead (mentor or coach) taking a very assertive role in the process. The lead may, for instance, direct the subject (coachee or mentee) as to the desired goals, or dictate what is the preferred action, and leave little room for debate. Although this can seem like a negative style, it can work well with certain personality types, or as an initial 'short burst' style of coaching to get things going.

2. Democratic

In this style the lead acts as a 'guide on the side'. The subject is encouraged to make their own decisions and the lead rarely, if ever, interferes. The subject's opinions and ideas are given equal weight with those of the lead, who may comment, but does not forbid choices.

3. Casual

As the name suggests this is a *laissez faire* style, which is also sometimes called 'lazy' coaching. In this style, the lead will allow the subject to make mistakes and find their own way out of them.

4. Solution-focused

This style is very concentrated on the goals that the subject wants to achieve, and some time is spent on defining these. The goals will tend to be seen as more important than the means of getting towards them, which can be quite flexible.

5. Holistic

Holistic, as its name implies, involves the whole person. In this style, almost nothing is off limits, and the lead and subject usually have to have a fairly frank discussion about boundaries before starting. A holistic lead may investigate your hidden motivations, and this can prove to be quite a challenging perspective. Having said that, knowing that the reason you shout at Year 9 might be connected to being shouted at when you were that age can be immensely helpful, and very quick progress can sometimes be made in this kind of work.

6. Challenging

Rather like authoritarian, this can be a bit fierce for many people. If you work with a challenging coach or mentor, you must be prepared to be questioned about your practice and your motivation on a regular basis.

7. Reflective

Reflective is similar to democratic in that it requires the subject to be able to participate fully in decisions. A reflective lead will encourage you to consider the impact of each stage of development and every action, reflecting on your practice and on the reasons for what you do.

8. Problem-solving

The problem-solving style means that the lead sets a series of problems – theoretical or actual – and encourages you to solve them by yourself. The problem-solving approach takes you forwards in terms of practice but encourages independence.

9. Non-directive

Like non-directive counselling, non-directive mentoring or coaching encourages the subject to find out the answers that they already know. It can seem similar to casual coaching, but it requires a great deal more of the lead, as it is difficult to avoid giving direction, even without intending to.

10. Supportive

Supportive supplies a 'safety net' for the subject, and focuses on positive reinforcement of their behaviour. In this style, the lead concentrates on what the subject is already doing well, and how to build on those behaviours.

Working to discover your own mentoring and coaching style

Tasks to complete

Task 1

Consider your reactions to the following situations, and choose which response feels nearest to your honest reaction.

1. A friend needs to assemble a piece of flat-pack furniture, and has asked you to help. Do you:
   a. Say you don't have the time or expertise, but you know someone else who can help?
   b. Get them to hold the first bit upright while you screw in the bolts; you've done this before?
   c. Wait and see what they would like you to do, while you count all the bolts and screws?
   d. Ask them to explain why they need your help, and at which stage they need it so that you can save time?
   e. Insist on reading the instructions carefully before you start so that you can be as useful as possible?
   f. Suggest you lay out all the pieces on the floor to see how they fit together before you start?

2. You have offered to be teaching assistant (TA) in a lesson for a colleague. The student you are working with seems stuck on a maths problem. Do you:
   a. Empathise – you always found maths hard as well – but don't interfere?
   b. Show the student how to solve a similar problem?
   c. Ask the teacher what they would like you to do – does the student have an individual learning plan?
   d. Explain the rule that will allow the student to solve the problem?
   e. Give the student a hint about the right answer?
   f. Ask what the student usually does when they are stuck?
3. As you are leaving work, a colleague asks you for directions to a place nearby to your home. You are in a hurry. Do you:
   a. Say you're not sure, and suggest they ask someone else?
   b. Explain the way verbally by describing easy-to-remember landmarks?
   c. Draw a quick sketch map?
   d. Suggest the person follows your car home and you'll show them the way?
   e. Ask if they have the postcode, and suggest they use Google maps to navigate?
   f. Quickly explain the way, and get them to repeat it back to you to make sure they remember?
4. Work is very busy, but you have promised to put up an open day display for your department. Do you:
   a. Stay late one night and finish it off so everyone gets a nice surprise in the morning?
   b. Ask your TA to do it – you'll manage in class without her for once, and it doesn't matter if it's not perfect?
   c. Suggest to a colleague that you work on it together, and you'll pay her back later?
   d. Tidy up your existing display so it looks smarter?
   e. Get your intern to do it as a useful learning exercise?
   f. Spend a lesson putting it up with the help of students?
5. You are trying to choose a new sofa. Do you:
   a. Go into the largest shop and choose the one that seems most comfortable?
   b. Look at the various options online before making a decision?
   c. Ask your best friend or partner for advice?
   d. Ask friends what they think makes a good sofa – where did they get theirs from?
   e. Spend a few weekends browsing in all the shops – it's a big decision?
   f. Check whether 'Which' have a guide for sofas and take their advice?

6. A colleague has volunteered to give an assembly, but has never done one before, and they confide to you that they are a little nervous. Do you:
   a. Invite them to come and watch you deliver an assembly?
   b. Tell them they will be fine and not to worry – everyone has to have a first time!
   c. Ask them how many assemblies they have seen, and which colleagues they find most interesting in terms of delivery style?
   d. Lend them an old book you have with some suggestions for assemblies in it?
   e. Offer to let them use one of your old assemblies that you know works well every time?
   f. Suggest that you do a joint assembly before they try one on their own?
7. A colleague whom you indirectly line manage is underperforming and improving only very slowly. In your discussion with their line manager do you:
   a. Ask if there are any external factors that are affecting the teacher's progress?
   b. Ask what steps they are taking with the colleague and how they are evaluating progress and improvement?
   c. Visit the colleague's lesson yourself to check how things are going?
   d. Suggest that you ask the colleague to come in and observe another teacher in a paired observation to help them understand some ways to move forward?
   e. Suggest that they move onto a pre capability six-week programme to offer more structured support?
   f. Invite the teacher to come and watch you to see how to do it?

Task 2

Select the words and phrases in the table below that you think you are most likely to use in a mentoring or coaching situation.

How likely are you to use this phrase?	Tick or cross
What you need to do is...	
If I were you...	
The most important thing here is...	
Why did you decide that?	
How would you like to approach this?	
It's up to you.	
It's your decision.	
I can't make that decision for you.	
What do we want to achieve?	
What do you want to achieve?	
Why do you think that you feel that way?	

How likely are you to use this phrase?	Tick or cross
When have you had that kind of feeling before?	
What have you done to solve this kind of problem previously?	
What is your motivation?	
What is the point of that?	
What is in the way?	
What is stopping you?	
Is this target helping you to move forwards, or are you struggling with it?	
What is stopping you from acting on that idea?	
What one change would make the biggest difference at the moment?	
Why do you want to achieve this?	
Who can help you with this?	
What have you already done to move forwards?	
When have you succeeded with a similar problem?	
What will the impact be?	
How will you evaluate what you are trying and know if you are successful?	
How did that make you feel?	
Have you tried..?	
You seem anxious.	
How do you feel about that?	
What are you responsible for here?	
What have you done well?	
What do you need to be able to succeed?	
It's important you're happy with that decision.	

Fig. 5 Phrases used in mentoring and coaching

Answers for tasks

For each question, look at the number allocated to your answer. The number is linked to one of the ten styles of mentoring or coaching discussed on pages 48–50. If you get the same number or numbers consistently, this may indicate that you have a preference for a particular style. If you get a range of numbers, then the style is likely to be dictated by your subject.

Task 1 answers

Note that not all numbers are represented in every question.

1. Assembling furniture: a. 4; b. 1; c. 3; d. 6; e. 9; f. 5.
2. Giving directions: a. 9; b. 1; c. 2; d. 8; e. 3; f. 7.
3. Being a TA: a. 3; b. 1; c. 4; d. 10; e. 2; f. 6.
4. Putting up a display: a. 10; b. 3; c. 2; d. 4; e. 8; f. 5.
5. Choosing a sofa: a. 1; b. 5; c. 10; d. 2; e. 7; f. 8.
6. Giving an assembly: a. 7; b. 10; c. 8; d. 9; e. 1; f. 4.
7. Underperforming colleague: a. 5; b. 2; c. 8; d. 7; e. 6; f. 1.

Task 2 answers

How likely are you to use this phrase?	Associated with style number
What you need to do is...	1
If I were you...	1
The most important thing here is...	1
Why did you decide that?	2/7
How would you like to approach this?	2
It's up to you.	2/3
It's your decision.	2/3
I can't make that decision for you.	3
What do we want to achieve?	4
What do you want to achieve?	3
Why do you think that you feel that way?	5
When have you had that kind of feeling before?	5
What have you done to solve this kind of problem previously?	5/7
What is your motivation?	6
What is the point of that?	6
What is in the way?	4/6
What is stopping you?	6
Is this target helping you to move forwards, or are you struggling with it?	7/6
What is stopping you from acting on that idea?	8/7
What one change would make the biggest difference at the moment?	8/5
Why do you want to achieve this?	4/7
Who can help you with this?	2/4
What have you already done to move forwards?	10
When have you succeeded with a similar problem?	10/7
What will the impact be?	6/1

How likely are you to use this phrase?	Associated with style number
How will you evaluate what you are trying and know if you are successful?	6
How did that make you feel?	9/5/7
Have you tried..?	1
You seem anxious.	9
How do you feel about that?	7/9
What are you responsible for here?	5
What have you done well?	10
What do you need to be able to succeed?	10/7/4
It's important you're happy with that decision.	10/3

Fig. 6 Mentoring and coaching styles as represented by phrases

Results

Answers are mainly style 1

You may favour assertive mentoring and coaching.

Advantages

Assertive mentoring and coaching does get things moving quickly. It can suit those who want to see rapid progress, and trust their lead absolutely. It is a time-saver, and a way of quickly sharing expertise. It also works well in groups, where a number of people have a clearly defined goal.

Disadvantages

This style puts a great deal of responsibility on the lead, and relatively little on the subject, and so is not so good when it comes to developing independence. Some people can find it oppressive and unhelpful as it tends to have the approach 'my way or the highway'.

Answers are mainly style 2

You may favour democratic mentoring and coaching.

Advantages

The sharing of goals and the lack of an autocratic style can suit many people who resist being told what to do – often a particular feature of teachers! The discussion involved means that the subject usually feels more ownership of decisions.

Disadvantages

The process is quite time-consuming as every decision has to be discussed and talked through so that all concerned understand the consequences. The lead's refusal to take sides on an issue may at times be frustrating for the subject.

Answers are mainly style 3

You may favour casual mentoring and coaching.

Advantages

Casual coaching or mentoring is very non-confrontational and can be helpful with someone who resists the whole idea of coaching. It encourages people to find out their own solutions to problems through a trial and error process.

Disadvantages

The failure of the lead in this method to direct where a subject is taking a less useful direction means that it is time-consuming and can be confusing for the subject, who may find it hard to distinguish useful from less useful actions.

Answers are mainly style 4

You may favour solution-focused mentoring and coaching.

Advantages

The focus on the end point tends to mean that this style is effective and engenders shared responsibility. Not being so worried by means leads to flexibility and change when something isn't going well.

Disadvantages

Concentrating on an end point all the time can mean that the process itself receives less attention than it should. A solution-focused lead can put their subject under considerable pressure if they are not careful.

Answers are mainly style 5

You may favour holistic mentoring and coaching.

Advantages

Looking at the 'whole you' may mean that this kind of style is particularly helpful to those who have personal or emotional problems that affect them at work. The larger perspective that this involves can lead to resolution in and out of the workplace.

Disadvantages

Considering emotional problems as part of work-based coaching or mentoring is a minefield and requires a very experienced and expert lead to do it properly. Setting careful boundaries to discussion is essential if the process is to remain work-focused and professional.

Answers are mainly style 6

You may favour challenging mentoring and coaching.

Advantages

For robust subjects, challenging mentoring and coaching is bracing and can be quick and effective. It takes no prisoners! With a trusted lead, however, and clearly established 'rules' about challenge it can be extremely effective.

Disadvantages

Constant challenge can be very taxing on both parties involved in the process. Though this is high-impact, it is also high-investment in terms of energy, and it can cause extra stress.

Answers are mainly style 7

You may favour reflective mentoring and coaching.

Advantages

Reflecting on actions is a key part of most useful CPD, and the emphasis on reflection in this method fits well with teaching practice. The time taken to consider impact and experience is well rewarded in terms of future planning.

Disadvantages

Reflective mentoring and coaching can sometimes feel as though it is not moving fast enough. Not all teachers enjoy having to come up with their own responses to problems, and can feel as though they are 'teaching themselves'.

Answers are mainly style 8

You may favour problem-solving mentoring and coaching.

Advantages

Problem solving is engaging and practical and often very attractive to leads, as it tends to divide the sessions up into short and readily achievable sections.

Disadvantages

This kind of work can feel remote from the actual situation in which you find yourself. At times it may feel as though you can solve issues in theory but not in practice.

Answers are mainly style 9

You may favour non-directive mentoring and coaching.

Advantages

It is effective for independent and reflective practitioners, but also good for those who find it difficult to accept other people's ideas or opinions. Skilful questioning elicits honest responses.

Disadvantages

This kind of mentoring and coaching can be very time-consuming, as it relies on the activity of the subject, and their engagement in the problems that they face. It can be difficult for subjects to accept the non-directive role of the lead, and they may feel unsupported.

Answers are mainly style 10

You may favour supportive mentoring and coaching.

Advantages

This style is helpful for those who may feel that they are unappreciated or who have lost confidence in their own practice. It is often a 'soft' way into mentoring and coaching that can then be shifted to another style. It is useful where there is an existing level of high competence.

Disadvantages

If the subject is stuck in systems of behaviour that really need to change, it can be hard to find the space in supportive mentoring and coaching to introduce new ways of doing things. It needs a skilled lead to be able to unpick strategies and introduce new ideas without altering the supportive relationship.

What happens if...

I got a mixture of answers?

Think about the categories you have learned about. Are the styles that you favour related? That is to be expected. Remember that there is a lot of crossover between styles. If there is a real outlier or two in your results, go back and look again. Why do you think you chose that answer? What does it say about your response to that particular kind of problem? Is it a situation that you find especially difficult?

Where do you go from here?

You may find that you are surprised by the results that you got after checking your answers to the quiz. It can be that your own perceptions of your coaching or mentoring style are different from the reality. Always remember that the label that we put on a style is just that – a label for convenience – and that your essential style has not changed. Also remember that there is a lot of crossover between styles. When I tried this quiz myself, the result was not what I would have predicted, but I thought that this was good, because it made me reflect carefully on what I had expected, and how I saw myself as a coach or mentor. However, if you are really surprised, then take a moment to consider why this is, and perhaps go back over the questions again to think through why you answered each one as you did.

Once you have considered the different styles of mentoring and coaching, reflect on your own experience of being coached or mentored. This could be in a work or a non-work context. You might think back to the last time you learned something new; taking up a sport or going to a gym are both situations where you might have experienced coaching. Bringing up a small child might have put you in touch with informal mentoring from family and friends. Think about these experiences, and consider which were positive and which were less useful. What made the difference to you? Can you connect them to any of the styles above?

When you have done this, remind yourself of any occasions in which you have experienced mentoring or coaching in a professional context. Think back to when you first entered the profession, and of the kind of support that you had then as a trainee or an NQT. At that time the training that you would have experienced would have related closely to the teaching standards, and aimed at making you secure in understanding them and fulfilling them. How did it relate to the ten styles that we have examined? Consider whether the support offered was helpful, or whether you felt that it got in your way. What experiences have you had since then that have helped you to develop professionally, and which have not been helpful? Do you still refer to the teaching standards when reflecting on your own or others' practice?

Bearing these ideas in mind, consider what you now know about your own preferences for mentoring and coaching, and how you like to be mentored or coached yourself. Is there a difference between the way in which you like to be treated yourself, and the way in which you lead others when you are supporting them, or are you just reproducing patterns without thinking about it? When you are taking the lead in a situation where you are supporting someone else, do you adapt to your subject in each case, or do you have a consistent strategy?

Chapter 3 takeaway

Reflection

Did you have a favoured style when you read through the different 'types'? Did the answers that you found out here about your own practice surprise you? How would you like to be seen as a coach or mentor? Do you think that you need to adapt what you do to become more effective?

Pass it on

Sharing your ideas with colleagues outside your school setting
Try and find a small group of colleagues outside your school who are at a similar point in career terms, and ask them about their experience of mentoring and coaching. If you don't already have colleagues outside school to talk to, try starting a twitter conversation using: #BloomsCPD, or start a conversation on TES talk, for instance.

Sharing your ideas with staff in your school
Arrange to meet with two colleagues in school who have mentoring or coaching experience, and ask them to reflect on or try out the 'styles' task questions with you. What style do they think you favour? Is this backed up by your results? What style do you think they use? Ask them to try out the tasks to see if you are right. This kind of thing does not have to be done formally, and can lead to energetic discussion about whether the categories are right – or what they miss out!

Share and tweet
Share your thoughts on the ideas explored in this chapter using: #BloomsCPD.

CPD book club recommendation

The Art of Coaching: Effective Strategies for School Transformation by Elena Aguilar. This book is both a guide and a personal account of being a coach which is enlivening and engaging.
(see Bibliography and further reading)

Blogger's corner

Have a look at the management mentors blog to see a business perspective on the differences between mentoring and coaching: management-mentors.com.

To do list:

- ❑ Try to reflect on your experiences of mentoring and coaching, and see if you can find examples from both outside and inside your professional life
- ❑ Browse the teaching standards. Which do you think connect to mentoring and coaching?
- ❑ Reflect on your own experience of both being a lead and a subject in mentoring and coaching. What styles have you experienced, and how successful did you find them?
- ❑ Tweet your ideas and experiences using: #BloomsCPD and see what others have said
- ❑ Read the management mentors blog: management-mentors.com.
- ❑ Read *The Art of Coaching* and consider which of the author's experiences you find most engaging

4 Getting to grips with the big ideas

Mentoring and coaching is an activity that takes up a significant amount of teacher time and so it is important that it is seen to have impact. One way of ensuring that you are having impact is by looking at the research basis for different strategies and getting an idea of how the main figures in the mentoring and coaching world go about their work.

It's important when you are thinking about mentoring and coaching not to confuse goals with practice. In other words, when you are trying to help someone become a more skilled teacher, you do not need to become expert on what it takes to be a more skilled teacher (as a coach or mentor, you should already have this skillset) instead, you need to be expert on how to coach someone else towards that goal. Of course it is important to know where they are heading and to be alert to the possible pitfalls, but the primary focus of this book is the process. This is not about giving people the answers, but about working with them so that they discover the answers for themselves.

Although mentoring and coaching is popular in schools, many of the principles and most effective practice is drawn from studies rooted in the business world. You will quickly see which of these are transferrable and which are too focused on the world of profit or loss to work effectively in a classroom context. Those which I have chosen to cover in this chapter have been selected because of their transferrable ideas – and because I have tried them out and they have worked! Many of the ideas that businesses produce about staff development are surprisingly applicable to teachers and schools. Like schools, most businesses are aware that their staff are their most precious resource, and that developing them is more effective than getting rid of them and starting afresh with untrained practitioners.

To read through all the key texts on mentoring and coaching would be prohibitively time-consuming – and as a busy teacher you don't have that time – so this chapter is designed to give you a quick overview of the key areas of research and some pointers as to further reading. If you like the sound of a study, you may want to investigate it in more detail; at other times you may decide that all you need is a quick refresher that a YouTube talk can provide. Wherever possible I've given you a video link that you can watch to quickly grab hold of the ideas.

Twitter and blogs are also good ways of keeping up to date with people's ideas about coaching. Often in a mentoring or coaching relationship, you can find yourself stuck in an impasse. Sometimes a 'quick fix' from a Twitter account can be just the thing that you need to get you moving – and at the very least can be an interesting point of discussion.

Throughout the chapter, after briefly describing the author's main ideas, I will give you some examples of techniques that have been developed from what they say. I can't recommend strongly enough that if you like these you go to the source and read it for yourself. This is a short-cut, but not a substitute for the real thing!

NFER on research evidence

Name: National Foundation for Educational Research (NFER)
Website: www.nfer.ac.uk
What to read: *Mentoring and Coaching for Professionals* by Pippa Lord et al.

Outline

This meta-analysis sought to evaluate the evidence base for the effectiveness of mentoring and coaching, using 13 different studies from schools across the UK. It analysed the challenges and the barriers to effective coaching found in different case studies.

Summary

This study collected together a number of studies so as to create an evidence base for the best practice in coaching and mentoring. It found that, contrary to expectation, new coaches seemed to be more effective than more experienced coaches. Its other findings were less controversial, but it clearly established that cultural change was needed for effective coaching or mentoring, with proper priority given to the practices established. It found that often coaching and mentoring took place in an organisational vacuum, where credit and support was not appropriately given, and that this lessened the effectiveness of any practice. Coaching and mentoring built into whole-school plans was discovered to be most effective.

What is its significance?

This groundbreaking study has been the starting point for many different mentoring and coaching programmes, providing as it does a rationale and a sense of how one might evaluate the impact of mentoring and coaching. It examines both different models (such as peer-to-peer support as opposed to expert-novice support) and approaches to mentoring and coaching where participants come from the same sector or from different sectors.

Putting it into practice

Strategy 1: New coaches are good coaches

This study found that those who were new to mentoring and coaching were more likely to report high impact. Despite preconceptions that suggested more experienced mentors and coaches would be more effective, it was found that those new to the practice were often more systematic and more diligent, as well as being more responsive to their coachees.

Strategy 2: Cultural change is key

Mentoring and coaching is not an isolated business, and in order for it to be effective, you will need to create a culture change where teachers start to feel comfortable in sharing good practice, and observing and critiquing each other. This may include making sure that there is dedicated time for mentoring and coaching, and that workload issues are properly taken into account.

Strategy 3: 'Unseen' practice needs to be identified

The research showed that although many people identified themselves as having been mentored or coached, that this was not always part of a clear programme, and that those who were providing the training were not often officially trained, or confident in what they were doing. When setting up mentoring and coaching, it is important to make sure that members of staff feel confident and supported in what they are doing.

Strategy 4: Joined-up thinking is key

It was found that mentoring and coaching were much more effective when they were linked to larger school improvement plans, or had a well-defined role in a given strategy. Linking to performance management targets, for instance, and thence to whole-school targets was seen as good practice, but was not always demonstrated.

Philippa Cordingley on working with students

Name: Philippa Cordingley, Chief Executive of the Centre for the Use of Research and Evidence in Education (CUREE)

Twitter handle: @PhilipaCcuree

Website: www.curee.co.uk/mentoring-and-coaching/effective-mentoring-and-coaching-emac-suite

What to read: 'CPDL that works for pupils as well as teachers' CPDL_that_works_for_pupils_as_well_as_TDT_OUP.pdf

Outline

CUREE draws together a number of mentoring and coaching resources to support school improvement. Now working closely with the Association of School and College Leaders (ASCL), it seeks to offer a number of proven and effective strategies for using mentoring and coaching to help with school improvement. CUREE also offers CPD resources and courses.

Summary

The overview of best practice for school improvement suggests that using mentoring or coaching can significantly help schools, as long as it bears certain guiding principles in mind. It emphasises that the most effective practice was found in schools where mentoring and coaching is highly personalised, where thought is given to the best match between mentor or coach and the person with whom they are working, and that shared objectives, and a collaborative approach are far more likely to build success than a 'top down' approach.

What is its significance?

The partnership with ASCL makes CUREE a very significant organisation, and it brings together a great deal of latest practice for school improvement. It suggests that mentoring and coaching is a key element in successful CPD, and that the conscious use of this is something that is likely to have a significant impact on teacher development.

Putting it into practice:

Strategy 5: Know the person you're working with

The research CUREE has gathered suggests that personalised mentoring or coaching is important – for the coach or mentor as much as for the person being coached or mentored – and that careful thought should go into matching up the two. Exercises designed to make you think about who you would find easiest to mentor or coach clarify what a difference this simple point can make.

Strategy 6: Shared understanding is essential

The learning suite sets out ten key principles that are seen as essential to effective mentoring and coaching, which focus on shared objectives and goals. Respect, mutual understanding and agreement are seen as a crucial foundation to any mentoring and coaching relationship.

Strategy 7: It's a two-way street

Not only mentors and coaches, but also those with whom they work need to be clear that they will need to develop certain skills in order to preserve the coaching or mentoring relationship. It is as important that learners commit to an open mindset and clear targets as it is that the mentor or coach holds to their professional standards of excellence.

Brian Tracy on eating frogs

Name: Brian Tracy

Website: www.briantracy.com

Twitter handle: @BrianTracy

What to read: *Eat that Frog!* by Brian Tracy

What to watch: Brian Tracy's webinar on 12-step method to setting and achieving goals (www.youtube.com/watch?v=eYokRtj655U)

Outline

Brian Tracy's book, *Eat That Frog!* discusses how to focus on the most important tasks that will add impact to your working day. Based on Mark Twain's saying that if the first thing you do each morning is eat a live frog then that will be the worst thing you do that day, this book encourages leaders and managers to tackle challenging tasks first and not avoid or evade them. It lists 21 key strategies that can help you to focus on achieving goals, and is helpful to use alongside a coaching plan.

Summary

This book is beloved by many leaders, because its advice is simple, effective and easy to swallow – to steal its own metaphor! Much of the book focuses on the need to organise, plan and prioritise your tasks, and have the courage to tackle them in order of challenge rather than order of perceived importance. Tracy's argument is that one's distaste for a task in fact indicates precisely the importance of the task, and the consequences of leaving it undone – as well as the likely time spent wasted worrying about it. He is excellent in terms of advice on time management and increasing effective actions.

What is its significance?

This is a classic and simple coaching text, and very effective indeed in explaining to people how important it can be to have a difficult conversation or manage time effectively. Its quick, bite-size style means that you can work with and explore one key idea at a time very easily.

Putting it into practice

Strategy 8: Tackle the hardest task first

This strategy is the key principle behind *Eat that Frog!* and underlies a lot of Tracy's coaching philosophy. Identifying the most challenging task will also, in most cases, identify the most important task, and the one which will be least effective if action is delayed. The task which has the most serious consequences if it is left undone will not necessarily be the one that you need to prioritise; conversely, time spent worrying about this task will be unproductive time, another reason to get it done quickly. Tracy asserts that in addition, the boost received from achieving this difficult task first will add confidence and vigour to your day and to your approach to other, subsequent tasks.

Strategy 9: Plan and prepare

Planning carefully for the day ahead or for a significant unit of time is time well used, and Tracy estimates that this can save the time used ten times over. Listing what you need to accomplish and then going through the list to prioritise the tasks is one of his key strategies.

Strategy 10: Focus on a single goal at a time

Another important idea for Tracy is that if you concentrate on a single thing, rather than multi-tasking, you are more likely to get that thing done effectively. Using all your energy on a single target or related set of targets, often by using an undivided section of time, is more productive than flicking around from task to task. He believes that by concentrating on a single task, and resisting the desire to be distracted through simple mantras such as 'back to work', you can reduce the time spent on a given task by up to 50 percent.

Strategy 11: The 80/20 rule

This idea suggests that out of a day's tasks, 20 percent will be more effective and important than the other 80 percent. The key to successful time management is to identify the key tasks which will be most productive and focus on them first. Prioritising in this way will stop you getting caught up in timewasting tasks that are less useful.

Strategy 12: Accept stress

Stress is a natural and inevitable part of human life, and to avoid it is impossible. Therefore it is essential not to run from stress, but to frankly approach it without fear, and find ways in which to manage it effectively. Visualising stress as excitement, for instance, will allow you to take advantage of the adrenaline produced by anxiety and make it productive, rather than allowing it to freeze you.

Strategy 13: Act like the person you want to be

Developing successful habits will help you to become a success. So pretending to be more confident than you really are, or more organised than you actually feel, can eventually mean that you end up being more confident or more organised. To start with you may feel fake, but as time goes on you will become more confident in the persona that you are projecting, until the habits you are trying to create become second nature.

Strategy 14: Use habits productively

Whatever you do repetitively has more force; when you do something again and again there is a natural inclination to keep doing it. Harnessing this natural human tendency can make you more effective – neglecting it can mean that you spend a large part of each day performing actions that are comforting but ultimately unnecessary. Spending time on low-value tasks is something that Tracy is absolutely against, viewing it as essentially damaging to the impact of your work.

Strategy 15: Manage your time carefully

Successful time management is key to working effectively with other people. Tracy advocates planning in advance (using what he calls the 90/10 rule – that is that the 10 percent of time spent planning will save you 90 percent of time thereafter when you are actually doing the job). He is especially adamant about focusing very clearly on priorities, and this is something that translates extremely well into educational coaching, as it allows us to focus on the impact of each action.

Sir John Whitmore on how to GROW

Name: Sir John Whitmore

Website: www.performanceconsultants.com

Twitter handle: @PCIntl

What to read: *Coaching for Performance* by Sir John Whitmore

What to watch: Dee Wilkinson: 'The GROW model in action' (www.youtube.com/watch?v=6f3X2PEsV-Q)

Outline

This book, though aimed at business leaders, outlines the GROW model of coaching and has many useful points for school leaders in terms of how to develop and encourage staff. It is highly practical and gives helpful examples, including HR issues as well as relationship development and team building.

Summary

The idea behind the GROW model is that a focus on the people with whom you are working is at the heart of successful coaching. Planning carefully and systematically, being realistic about strengths and weaknesses, and making reasoned choices are all important. The key idea that you may have to choose between two good things is crucial when it comes to planning a way forward.

What is its significance?

This is one of the most famous coaching texts, developed initially in relation to the basic coaching ideas formulated in *The Inner Game of Tennis* (see p. 10). It has been immensely influential and inspired many other writers and researchers, but remains popular because of its accessibility and directness. In the later editions, it has taken on the changing nature of leadership, and is less focused on a 'top-down' model, and more interested in distributed leadership, making it even more useful for school coaching work.

Putting it into practice

Strategy 16: Put people first

A focus on people is at the heart of this coaching model, and it emphasises time and again the crucial importance of communication and modelling when it comes to good practice. Getting people on board with a coaching programme is paramount in this model, and ensuring that there is a good match both in temperament and in intentions between those who work together is emphasised. The idea of being flexible and responsive to others is also highlighted.

Strategy 17: Plan and plan again

Just like Tracy's frog-eating, planning is highlighted as a key element in a successful programme. The G of the GROW model stands for establishing clear goals at the outset, and establishing exactly what you want to achieve. Clear communication between coach and coachee is essential here in order to clarify the 'route map' forward.

Strategy 18: Be realistic

The R of the GROW model stands for reality, and it is essential for success. Being clear-sighted about the difficulties and obstacles in the way of your coachee is an important principle to establish if progress is to be made. Whitmore indicates that many coaching relationships fail because of misplaced optimism, and a failure to appreciate the challenges ahead, leading to participants becoming disheartened and giving up. 'Tough love' is in effect the way forward here.

Strategy 19: The choice is yours

The O of the GROW model is for options, and the model emphasises the way in which participants need to be able to see that there is no such thing as a simple choice. All choices will have advantages and disadvantages, and you may in effect end up choosing between two good things. Being able to project forward and imagine how different options will work out can be a powerful tool in a session to help make a decision where there is not a clearly-defined best outcome.

Strategy 20: Be decisive

The W of the GROW model was initially 'will' but has also been defined as 'way forward'. Both suggestions indicate a key part of this model, which is putting oneself wholeheartedly into any decision made. Taking time to consider options can actually allow for greater decisiveness, as the time spent planning and deliberating reduces uncertainty and allows for greater commitment and determination in this key final aspect of the coaching process.

Michael Bungay Stanier on good habits

Name: Michael Bungay Stanier

Twitter: @boxofcrayons

Website: www.boxofcrayons.biz

What to read: *The Coaching Habit* by Michael Bungay Stanier

What to watch: Michael Bungay Stanier: 'Do More Great Work' (www.youtube.com/ watch?v=9PFYnDGDJqw); 'The Coaching Habit Videos' (www.boxofcrayons.biz/the-coaching-habit-videos)

Outline

Stanier takes as one of his starting points the idea that the majority of coaching is ineffective, in part because it is too ambitious in terms of what can be accomplished, and sets out grand programmes for reform. His assertion that you can coach in ten minutes a day puts good coaching practice within the reach of even the time-poor, and his habit of pointing out simple ideas and cures which – once pointed out – seem blindingly obvious makes his advice very easy to take.

Summary

The idea behind *The Coaching Habit* and the idea of doing 'great work' (as opposed to merely good work) is that habits are a powerful and often underused tool when it comes to changing undesirable behaviour. Stanier examines many ways in which traditional working habits can act against good practice, and considers ways of forming better habits, in particular through questioning that can reveal how unproductive habitual behaviour can be. His idea of 'micro-habits' – that is small but highly effective changes to behaviour – is especially useful for those working in educational contexts.

What is its significance?

Stanier is keen on making sure that people do what he describes as 'great work' rather than time-wasting and pointless work. In this he resembles Tracy in his focus on sharply picking up what is most effective. He is eloquent about how hard it can be to change learned and habitual behaviour, and his practical focus on the details of change have made his ideas very popular indeed.

Putting it into practice

Strategy 21: Start small

Stanier talks about 'micro-habits' as effective ways of changing behaviour. He thoughtfully analyses what it is that stops people from changing the way that they behave, and focuses on the difficulty of changing embedded practice, which becomes automatic, suggesting that over 45 percent of everyday practice is based on habitual actions. His suggestion is that you centre new habits around tiny repetitive changes, 'micro-habits', which help to anchor your new resolves.

Strategy 22: Ask the right questions

Stanier focuses on questions and questioning as a central part of effective coaching and effective leadership. He gives 'What's on your mind?' as an example of an open question that treads the fine line between being too broad and too narrow. He outlines certain types of key question that can open out discussions and help move on coaching that has stalled, as well as ones (such as 'What was most useful?') that can conclude it on a high. One of the most useful parts of *The Coaching Habit* is these quick-reference questions.

Strategy 23: Try the three Ps

The idea that there are three Ps – Project, People and Patterns – that can be used to structure a coaching conversation is a simple but brilliant one. Easy to remember, the three Ps can be used as different facets of a problem to explore what might be the barriers in the way of moving forward. Stanier maintains that recognition of patterns in behaviour can be a liberating moment in a coaching conversation.

Strategy 24: Shock and AWE

The idea of the AWE question – in other words, asking 'And what else?' is typical of Stanier's style. It is a small but powerful cue, moving along a conversation, picking out what is essential and what other options might exist. He cites an interesting study by Paul Nutt, which evaluated 161 decisions made in organisations (see 'Why Decisions Fail: Avoiding the Blunders and Traps that Lead to Debacles'). He found that in 71 of these the preceding thinking process was binary – that is it was simply a choice between two options. The point made is that this is a preparation process for making decisions, which is no better than that used by untrained teenagers, and has a failure rate of more than 50 percent. So briefly, asking a simple binary option (should we do this or that?) is more likely than not to come to the wrong decision. Adding in the AWE question reduced this failure rate by nearly half.

Strategy 25: Resist having all the answers

In a coaching relationship it is easy to not listen because you are secretly thinking about what you are intending to say next – and actually this can result in putting advice in the form of questions, which may be unhelpful. In a leadership position, it can be hard not to feel responsible for results, and therefore not to push forward the coaching process in an artificial way. Stepping back and letting people evaluate for themselves what are the barriers, or what is their greatest challenge not only saves time, but it also allows you to step out of the role of leader or manager.

Strategy 26: Be able to say no

Being able to choose what you are saying no to, Stanier maintains, is as important as knowing what to say 'yes' to. Especially thinking about what you are actually excluding from your plans going forward, and what this might mean. Saying 'no' can often be a problem for both coaches and mentors and those with whom they work; many high-achieving people have the sense that nothing will get done unless they do it themselves, or that they have to double-check things done by other people. It can be right that things will not be done as well if you do not do them – at first – but learning to let go and to say 'no' can also give you space to let others grow and develop.

Jenny Bird and Sarah Gornall on expressing yourself

Name: Jenny Bird and Sarah Gornall

Twitter: @JennyBird17 @CoachingClimate

Website: www.coachsupervisor.co.uk (Jenny) and www.coachingclimate.co.uk (Sarah)

What to read: *The Art of Coaching* by Jenny Bird and Sarah Gornall

What to watch: An interview with Sarah Gornall: https://www.youtube.com/watch?v=2LZHJxf4scc

---

Outline

Bird and Gornall's ideas are based on a very straightforward premise – that as experienced coaches, they often used, and encouraged their clients to use, visual representations of ideas in order to help with the coaching process. *The Art of Coaching* is a systematisation of ideas delivered through coaching sessions, presentations and lectures which explains how visual art can be an essential tool in the coaching process.

Summary

Visual ideas are powerful learning tools, and Bird and Gornall investigated how they could be used in a coaching context, demonstrating that they substantially increased the effectiveness of sessions, and the subsequent longevity of the changes brought about. The images range from simple diagrams to more complex pictures, and the process seeks to tap into the coachee's own creativity so as to create memorable focuses for progression.

What is its significance?

What Bird and Gornall do is demonstrate a range of standard coaching techniques, but show how using visual cues can dramatically increase the effectiveness. This involves, as they freely admit, some standard diagrammatic representations brought in from other sources, but also many of their own – the do-it disc in particular being one of the most innovative.

Putting it into practice

Strategy 27: What you draw expresses what you feel

We often use the language of visual imagery to express our understanding of someone else: 'I get the bigger picture'; 'I think that we can see where you're coming from'; 'Do you like the look of that plan?'. It is a relatively small step to take this forward to a stage where you literally illustrate how you see ideas developing. Research suggests that using visual imagery reduces the energy needed for processing information and allows more time for thinking in detail about a problem. Of course it is also a method that works well in groups, to break down barriers and to explore how others visualise an issue.

Strategy 28: Talk into art into writing

When people find it hard to express themselves then art can be a way of breaking down barriers. Asking a person you are coaching or mentoring to draw a literal map of where they think they are heading (with mountains, hazards, rivers to cross if you like – as well as sanctuaries and shelters) is an enormously empowering tool with which to start off a series of sessions. The initial adaptation of discussion into artwork can then be annotated with written plans, turning talk into art and then into writing.

Strategy 29: More than words can say

When working with people for whom English is not a first language – or with people who find it hard to express themselves fluently in words for whatever reason – art is a way of sharing ideas without the pressure of being accurate or articulate. Art is also something that can bring out subconscious tensions and anxieties (see the 'map' model below) in a non-threatening way. As the authors say, of any image 'its value lies in the sense the client makes of it'.

Strategy 30: The do-it disc

The do-it disc is a strategy that evolved from being denied permission to publish a famous grid organiser – thinking their way around this, Bird and Gornall came up with a more effective model. The disc is divided into four segments, one labeled 'influential and important', one 'urgent and important', one 'not *my* urgent' and the final one with 'the three Rs' of rest, review and restore. Gornall and Bird worked out that when they were performing tasks which are sometimes labeled as 'distractions' by other writers – such as answering non-urgent e-mails, for instance – they were actually taking a vital break from the process, and in the interim allowing themselves to reflect on what they were doing and refresh their thinking. The inclusion of this element in the disc distinguishes it from many other more driven models, and it can be an extremely effective way of working with those who find it hard to give themselves release time.

Julie Starr on taking time to cultivate conversations

Name: Julie Starr

Twitter: @juliestarrcoach

Website: www.starrconsulting.co.uk

What to read: *The Coaching Manual; The Mentoring Manual; Brilliant Coaching* all by Julie Starr

What to watch: Julie Starr: 'The Coaching Conversation' (www.youtube.com/watch?v=ydJsrxaW_q4*)

Outline

Starr advocates a highly collaborative and emotionally intelligent form of coaching and mentoring which can be adapted readily to an educational context.

She is interested in the ways in which relationships between coaches, mentors and those with whom they work are affected by some of the complex matters that underlie the need for coaching or mentoring in the first place.

Summary

Julie Starr's ideas focus on very practical examples and ways of improving coaching and mentoring. She is keen on establishing effective processes and in building productive relationships between coaches, mentors and those with whom they work, seeing this as the foundation of all effective coaching and mentoring work. In her eyes, systems and processes enhance this relationship, and quick fixes are to be avoided.

What is its significance?

All Starr's books are characterised by an intense practicality. They supply examples and guidelines, and lay out ideas in a form that makes it very easy to draw on them to create your own systems and processes. Although she deals with complex content, she does so in a way that makes it straightforward to understand.

Putting it into practice

Strategy 31: Coaching is like gardening

A really helpful image that Starr highlights on her blog (www.starrconsulting. co.uk) is that of coaching or mentoring as gardening. In the same way as one takes time in gardening to plan, to develop, to weed out things you don't want, and cherish those you do, so as a coach you should be a gardener. Thinking of the person you are working with as a garden where certain aspects might flower more readily than others, allows you to keep your mind on the bigger picture while working through points of stress.

Strategy 32: Informal conversations can be coaching opportunities

Not every coaching conversation has to be one which is formally set up and where time is assigned for that specific purpose. Given her focus on the relationship between coach and coachee, it is no surprise that Starr maintains that sometimes the most important conversations can take place in informal contexts – such as 'watercooler' conversations. The main point of a coaching conversation is how it makes the coachee feel – if they have a long session, but if it is ultimately unproductive then it is just so much wasted time. Conversely, a short encounter can provoke a thoughtful response – with the coachee signalling that this was significant with comments such as 'That really made me think' or 'It clarified my ideas' or 'I think I know where I'm heading now with that plan'.

Strategy 33: The mentoring map

The image of a map as a way of talking through progress in a mentoring relationship is formalised by Starr. Here, though, rather than being a way for the person being mentored to think through their pathway, it is a tool for the mentor, to explain and think through the idea of the mentoring journey. A really helpful bit of self-reflection which can also work in a coaching situation – and you can draw it as a picture if you have been taken with the ideas from *the Art of Coaching*! (pages 74–75).

Strategy 34: What's worth having is worth working for

Unlike some of the 'quick fix' life coaches of the business world, Starr is firmly on the side of taking time when mentoring and coaching. Planning thoughtfully is key, but so too is being resilient, and being prepared to deal with the difficult times. It is important to emphasise that sometimes change can only come through patience and time, and that going outside your comfort zone is a key part of this.

Strategy	Description
1: New coaches are good coaches.	You don't have to be experienced to be effective.
2: Cultural change is key.	Change has to go right through an organisation if it is to be effective, so give proper time to coaching and mentoring.
3: 'Unseen' practice needs to be identified.	Leaders should notice and value the good being done informally, and formalise it to make staff feel confident and supported.
4: Joined-up thinking is key.	Make sure coaching and mentoring is part of larger planning and performance management targets to unite effort and avoid re-inventing the wheel.
5: Know the person you're working with.	Match mentors and coaches carefully with those with whom they work; it's a key relationship and should be taken seriously.
6: Shared understanding is essential.	Buy-in from both partners about the process is fundamental to success.
7: It's a two-way street.	Both mentors and coaches and those with whom they work must be open to change.
8: Tackle the hardest task first.	What you fear doing will be the task that should not be delayed.
9: Plan and prepare.	Time spent planning is never time wasted.
10: Focus on a single goal at a time.	Work through one thing before moving on to maximise effectiveness and completion rates.
11: The 80/20 rule.	20% of tasks each day will be the most important and effective. Focus on them first.
12: Accept stress.	Stress is unavoidable; don't fear it, think of it as excitement.
13: Act like the person you want to be.	Mimic the behaviours of success to make them into habits.
14: Use habits productively.	What you do repetitively has power – don't waste time on pointless activity.

Strategy	Description
15: Manage your time carefully.	If you spend 10% of time planning, this will save you 90% of time when you do the task.
16: Put people first.	Communication and modelling is key to good practice.
17: Plan and plan again.	Time spent planning will be richly rewarded.
18: Be realistic.	Avoid misplaced optimism, and look clearly at challenges ahead.
19: The choice is yours.	Take time thinking through choices and appreciating consequences fully.
20: Be decisive.	Take time deciding, but commit to decisions once made.
21: Start small.	Micro-habits and small changes are effective routes to success.
22: Ask the right questions.	Have a few key questions to hand that will open out conversations; don't be afraid to use a script.
23: Try the three Ps.	The three Ps – Project, People and Patterns – can be used to structure a conversation around goals, who is involved, and patterns of behaviour to encourage or avoid.
24: Shock and AWE.	Never give yourself a choice of two. Always ask 'and what else?' To loosen up thinking.
25: Resist having all the answers.	Leave time and space for reflection, and don't feel you always have to know how to solve everything immediately.
26: Be able to say no.	Gain control by knowing what you can refuse to do as well as what you can do.
27: What you draw expresses what you feel.	Using visual imagery reduces the energy needed for processing information and allows more time for thinking in detail about a problem.
28: Talk into art into writing.	Talking through ideas, expressing them as art, then turning the drawings into notes.
29: More than words can say.	Art is a way of sharing ideas without the pressure of being accurate or articulate.
30: The do-it disc.	Including rest and refreshment in a model of organisation.
31: Coaching is like gardening.	Little and often maintains the coaching relationship.
32: Informal conversations can be coaching opportunities.	Take opportunities when they are offered to build a relationship.
33: The mentoring map.	Draw a literal routemap for how you want to go and where you want to get to.
34: What's worth having is worth working for.	Change comes through patient work; don't be afraid of challenge.

Fig. 7 A list of the key strategies

Chapter 4 takeaway

Reflection

Which of the different experts listed in this chapter did you think you would like to explore further? Was there something that struck an immediate chord, something you have already used, or something that you found straightaway appealing? Think back to when you have been coached or mentored. Which strategies are most like those that you experienced?

Pass it on

Sharing your ideas with colleagues outside your school setting
At the next opportunity you have, take one coaching or mentoring technique from this chapter (such as strategy 8: tackle the hardest task first, or 'eat a frog') and use it to start a conversation with a colleague from another school. Which strategy have they found most useful? Where did they find it from? Try starting a Twitter conversation using: #BloomsCPD, or start a conversation on Facebook or on the Guardian Teacher network.

Sharing your ideas with staff in your school
Instead of a 'teaching tip' at a briefing or staff meeting, ask if you can share a 'coaching tip' with staff. Choose one of the more innovative strategies, such as strategy 27 (what you draw expresses what you feel), and invite staff to use it in their next line management meeting. Ask for feedback the following week.

Share and tweet
Share your thoughts on the ideas explored in this chapter using: #BloomsCPD.

CPD book club recommendation

Eat that Frog! by Brian Tracy
(see Bibliography and further reading)

Bloggers' corner

The performance coach blog gives a regular update on different types of coaching theory and is a fascinating read! Check it out at www.theperformancecoach.com/uk/performance-coach-resources/blog.

TO DO LIST:

☐ Browse through the selected videos, and find one that you think you would be happy to share with colleagues. What is it about it that makes it helpful for CPD?

☐ Choose your own ideal coach or mentor. You can use any historical character you like. Then choose your ideal person to coach or mentor in the same way. What similarities or differences do you notice?

☐ Draw your own map of what you think it would look like to be a coach or a mentor – remember to plot the pitfalls and obstacles in your journey as well as the milestones!

☐ Go to Twitter and choose one of the people mentioned in this chapter to follow. Respond to one of their tweets

☐ Tweet your own ideas and experiences using: #BloomsCPD and see if your new twitter connections respond

☐ Read the performance coach blog: www.theperformancecoach.com/uk/performance-coach-resources/blog

☐ Read *Eat that Frog!* by Brian Tracy

5 Putting it into practice

Moving from theorising about mentoring and coaching to actually starting up a series of meetings with someone that you are intending to coach or mentor can be a big step and one that requires more preparation than you might think. Remember the 90/10 rule noted in **Strategy 15: Manage your time carefully** (page 69), and don't neglect to put more work into the planning stages than you think you might need to; it will reward you richly.

The six-part planning tool

One way of organising your time is to use a six-part process for planning and preparing yourself for your new role as a coach or mentor. This should ensure that you don't miss out any important stages, and is a helpful way, I have found, for structuring and managing the process.

1. Before you start
   - Plan your mentoring and coaching
   - Keep records of what you do
   - Establish time limits for yourself
   - Establish clear boundaries
2. Starting off
   - Be clear about expectations
   - Check your credibility
   - Establish the relationship
3. Target-setting
   - Prepare to set your targets
   - Set SMART targets
   - Create productive habits
4. Maintaining momentum
   - Ask questions
   - Use mirroring
   - Use modelling
5. Dealing with problems
   - Set interim goals
   - Address recurrent patterns
   - Address barriers to progress
6. Recognising success
   - Know when to stop and celebrate what has gone well

What follows is a detailed explanation of each stage of the six-part planning tool with references as to when you might use the strategies identified in the previous chapter.

Before you start

Plan your mentoring and coaching

Planning, as many mentoring and coaching experts will tell you, is essential if you are to use your time, and that of your coachee or mentee, productively. You need to ensure that you have marked out time for your sessions, as described in **Strategy 9: Plan and prepare** (page 68), and planned carefully what the aim is for each session. This is the kind of reflective planning that involves you rather than the person with whom you are working. It can seem slightly self-indulgent to give yourself this time, but it will save you time in the long run!

You may find it helpful to create a map of mentoring, described in **Strategy 33: The mentoring map** (page 77). This means that you work out visually where you would like to be at the end of the sessions. Using a visual representation can help you to consider possible pitfalls and obstacles realistically, and also work out what support might be available if problems arise. I once mentored someone who was a considerable artistic talent; seeing her own depiction of how she saw her career journey really helped me to keep it fresh in my mind, and made her problems and worries extra-real to me.

Be confident: remember **Strategy 1: New coaches are good coaches** (page 65) and don't lose your first freshness and enthusiasm. Nonetheless, before you start a series of mentoring or coaching sessions, and before even your first conversation with your coachee or mentee, take a little time to work out the following:

- Are you coaching or mentoring? Are you clear about the difference? If not, look again at Chapter 1 (page 65).
- What is the objective of the sessions?
- How many sessions are you planning for?
- What will be the time limit?
- What will the frequency of your sessions be?
- Will they always have the same format, or will this vary? If so, why?
- Will others be involved in the sessions? If so, who invites them?
- Are the sessions tied to any standards in particular (e.g. the teaching standards or leadership standards) that you can use to help you track your progress?
- If they are not, then how are you going to measure progress and show the impact of what you are doing?
- Are any colleagues engaged in similar activity? If so, are you going to be able to share practice with them?

Keep records of what you do

It is extremely important to keep notes on your coaching or mentoring – as much for the person you are working with as for yourself. It may sound overly formal, but often having a rough agenda for each meeting will be helpful to start things off, and this will also be helpful when it comes to keeping notes of what you have done. Be aware of **Strategy 3: 'Unseen' practice needs to be identified** (page 65). Notes on an agenda are an acceptable form of record, though they can be a little thin. Always make sure that you have more than one copy.

If you are formally mentoring someone (for instance, for initial teacher training) it is likely that there will be specific forms and procedures that you will need to follow. Make sure that you are rigorous about keeping to these. Similarly, if your school has an existing system of record keeping, make sure that you know about it, and keep to it.

If you do not have a formal format available, it is good practice to write up a brief account of the main points covered and send it in an e-mail (e-mails are indestructible – so good evidence if you need it) which your mentee or coachee can then reply to if they need to amend the account, or add to what you are saying. Make sure that your mentee or coachee is aware of this practice and is happy with it.

Establish time limits for yourself

Mentoring and coaching can both take up far more time than is initially allotted to them. Remember **Strategy 11: The 80/20 rule** (page 68) and stick to focusing on those activities that will be most productive. As both mentoring and coaching are relationship-based activities, it is easy to get drawn in and spend far more time than was planned working with someone. Of course in many ways this is good, but it is something that you need to guard against so as to protect yourself – and the other aspects of your role. Always consider **Strategy 15: Manage your time carefully** (page 69).

To do this, ideally you should plan sessions that have a clear start and end time which is signalled by the start of another activity (such as a lesson) that one of you needs to get to. You may find that you need to practise winding up a conversation, and feeling comfortable about strategies with which to do this. For instance, you might use the phrases below:

- Looking ahead to next session, what are your priorities?
- How can we best use the last ten minutes of this session? Would you like to continue with this discussion?
- Can we sum up what we've agreed today?
- Thinking about what we've discussed, what has been most useful?
- Before we finish, can we broaden out this discussion a little?
- With the limited time that we have left, what's the best direction to take this in?

I worked with a colleague once who, although delightful in many ways, had very little sense of timing, and found it hard to stick to boundaries when it came to mentoring meetings, even when I made it clear what the timings were. I actually went so far as to ask a discreet colleague to interrupt us with a reminder of where I should be next so as to bring a natural end to the session without always feeling as though I was cutting off the conversation.

Establish clear boundaries

Make sure that your relationship remains professional at all times. This does not contradict **Strategy 32: Informal conversations can be coaching opportunities** (page 76); there is a difference between a lack of formality and a lack of professionalism. It can be convenient to plan coaching or mentoring sessions to coincide with a coffee break, but be careful that this does not blur the boundaries and become more about friendship than about mentoring and coaching. If you present yourself as a friend, it is then very difficult to re-establish the professional boundaries when you need to.

In terms of communication, maintain a certain degree of formal distance. It is really tempting to give your coachee or mentee your mobile phone number, for instance, but this is simply an invitation to work out of hours, and be interrupted when you are busy elsewhere. E-mail is a far better means of communication – apart from anything else, it will require the person contacting you to formulate their ideas, or explain their problem, in writing, which itself can be a step towards solving it.

I once had a mentee who continually sent long e-mails that I found took up a lot of time to answer. Often, I would answer them only to find that the person concerned had already asked for advice from someone else, or solved the problem by themself. To cut down this process, I asked the mentee to draft e-mails to me, but not send them and then to bring them to our next session to discuss whether or how they had managed to resolve the problem without interference from me. This meant that we could have a really productive discussion, either about the strategies they had come up with to deal with the problem, or – when they had not solved it independently – to use the e-mail drafts as the basis of a discussion as to how to move forward.

Always be aware that the coaching or mentoring relationship is one that ultimately requires you to step back. You need to be prepared for when the person with whom you are working becomes independent of you, and aware that you will block them from doing this if you do not set limits to the relationship.

Starting off

Be clear about expectations

Whether you are coaching or mentoring, make sure that the person that you are working with is clear about your relationship and what you are doing in the sessions. You will need to discuss what they would like to achieve, what they need to achieve (especially if you are working towards a particular set of professional standards) and how you will both know when this has been achieved. In short, follow **Strategy 5: Know the person you're working with** (page 66).

What happens if...

I have a personality clash?

It is important to work out what lies behind a so-called 'personality clash'. Is it a difference of expectation? Are you bringing previous events to the table? Honesty is important here, and can be the basis of a real change, for you as well as for the person you are working with.

Using **Strategy 28: Talk into art into writing** (page 74) can be really helpful when it comes to these initial sessions. Asking your coachee or mentee to draw a map of where they would like to go is a productive and fun way to start a session. One way of structuring this is to frame it as a quest – to the Emerald City (*Wizard of Oz*) perhaps, or to Mordor (*The Lord of the Rings*) – and then ask them what might take the place of the flying monkeys or of the Balrog. A really pertinent question here is, 'What would success look like?' How will you both be able to tell when it has been achieved?

Another useful strategy based on the ideas of strategy 28 can be to use a series of images to ask the person with whom you are working to discuss the style of coaching or mentoring that they prefer. Collect a series of pictures as follows:

- adult holding a child's hand
- rugby team
- skydivers
- shepherd with sheepdog
- mother duck with duckling
- conductor and orchestra
- ringmaster
- green shoots of plants
- gardener pruning
- three-legged race
- bees in a hive
- someone handing over a wrapped present
- students in an exam.

Ask the person you are working with to look through the images and select the three that they think represent a good coaching or mentoring relationship, and then the three that represent a bad coaching or mentoring relationship. This is a really good way of establishing how your expectations may differ from theirs, but creating a non-confrontational context in which to do this.

When I initially used these images for one session with a small group of people who were interested in professional development through coaching, I was really concerned about the selection of images that were chosen by a quite experienced teacher. I realised that my own ideas of this teacher's competence were actually based on reputation rather than fact; the images selected suggested that he had quite a negative idea of how people learn which might lead to real problems in the classroom. Questioning and talking about the images led to a much deeper discussion about teaching and learning, and ultimately to a couple of observations (me of him and then him of me) that sparked a really fruitful line of development.

Check your credibility
Mentoring

It is important to ensure that your mentee is happy to have you as a mentor, and that they have a professional respect for you and your achievements. It may sound shallow, but if they do not respect what you have achieved professionally, then they are unlikely to see you as a helpful guide for their own professional development. Often, in a school context, members of staff do not necessarily know the details of each other's CVs. It can be helpful, as a first conversation, to talk them through your own career experiences, and how you got to your present post. In the process, you may be able to talk about a mentor and make it clear how helpful the relationship was for you.

For instance, I once worked as a mentor to someone who had come into teaching late. They were anxious about not being the same age as their contemporaries on the training course, and felt that they would not be able to catch up. When they made a comment that referenced me directly as being someone they thought had huge experience, and could not understand their anxieties, I asked them to talk me through their experience of the school, and write down all the names of the staff they had worked with closely or seen teach. When they had done this, I asked them to identify all those who they felt were real experts at their jobs. Then I asked them to see if, from that list, they could identify those who had trained straight after university, and those who had taken a career break, or who had moved into teaching after another career. They were amazed to find out how many staff, including myself, had not actually come into teaching straight after university, and reassured by the number of different routes that they could see had been perfectly successful.

Coaching

It's important, if you are a coach, that you have credibility with your coachee, and so if possible make sure that they have the opportunity to see you exercising the kind of skills that you are coaching them in. Ideally, therefore, if you are for instance coaching someone in conflict resolution, they would need to have the opportunity to shadow you so as to see you exercising your skills. This may be an activity that you need to repeat on a regular basis. Other ways of establishing this crucial respect for your judgment is for your prospective coachee to watch you working with someone else – or to see you observing someone, and to share their reflections on what they have seen.

Establish the relationship

Although it is important to maintain professionalism, it is also important that the person with whom you are working feels that you are approachable and will listen to what they have to say. Bear in mind **Strategy 6: Shared understanding is essential** (page 66) and make sure that you have shared goals and confidence in your ability to work together. To do this, you really need to get them to be prepared to open up to you to some extent. Initial ways of breaking the ice that encourage people to be reflective are easily found. Here are a few of my favourites:

- **First day at school** – imagine that you are the teacher writing a report on your first day at school. What would they say about you? What was it like for you? What did you learn? How has it been different/the same as the learning that you have experienced since then?
- **Six words** – describe yourself/your goals/your ambitions/the person you would like to be in six words.
- **Best friend/worst enemy** – if I asked your best friend to sum you up in a sentence, what would they say? If I asked your worst enemy the same question, what would they say? (I've used a variant of this as an interview question!)
- **Five Cs** – this works well in group icebreakers as well. Ask the person you are working with to write down the word or name that best reflects their personality from the five Cs list:

  1. A cartoon character
  2. A colour
  3. A country
  4. A cuisine
  5. A car

For instance, I might choose Roadrunner, Purple, Ireland, Mexican and Jeep. Make of that what you will, but it's a good basis for discussion.

- **Room 101** – named after the TV show, this asks the person you are working with to name three things/issues/problems that they would like to remove from the world altogether by putting them into 'Room 101' (the room that hides our darkest fears).

Although these kind of starters can sometimes feel a little artificial, one very important thing that they can do is to establish that this is a different space – that what you do here is distinctly different from what you do in a line-management conversation, for instance, and different from a friendly chat in the staffroom. Establishing this is an important part of starting the coaching or mentoring journey. For further ideas for icebreakers – for groups as well as for individuals – try www.portfolio-info.co.uk/ice-breakers-and-activities.

Target-setting

Prepare to set your targets

Setting targets and goals is one of the most important parts of coaching or mentoring. Remember **Strategy 4: Joined-up thinking is key** (page 65), and try to ensure that the goals are tightly tied into the school or department improvement plan. Setting targets is also one of the points where the difference between mentoring and coaching becomes most clear.

Mentoring

In most instances, when mentoring, you will be aiming to achieve an agreed career transition. This may mean that you are helping someone through their time training as a teacher. It may mean that you are working with them in their NQT year. Alternatively, you may be helping them to take on a whole-school responsibility, or supporting them in applications for leadership posts.

Whichever role it is that your mentee is seeking, it is your responsibility as a mentor to establish that this is a realistic goal, and that the time frame they are considering is sufficient for the amount of work that is necessary. It is obviously overambitious for someone in their first year of teaching to aspire to be a senior leader within a year, but it can sometimes be equally overambitious for people to move forward in their career if they have not taken the necessary preparatory steps. It can be harder for a subject leader in a small subject, for instance, to hear that they cannot move into senior leadership as quickly as the head of a core subject, as they may not appreciate the greater range of management strengths that come from that larger role. Part of what you will need to do is start from a realistic point.

It is therefore particularly important to start the mentoring process by talking through the expectations of the person you are working with, and their route towards a final desired goal. It may be that you will have to say to them that they will have to temporarily lower their sights – or that you will not be the person who can accompany them on the whole journey. It may indeed be that you will need to pass them from mentor to mentor, but you must establish what your role is, and your remit before you start.

Coaching

In coaching, your goals are equally important, but generally they are easier to define. Because by its very nature, coaching is put in place when someone needs to develop specific skills, you will often find that your coachee's expectations are fairly clear from the outset, and that they are well aware of what they need to develop.

Where this is not the case, it is often when the coaching relationship has been set up as part of a wider programme of support for someone. It can be hard for a teacher to feel that they need support – they may disagree with the judgment that led to this, or have an antagonistic relationship with the line manager who set it up – and this is something that you will need to get over before you start.

One very helpful way of working through this kind of initial reluctance is to talk through the kind of situations in which people have previously needed support – or more generally, what life events can lead to a need for support. For instance, talking about the transfer from school to university, and what support you would have wished to have then, can be a way into admitting that change is a trigger for support and does not equate to a negative judgment about someone's ability.

When setting targets, they will differ depending on whether you are coaching or mentoring. If you are mentoring, your targets will likely be long-term (for instance, to get QTS; to get a promotion) and you will need to have some interim targets, whereas for coaching they are more likely to be short-term to start with, though may be closely linked together and progressive. Whichever you do, remember **Strategy 10: Focus on a single goal at a time** (page 68) and don't try to do too much too quickly. Multiple targets needs to be carefully planned and staged if they are to be productive.

Set SMART targets

When target-setting the key idea of SMART targets should always be borne in mind. This establishes the idea that targets should always be:

- **S**pecific
- **M**easurable
- **A**chievable
- **R**ealistic
- **T**ime-limited.

An initial discussion about each element is a very good way of starting off the first coaching or mentoring session, and will save you a lot of time later. It is key to ensure that the person with whom you are working understands how to set a SMART target, or you will waste a lot of time.

Specific

A local Washington radio station had the bright idea of ringing up all the embassies to ask each ambassador what they wanted for Christmas. The UK Ambassador was a little surprised by the question, and not sure if he was allowed to accept gifts, but after some pressing, reluctantly gave a suggestion.

On Christmas Eve they broadcast the show, and he listened in increasing trepidation: 'The Russian Ambassador would like all the West to appreciate the wonderful strength of Mother Russia'...'The Italian Ambassador would like better communication between nations'...'The German Ambassador would like all countries to share Germany's financial strength'...'The Irish Ambassador wishes for peace between all countries'... Finally, the presenter concluded, 'And the British Ambassador? Well, the British Ambassador would like a small box of crystallised fruits'.

General targets are rather like general wishes, and are surprisingly popular. Sometimes people will say something like, 'I want to be a better teacher' or, 'I want to get really good at behaviour management', without really seeing how vague and hard to work with these targets are. You need to turn each target into a box of crystallised fruits.

Try looking at these 'wide wishes' and compare them to the Christmas wishes in the story above – 'I wish for world peace', or 'I wish that everyone would be nicer to each other'. Then ask the person you're working with how would they make *those* targets more achievable. What would be the first step towards world peace? What is specific that you could do to help everyone become nicer to each other? Then apply the same logic to their own targets. Specific targets needs to be both clearly defined and understood and agreed to by all involved.

Measurable

In the same way as specific targets are easier to plan with, targets that have no measure of success are impossible to succeed with – or to fail with. To say, for instance, that your target is to improve attendance without making clear exactly how that improvement will be measured makes the target almost meaningless. You may well end up with a tiny 'improvement' which is technically successful but which has not actually managed to implement the change that you really want to see.

Attainable

For a target to be measurable, it also has to be attainable. To achieve 0 percent absence in attendance data is probably impossible; to achieve 0 percent *unauthorised* absence might be. Creating milestones is one way of breaking down a big target into units that are achievable. Working on a flight path might similarly help. Make sure that you are using national measures of comparison, or comparisons against equivalent schools (easily found on the OFSTED website) to help you make targets more meaningful.

Realistic

Making sure that a target is realistic is part of working effectively with someone you are coaching or mentoring. As noted in **Strategy 18: Be realistic** (page 70), try to ensure that you are clear-sighted about the obstacles that may be ahead of you. A good way of doing this is to start a SWOT analysis (Strengths, Weaknesses, Opportunities, Threats) of the issue under consideration. This means that you divide a page into four quadrants, and write the letters S.W.O.T., one in each section. Then look at the Strengths, Weaknesses, Opportunities and Threats and make notes in each quadrant as appropriate. A SWOT analysis can be done regularly to track progress towards a specific goal.

Time-restricted

A target cannot run forever, and part of your work as a mentor or coach is to help the person you are working with see how quickly they may need to move in order to work towards their goals. On the other hand, they need to remain realistic about how much can be done in a limited amount of time. This is where your greater experience will be particularly helpful in trying to help them evaluate how long a task will take, and how realistic it is to complete a target within a particular timeframe. There is a balance to be struck here in terms of being realistic and being aspirational. For instance, to plan to complete a department improvement plan from scratch within a week risks that it would not be done carefully enough, would not have buy-in from the team, and would potentially result in a lot of burning the midnight oil. To plan for it to take a term, however, would mean that it would be out of date as soon as completed. On the other hand, to raise attendance in a research group of Pupil Premium students might be something that you would monitor every week, but would not expect to see evaluated more than once a term.

Create productive habits

When working towards targets, you may find that the person you are working with finds it difficult to change their previous behaviour. This is the time when it may help to talk about the nature of habits, and how to change them. Have a discussion about habits, focusing on **Strategy 14: Use habits productively** (page 69). Help the person with whom you are working to make a small change – such as restricting time spent dealing with e-mails – and see the value in daily repetition. Using micro-habits, as described in **Strategy 21: Start small** (page 72), is a good way of working initially. Making a tiny change, such as altering the order in which you do things, using a different colour board marker, or even wearing different clothes can start off a whole series of more productive habits in your working pattern.

Another strategy that can be very helpful when initially working towards targets is **Strategy 13: Act like the person you want to be** (page 69). Discuss things such as body posture or tone of voice, and how they affect how others perceive you. Discuss ways in which you can 'put on the clothes' of a more confident person, projecting the persona of someone successful at achieving your key targets. This works with literal clothing as well. It is interesting how powerful clothes can be in terms of projecting an image, and also how resistant people are to suggestions that they should change the way that they dress to prepare for a particular role. Several times I have encountered excellent potential leaders who either do not understand the impact clothes make, or have, as it were, ideological objections to their importance, and so will not change their manner of dress when they aspire to a new role.

One teacher I worked with was really resistant to the idea that he should start to wear smarter clothes to match his leadership aspirations, maintaining that the nature of his (practical) subject made this impossible. When I suggested that he could bring in a jacket to wear out of class, when taking assemblies and so on, he felt that this was asking him to 'fake' a personality he didn't want to have with the students, and clearly felt it was not a piece of useful advice. I left the discussion at this stage, but on another occasion, when he was wearing a smart suit for parents' evening, asked him why he felt that it was appropriate to wear a jacket for this occasion. He thought about it, and then explained that it had to do with respecting the parents, and representing the school. I pointed out that as a future leader, he might need to meet with a parent any working day, and would have to represent the school. In addition, what message would it send the children, I suggested, if he only wore a jacket to meet their parents, and not to meet them? Following our next session, when we discussed the idea further, he started wearing a jacket on a regular basis, and evolved a smarter style that he still felt comfortable with every day.

Maintaining momentum

Ask questions

Questioning effectively is a key part of running mentoring sessions, as **Strategy 22: Ask the right questions** (page 72) makes clear. As soon as you start, you will find yourself asking questions to establish the relationship, a classic 'What's on your mind?' being the ideal way of opening out a session.

Make sure that you consider carefully the extent to which you are asking open and closed questions. The idea of the AWE question described in **Strategy 24: Shock and AWE** (page 72) can be extremely useful in moving a conversation along, and directing the person with whom you are working to consider other options, and asking similarly open questions such as the following:

- What has gone well this week?
- Why did that matter?
- What would you like to have happened in that situation?
- What do you think is stopping you?
- If you weren't afraid of the consequences, what would you do?
- What are the advantages of this problem?
- Who might be able to help you and how?
- What might make a difference next time?
- How is this affecting your energy levels?
- What is your instinct about this situation?
- Is your target helping you move forward, or have you become stuck?
- Who is benefiting most from this situation?
- What are you willing to do to improve this situation?

Open questions are best for eliciting emotional responses, but sometimes you will also need to ask closed questions, about data for instance, which will demand a very different kind of response. Make sure that the session does not become simply a counselling session in which the person you are working with takes the opportunity to complain about their colleagues or the circumstances of their work, and doesn't really reflect on their own practice. Try focusing them by asking precise questions, e.g. 'What did you find most useful?', 'Which strategy worked best?' or even, 'Is this what you want us to spend our time on this week, or are you just offloading?'

One way of focusing a discussion more sharply is by using **Strategy 23: Try the three Ps** (page 72). Focusing on precise ideas, especially on patterns and what they might mean, is a good way of avoiding conversational drift, which is a waste of your session time.

Use mirroring

Mirroring is a useful strategy in the early stages of a coaching or mentoring relationship, which can help participants feel at ease with each other. It is something that people often do naturally by imitating the non-verbal signals of another person, and research suggests that it can make people more successful with job interviews by building rapport. Often mirroring occurs when someone of lower status is unconsciously trying to align themselves with someone of higher status, and it frequently goes unnoticed by both participants. Do beware – once you start to notice how you are mirroring, or being mirrored it can be hard to take it seriously. I once had a colleague who was a veritable chameleon when it came to mirroring others, and it was almost irresistible to change position in a meeting and see if he would copy you – very distracting!

However, as a coach or a mentor, you can consciously use this reaction to help support your relationship. Knowingly adopting a relaxed posture, speaking quietly and breathing slowly, can offer cues to the person with whom you are working which will help them to relax themselves. Similarly, when coaching someone in a classroom situation, suggesting that they initially mirror your stance or body language with students can be a good way of focusing them on the non-verbal signals that they are themselves sending out without realising it.

Use modelling

When working as a coach or mentor, it is important to ensure that you are modelling both professional behaviour and the good practice that you want to see. One of the important things you will need to do is remain focused on the objective of your sessions. Remember that your time is valuable, and so is that of the person that you are working with. Some informal conversation is helpful as an icebreaker, but if you do not focus on your agenda each session, soon your conversations will lose momentum and become little more than friendly chats. Don't be afraid to use very precise cues to keep on track, such as:

- 'It's good to know how your week has gone, but can we look again at our plan?'
- 'Thank you for letting me know how things are going. I'd now like to start on...'
- 'I appreciate that it has been difficult for you; can we make another time to discuss it, so that we don't use up our session time?'
- 'How do you think that links to what we have been working on?'
- 'Which target did that affect?'
- 'So why has this come to the forefront of your agenda?'
- 'Let's look at what we've worked on so far...'

When it comes to sharing good practice, remember that seeing other people is one of the most powerful tools that you can use. Ultimately your aim in school should be in line with **Strategy 2: Cultural change is key** (page 65). You are aiming to ensure that the kind of modelling that you can provide for the person with whom you are working can be provided by many colleagues, and not just you. To this end, encourage them to go and watch others teach – even for a starter or a plenary – so that they get a much wider perspective of how good practice can be varied and still be high quality.

Dealing with problems

Set interim goals

It is unlikely that you will find that your coaching or mentoring will be straightforward and easy – if that were the case, the person concerned would be able to help themselves – and so it is always worthwhile re-evaluating what you do and setting interim goals. This can be as simple as focusing on the progress of a group of three students within a class, when the overall goal is the progress of the entire class, so as to make the ultimate target more accessible.

Setting interim goals does not mean that you forget about your overarching target – far from it – but they can grant a small measure of success to the person with whom you are working, and this can be immediately helpful. Imagine, for instance, that you are trying to deal with the simple target of being able to know all the names in the class that you are teaching (a genuine target for someone I mentored). Names have immense power, and are key in behaviour management, but especially for new teachers it can seem overwhelming to have to know them all in the space of a week or so. As a result they can sometimes give up. I once worked with an experienced teacher who thought that it was acceptable to not know all the names of the students they taught by Christmas; unsurprisingly, behaviour management was an issue for them.

There are strategies you can use to learn the names of a whole class in a single lesson, but where these fail to work and the teacher is still struggling, it may be worth setting an interim target. Instead of emphasising the importance of the task, and risk making the new teacher more stressed, work out how many names they already know. The chances are they will have picked up on some as a starter. Congratulate them on this, then set an interim target that at the end of each lesson they will have learned three more new names, using them repeatedly in that lesson to target students for questioning and reward. This is not overwhelming, but by the end of four more lessons they will have 12 names as well as those they knew initially. Every time I have tried this strategy, the teacher concerned has ended up knowing all the class names before the end of the four lessons – simply because they found it easy to exceed the target of three names a lesson once they started. Interim goals often work in this way, and encourage those you are working with to experience success – the first step towards actively seeking more change. .

Address recurrent patterns

Recurrent patterns in mentoring and coaching can often mean that you will find yourself dealing with what seems like the same problem over and over again – and becoming fatigued by the apparently never-ending pattern whereby the person you are working with does not seem to learn from their previous mistakes. This can be frustrating, and unless you take steps to work with it, can lead to a lack of progress.

I remember working with someone who was wonderful at expressing verbally why shouting was not a good behavioural management strategy. She was able to clearly and eloquently explain why it was ineffective, but found it impossible not to raise her voice at students. Often she would use a rather loud and sarcastic tone of voice, quite different to her normal speaking voice, which would rile students up immediately, and then she would be dismayed at their reaction to her perceived aggressiveness. She found it hard to accept that her tone of voice was integral to their reaction until one day (with her permission) I recorded her, and played her own voice back to her. She became immediately much quieter in tone, and much more aware of how sarcasm sounded in the classroom.

Similarly, working with someone who had problems working with a specific group of girls, I noticed that when she described them she talked about them in terms which were very negative (for instance loud, whiny, whingy, bitchy), in contrast to the ways in which she talked about the boys in the same group who showed equally challenging behaviour, describing them as bouncy, funny, or lively. However, she was resistant to the idea that she was being unfair or biased, maintaining that she treated them in exactly the same way.

As a result, I spent a lesson observing and recording how often she spoke to the girls to praise or blame, and comparing this to how often she spoke to the boys in the class to praise or blame. The results showed that she generally blamed or reprimanded the girls and praised the boys, even when they were demonstrating similar behaviour. She was genuinely shocked by the difference between the two. The disparity I showed her encouraged her to keep her own tick record of questioning and rewarding on a seating plan, and transformed her relationship with the class.

One way of being less frustrated by patterns of recurrence, is to use the recurrence as an active theme in your next session. Discuss why it is that this problem is repeating. Can the person you are working with identify the pattern? Can they understand it when you explain why you see it as a pattern? At this stage you may find **Strategy 27: What you draw expresses what you feel** (page 74) very helpful. Often a visual representation of the idea of the pattern can help to find ways out of the pattern.

One helpful visualisation for this process is that of weeds in a garden. **Strategy 31: Coaching is like gardening** (page 76) expresses this well. Sometimes it is impossible to change something (especially something as integral to someone's sense of self as their attitudes towards gender, or their tone of voice) in a single session. You will need to come back to it again and again, but each time you should find the weed grows less strongly. Don't forget to concentrate on the flowers as well as the weeds!

Address barriers to progress

One of the main barriers to progress in mentoring and coaching is perceived stress. Use **Strategy 12: Accept stress** (page 68) to help the person with whom you are working understand that it may be impossible to get rid of stress. Perceiving the physical markers of stress – increased heartbeat, faster breathing, queasy stomach – as those of excitement is a powerful way of visualising away anxiety. Similarly, talking through which other situations are stressful, and how you cope with them, can help to deal with recurrent stress.

I worked once with someone who always felt anxious walking into class. We talked about other stressful situations that he encountered regularly, and he confided how he also felt anxious and guilty – without reason – if he saw a police car when driving, but then felt relieved when it passed him without any confrontation. We harnessed this experience to use the slightly ridiculous visualisation of a miniature police car driving down the corridor at school to defuse his stress. As soon as the tiny imagined car had passed, he felt a surge of relief and walked into his classroom.

One of the biggest barriers to progress is a lack of faith and a lack of confidence. It can be almost impossible for some people to believe that they are going to be able to succeed, especially if they have had a previously unhappy or unsuccessful experience. It is really important to take time when you are working with people like this. Remember **Strategy 34: What's worth having is worth working for** (page 77) and take your time to work through the issues.

Ask your coachee or mentee to talk through a successful experience. This could be anything where they have achieved something, despite an initial lack of confidence – from changing a nappy to cooking a meal – as long as it is something where they achieved success. Use **Strategy 16: Put people first** (page 70), and never forget that the person with whom you are working is a three-dimensional person with a life and an ability to succeed outside school. Use that success that they will have somewhere in their past to fuel their success in the future.

Recognising success

Know when to stop and celebrate what has gone well

An important part of mentoring and coaching is being able to recognise when it is time to back off and let the person you are working with 'fly free'. Stepping back from the relationship is a key part to concluding the process, allowing you to work productively with the next person. It is really important that you consider **Strategy 26: Be able to say no** (page 73). This is important modelling for the person with whom you are working as well. A persistent problem for high-achieving individuals is the sense that nothing will get done properly if they do not do it themselves. Watching you learning to let go can be a powerful tool towards helping the person with whom you are working to let go as well.

Often a coaching or mentoring relationship means that you are seen as having all the answers; this is not good either for you or for your partner. **Strategy 25: Resist having all the answers** (page 73) is invaluable to help you at this point. In particular, be careful about the kind of questioning that you use at the point at which the relationship is ending. Make sure that you step back, and allow the possibility of change.

Finally, always remember to use **Strategy 7: It's a two-way street** (page 67). You will find that you may change during the mentoring and coaching process as much as the person with whom you are working, and that is the way that it should be. As in **Strategy 2: Cultural change is key** (page 65), all mentoring and coaching, to be effective, should ultimately change practice more widely within the school, and that includes your own practice.

Chapter 5 Takeaway

Reflection

Which section of the mentoring and coaching process do you find most demanding? Is it the planning, the target-setting or maintaining the ongoing momentum? Think back to when you have been coached or mentored. Which parts of the process do you feel worked, and which were less successful? How would you change this?

Pass it on

Sharing with colleagues outside your school setting

Try starting an Instagram conversation using an image that you think represents good teaching and learning. You could also share this using: #BloomsCPD.

Sharing with staff in your school

Ask for a slot in which to talk about setting SMART targets with staff and students in your next staff meeting – this is especially good at or around performance management time! Make sure that all staff are clear about what a SMART target is, and how to set one. Ask for feedback the following week.

Share and tweet

Share your thoughts on the best ways to plan coaching or mentoring sessions using: #BloomsCPD.

CPD book club recommendation

The Art of Coaching by Jenny Bird and Sarah Gornall
(See Bibliography and further reading)

Blogger's corner

This Texas-based blog focuses on mentoring and coaching, and has some brilliant insights, good for dipping into: ael.education/blog/category/teacher-coaching-mentoring.

To do list:

- ☐ Select your own images of mentoring and coaching and make them into a PowerPoint slideshow preparatory to printing them out as sort cards for strategy 28 (print six to a sheet as handouts)
- ☐ Start an Instagram conversation through one of your selected images, or share it on Pinterest to start a conversation about what image might best symbolise good teaching and learning
- ☐ Ask for a staff meeting slot to discuss SMART target-setting
- ☐ Tweet your own ideas and experiences about planning coaching and mentoring sessions using #BloomsCPD and see if your new twitter connections respond
- ☐ Read the AEL education blog, and leave a comment on the site
- ☐ Read *The Art of Coaching* by Jenny Bird and Sarah Gornall

6 Evaluating progress

Evaluating progress in mentoring or coaching can be difficult. It is tempting sometimes to go for subjective evaluations – the positive feedback from a good relationship with the person you are working with is very endorsing – but of course this is not necessarily an accurate measure of progress with the original objectives. 'Soft' data is easy to come by in mentoring or coaching, but although it has its place, it is the hard data of progress and targets that is most helpful.

Consider what impact would look like for you. This will take just as much planning as anything else. For instance, if you are working on improving attendance, clearly improved attendance would demonstrate impact. But how will you measure this? What percentage point would show real impact, and not be dismissible as ordinary variation? Do you need to look at variation in previous years to give you this information? For which groups will you measure impact? Can you cut and slice the data to look at Pupil Premium students, more able, SEND, girls and boys, EAL students? What other categories would be useful? Having a plan for how you are showing impact can make the data that you gather much more useful.

When evaluating progress in mentoring or coaching, it can therefore be useful to look again at the six sections of planning in the previous chapter (page 82) and work through each, considering which have proved most challenging, and considering the below questions for reflection at each stage, perhaps RAG rating them in Red, Amber or Green to measure their success. On the one hand, you should then have the clear evidence of progress that your records should provide, but on the other, if progress is slowed or stalled, going through these questions and pointers can sometimes help to work out exactly what has stopped things moving forward.

1. Before you start

Have you effectively planned your mentoring and coaching sessions in outline?

You don't need to have planned every word of what you are going to say, but it does make sense to have a 'map' of where you are heading with the mentoring or coaching sessions. Have you written your own plans, or are you acting from someone else's template (as when mentoring trainee teachers)? Whichever you choose, you should ensure that at the root is a set of standards – usually the teachers' standards – that they draw on.

It is possible to use the outline plans of another coach or mentor who has done similar work, though, as with teaching a lesson, it is likely that as you become more experienced and develop your own style, you will find it harder to work to someone else's plans. On the other hand, if you are not an experienced coach or mentor, then a good set of plans can be really supportive; don't be afraid to ask for help at this stage.

Planning does not have to be complex, but it should be broken up into points; when reviewing, look carefully at how easy it has been to follow them, which points have been helpful and which you skimmed over. For instance, you might decide that for the first session you would plan as follows:

- Discuss reason for sessions.
- What has prompted the set-up of this course?
- How does X feel about that?
- Do they agree the sessions/objectives are necessary?
- Set up ground rules for the relationship/contact details/boundaries and establish rough outline plans and objectives.
- Look through 'map' of plans that X has worked on.
- Draw in and discuss obstacles and challenges, barriers and helpers. Try and articulate targets together.
- Work on SMART targets and talk through potential timescales.

Using this as a guide, you can then evaluate in retrospect how helpful the planning has been, as below:

- Discuss reason for sessions. *Good we discussed performance management.*
- What has promoted the set-up of this course? *Dealt with above.*
- How does X feel about that? *Dealt with above.*
- Do they agree the sessions/objectives are necessary? *Dealt with above.—but important question.*
- Set up ground rules for relationship/contact details/boundaries and establish rough outline plans and objectives. *Perhaps start with ground rules?*
- Look through 'map' of plans that X has worked on. *Better later.*
- Draw in and discuss obstacles and barriers, challenges and helpers. Try and articulate targets together. *Ok, but need desk space.*
- Work on SMART targets and talk through potential timescales. *Should have started with this.*

Fig. 8 First session evaluation

How can you check what is working well in this area?

- Look through your first plans, following your initial session, and see from your notes how far you diverged from your original idea about what would happen in the session. This is not necessarily a bad thing, but it may suggest that you need to readjust your planning.

- How realistic have you been about timings? Did the session finish early or overrun? You may find that you need more time to cover all the objectives outlined above for the first session. Your subsequent sessions should take account of this if there is a change.
- Ask the person that you are working with to tell you what they thought was the focus of the first session. Does it agree with your planned focus?
- Tick or cross the parts of your plan that you thought went well or did not seem helpful; it's a useful reference for the future.

Are you remembering to keep records of all your sessions?

Keeping careful records of your sessions is really important in mentoring or coaching; it is a way of showing that you are making progress, and something that you can use later on to reflect on with the person you are working with. You will need to decide how you are keeping records. Your school may have a template, or you may need to devise one. At its simplest, a shared e-mailed agenda can be a record, but it is generally more helpful to have a system that includes action points, interim evaluations, and points moving forward.

Do be careful how you keep records. Do it subtly, and ensure that the person with whom you are working is comfortable with your methodology and the private nature of the discussion. I once had to deal with an informal complaint from a colleague who felt that her mentor was not paying attention in their sessions as he was 'always tapping on his computer'. It transpired that this was simply his way of recording the sessions but that while he felt he was being professional and meticulous, his mentee felt that it gave a very unfriendly impression which did not help the dynamic. The mentor emphasised that it was a more effective use of time, while the mentee said that she felt that he was writing up a report for someone else and not thinking about what she said.

After discussion and some gentle mediation, where both concerns were shared, we agreed that he would instead talk with her face-to-face, and come out from behind his desk. Changing the room where the mentoring took place to one without a computer helped to manage this, and created a more comfortable environment. It was agreed that he would jot down handwritten notes in a slightly shorter session each time, to give him additional administration time, and then send an e-mail with a brief record of the session to ensure that both parties had an agreed sense of what had been covered. After this, the sessions proceeded without further trouble.

Scenario

J and K are working together on J's behaviour management skills, and part of the programme entails that he keep careful records on SIMs. An incident occurs where J feels that he did not deal well with a student's behaviour, and this is discussed in a coaching session. K remembers that J mentioned a run-in with that student some weeks earlier, but there is no record on SIMs of the incident. Fortunately K's record of the conversation reminds J of the incident and he remembers that he did forget to log it. Discussing the connections means that he realises why record-keeping is important.

Fig. 9 Example scenario

How can you check what is working well in this area?

- Do you have clear actions following each of your sessions that are communicated to the person with whom you are working?
- Have you discussed the record-keeping with the person with whom you are working?
- What sort of filing system do you have for records in general? Are you a careful, colour-coded record keeper, or a bit scrappy? A new project is the time to organise yourself, so choose a particular colour file for your mentoring or coaching work.
- Create an e-mail folder for all mentoring and coaching communications, as a way of keeping them all in one place for easy reference. If you use Outlook, you will be able to save these as PDFs and print them out or store them with minimum fuss.

Do you feel that you have sufficient time to work on your mentoring and coaching?

How have you signalled your mentoring or coaching time? Is it marked out on your timetable in SIMs or whichever electronic management system your school uses? You will need to make sure that your time is protected; alert others who may feel that they have calls on your time that you are busy in these sessions. Avoid 'time creep'. If mentoring or coaching time is on the timetable, don't be tempted to let it be nibbled away by finishing off an e-mail or arriving late from a lesson.

How can you check what is working well in this area?

- Always be sure that there is a visible clock in the room where you are working so that you are both clear about timings.
- Use the alarm on your phone as a way of controlling time management, e.g. to indicate when there are five minutes left before the end of your sessions. This is also helpful as a cue for finishing up a session – with someone who takes a while, set the alarm ten minutes before the time you want to finish, or set it halfway through to make sure you divide up the time efficiently.
- Make a note of the time that you spend on mentoring or coaching during the day, using a stopwatch or phone timer. It soon adds up – you may find it is more effective to use this time all at once rather than in dribs and drabs.
- If you have a number of tasks to do with regard to mentoring or coaching, write them in a list, then work through the list at a designated time, and record how long it takes.

Do you feel comfortable with the boundaries that you have set?

Boundaries are really important in mentoring and coaching. Even if someone is your friend and colleague (you might say, especially if they are your friend) you need to make sure that you don't overstep the line, because this will make them less able to work with you when it comes to anything that is not praise. An honest mentoring or coaching relationship relies on the ability of the coach or mentor to speak truthfully to the person with whom they are working without anxiety about the upshot. If you start off with too close a relationship this can be hard to achieve. Planning carefully, establishing the expectations of both parties and ensuring that you are very clear about how sessions are run can overcome this potential problem.

After the first few mentoring sessions, take a little time to re-evaluate how things have gone so far. Do you feel that the relationship is progressing well, or is it taking up a lot of time and emotional energy? What in the way that you are working is making you feel energised, and what is making you feel drained?

How can you check what is working well in this area?

- Do you strongly identify with the person with whom you are working, seeing them as a younger version of yourself, or of someone you know?
- Do you socialise with the person you are working with outside school? While you are mentoring or coaching them it may be an idea to limit social contact to avoid crossover.

- Have you told the person you are working with any personal information about yourself? Have they confided personal information in you? This can be a warning sign that you are transgressing professional boundaries. How is this information related to the work you are doing together?
- How have you organised the space in which you are mentoring? Be careful about the physical context as it will affect the mental space in which you negotiate, e.g. if you sit in armchairs, this will suggest it is an informal non-working space. If you are sitting opposite each other across a desk, it will suggest an interview. The best positioning is probably at right angles on two edges of a table, that way you can work or look at the same document on the table, but are not staring into each others' eyes, and it is no effort to look away for reflection without seeming rude.

2. Starting off

Have you established clear ground rules?

If you are not an experienced coach or mentor, you may find that you need to reaffirm your professional boundaries strongly, setting out clear guidelines about what is on and off limits for the duration of your sessions. Think especially about the space in which you meet, and the times at which you meet.

If you are uncertain about how you should operate within these rules, imagine that you are a doctor, and that you meet a patient who you know socially. In general, doctors are encouraged in this situation to avoid treating their friend if at all possible. Nonetheless, if this is unavoidable they will, but will take extra care about boundaries. Do the same. Imagine how uncomfortable you might feel going to the doctor about an intimate problem, and are met with chat that suggests your relationship is other than professional.

If I am working with someone I already know, I will actually introduce myself formally in the first session. It usually raises a laugh, but also makes clear the point that I am not going to bring to the session my previous knowledge about this person. A similar signalling of professional behaviour is crucial at the start of your work.

No matter how tempting, try not to arrange informal meetings after school in a café – the surroundings will immediately affect what you can discuss – and in addition it is not likely to be a confidential and secure environment!

How can you check what is working well in this area?

- Have you had a clear 'agreement' about the content and purpose of sessions? Write this down and refer back to it if you feel that the ground rules you have established are becoming unclear again.
- Use a diagram as a focus when discussing which areas are on and off limits. Talk through scenarios, asking 'What would you do if...?' to clearly establish your role as mentor or coach rather than instructor.
- Have you given the person you are working with access to contact with you that you do not give to other colleagues (e.g. made them a Facebook friend, given a personal phone number or home address)? This can blur your professional boundaries.
- How does the relationship you have with your coachee or mentee compare with other relationships that you have at work, e.g. with your line manager? Reflect and consider whether you would be comfortable with having the same kind of relationship with another colleague.
- Are you worrying about issues raised in your sessions at other times? For instance, do you feel the urge to discuss ideas continually with your partner or friends? Are concerns keeping you awake at night?

Is the person you are working with confident about your expertise as a coach or mentor?

Credibility is a difficult matter. It can be tough to establish if the person that you are working with feels confident about your competence, because the nature of the relationship will tend to mean that they are courteous and polite to you, and are unlikely to challenge your expertise. This is fine initially, but if they are to have real confidence in your ability to help them progress, then they will need to feel complete trust in your capacity to help them – and this in turn means that they value your experience and knowledge.

You may not feel entirely comfortable about sharing your expertise. This seems to me a problem that teachers often suffer from, perhaps more than other professions. Perhaps we are taught to be self-deprecating and modest as public servants, and also taught to emphasise the vocational nature of our job rather than highlight our own skills. Indeed, I remember a colleague telling me how in feedback for a job in a church school they had been told that they had over-emphasised their own skillset, and that the school felt that they were not 'modest' enough about their abilities. Not a perspective that I think they would have encountered in quite this form in a different field.

One way to open up to the person with whom you are working is to talk them through your own career. Discuss how you have come to your present position – just as though you were being interviewed for a job – and ask the person you are working with to question you about your qualifications. Once they get into the spirit of the game, you will be surprised and intrigued by what they ask.

How can you check what is working well in this area?

- Have you given the person you are working with a chance to discuss your own career path? As an ice breaker play asking 20 questions about their career, and get them to ask 20 about yours.
- Have you talked about your own coaching or mentoring experiences? From the other side of the desk, as it were?
- Talk to the person with whom you are working with about what they think constitutes an ideal coach or mentor. How close are you to what they would like, and what can you add to the discussion that they have not thought of? For example, if they say 'I would like a mentor who has applied for and failed to get a job at senior level, so that they understand my feelings' try asking them 'would it be helpful to have a mentor who has interviewed candidates at a senior level and knows reasons why they might not be chosen?
- Share your (edited) CV with the person with whom you are working. Ask them to RAG rate your experiences in terms of which areas they think will be most helpful to them. What experience have you had that you have not included in your CV, and why?
- If you have a specific qualification in a particular area that the person you are working with may not know about (for example counselling), talk to them about it, and tell them what led you to take it on.
- Ask the person you are working with to look at their CV. What skills and talents does it show that would lead them to be able to mentor others? People are often surprisingly unconfident about 'reading' a CV deeply.

Have you established a positive mentoring or coaching relationship?

Be aware that a mentoring or coaching relationship inevitably involves some intimacy, because of the nature of the work being done. Do not be afraid of this, but be conscious that you may need to reaffirm professional boundaries to be most effective.

In particular, be careful to check that what you think you have said to the person with whom you are working tallies with their understanding of what you have said. Many misunderstandings arise because, though there is good will on both sides, people have different expectations of the coaching or mentoring process. Make sure that you both understand the ground rules early on to make the relationship more comfortable.

Having a particular working space that you use for meetings will help with this – especially if you have to switch roles. As far as you can, make the room a sanctuary, so that it is a comfortable and uninterrupted place – at least during sessions. Have a 'do not disturb' notice on the door, switch off phones, and make it clear only a genuine emergency interrupts your time.

If you are working with someone who is at risk of disciplinary matters relating to performance, such as the capability procedure, for instance, or who is under pressure from other sources, then use your authority as coach or mentor to catch those pressures on their behalf. State very clearly that all problems or issues arising should come through you, and not go directly to the person you are working with. This will have many benefits, but most importantly, perhaps, will allow you both to be in the position of a protector and guide, thus creating more trust between you and the person with whom you are working – and also ensure that you have all relevant information when you are dealing with a particular problem.

What happens if...

I feel that the person with whom I am working has moved beyond professional boundaries?

Seek help from your own line manager, and identify the area where you feel that things have gone too far. Clarify your expectations with the person with whom you are working and explain the boundaries again. Emphasise that the rules are there to help them, and to ensure that they get the best out of the sessions, not because you don't want to be their friend!

How can you check what is working well in this area?

- Ask the person with whom you are working to repeat back to you what you have said to see if they have fully taken it on board.
- Check your timings – are you both arriving at sessions on time? This is an important signal of how important you find a session, so constantly arriving late creates a bad impression. If there are genuine reasons why it is difficult, it is better to change your start time to five or ten minutes later – and keep religiously to it.
- Agree the importance of sessions, and as a result enforce the 'no interruptions' and 'no-phone' rule (harder than you might think!)

- If you are concerned that the relationship is not sufficiently focused on the objectives, then ask specific questions which encourage self-reflection such as:
  - What do you think you can do to move forward here?
  - What do you think went best in that lesson?
  - What was the most useful point we discussed today?
  - What other strategies could you use to resolve that issue?
- Such questions will tend to ensure that the relationship is re-established and the balance between discussion and progress restored more equally.

3. Target-setting

Have you established clear targets?

Setting effective targets is the key to effective mentoring and coaching. A good target will act as a route map for you when it comes to moving on practice. If your targets are unclear, then you can waste a huge amount of time working away on tasks that are ultimately unfruitful in terms of evidencing progress. If you feel that there are areas that the person with whom you are working wants to develop, and they do not relate to the stated targets, then it may be time to reflect on why this is and redefine your targets.

Having said this, it is often the case that people will create 'busy work' for themselves in areas where they already feel confident, and that this is why the work does not connect well to targets. Picking up on this at an early stage is essential for good coaching and mentoring. Your job is to push the person with whom you are working out of their comfort zone – otherwise you would not be needed.

How can you check what is working well in this area?

- Look through each of the targets that you have set with the person with whom you are working, and get five different coloured highlighters, one for each letter of S M A R T. Highlight in the relevant colour each element you can find within the wording of the target. Are you missing anything?
- Use comparison when it comes to creating and evaluating targets. Try and translate them into more everyday terms, especially if you use the term 'progress' which many teachers understand or interpret differently.
- For instance, if a target is to improve the progress of EAL children in a specific teaching group, compare this to something like improving your progress around the supermarket. What would increased progress look like in this context? Picking up more items? Sticking to a list? Getting it done more quickly? Buying cheaper products? In the same way, you should be precise

about the kind of progress you want your EAL students to make. Is it to understand more vocabulary terms related to your subject? To be able to access a test on subject knowledge if you translate the test? The more precise your description at this point the easier it will be to evaluate later.

- Compare the targets that you are working with, with a set of targets that you have used on another occasion, so as to model good practice. Talk through the way in which you have worked through the milestones leading to achievement of these targets as a paper exercise.

How are you monitoring your targets?

Once you have set realistic targets, monitoring them closely is the next step. It is really important that when you do this you evaluate how they may need to be adjusted or shifted in the light of changing circumstances. For instance, you may find that a target is achieved more quickly than you had expected, and that a more aspirational target needs to be created; alternatively, personal circumstances may interrupt progress – illness for instance – which means that you could need to readjust these targets. Ideally when you target-set you would consider these possibilities as part of the target-setting process, and perhaps set a range of achievement rather than a single number to fulfil.

Monitoring of targets will require you to access some form of data, and again it is important that to do this you have clarified which kind of data will be acceptable. It can be tough if a target for progress which you have agreed to as being monitored by achievement data is then supported by student voice – however lovely that feedback, it is not the feedback that you originally planned, and you need to be careful not to accept it – unless of course you are going to decide to change your data set (which is not advisable, where you have carefully set targets in the first place). Instead, consider how the additional data can support an area, or enhance evaluation, but do not allow it to take over.

How can you check what is working well in this area?

- Be ruthless about the nature of the data that you accept as evidence of progress. Look back at the M part of your smart targets, and check that the data you are dealing with matches what you had planned. Discuss thoroughly with the person with whom you are working the data required, and make it clear why you have chosen one particular kind of data.
- Consider different ways of monitoring; for instance don't feel that you have to observe a whole lesson – it may be quite enough to observe a starter, or a plenary, or look at a particular session of group work. The advantage of this is that it does not distract you or the person with whom you are working from your precise short-term goals.

- Use data that comes from other sources – don't feel that you have to be responsible for collecting it all. For instance, it is perfectly acceptable, if you are working with someone who is concentrating on marking, to ask that some of their students be included in the next marking drop. Then the evidence can be evaluated by someone else – which is important to ensure objectivity about progress.

Have you created productive habits?

If you are not careful, mentoring and coaching can turn into a cosy chat, which although useful as a stress-reliever, is unlikely to be of good value to the school in terms of the person with whom you are working making good progress. Being organised about the ways in which you start and finish your sessions – in effect regarding them as a lesson to be planned – can really help with this. Routines and habits are, as Shakespeare so wisely said, either monsters or angels – either way they are powerful.

If you have more than one coachee or mentee, this becomes easier, as you can compare sessions, and this will tend to lead to a standardisation. If you are working within an established system (such as mentoring university students) then again you can compare with others doing the same task so as to help you be consistent.

How can you check what is working well in this area?

- Write a list of the habits that you are practising, and RAG rate them depending on whether they are productive, and time-saving, or time-wasting (make sure that this doesn't itself turn into a time-wasting habit).
- Agree which routines are important and which are not. Check these against your original plans
- Compare your sessions with others who are coaching or mentoring. Compare notes about what you do in sessions (maintaining confidentiality) to get a sense of how others use their time.

4. Maintaining momentum
Are you asking the right questions?

Just as when you are asking your students questions, take a moment to refresh your style, and check that you are asking the right kind of questions. What are you trying to achieve? You will need to change the nature of questioning as you progress through the stages of coaching or mentoring someone, moving towards their ultimate independence.

Do not fall into the trap of feeling that you need to intuitively know what kinds of questions to ask – don't be afraid of using a script like the one below to prompt you, and jog you out of your comfort zone.

How can you check what is working well in this area?

- At the early stages of coaching or mentoring, try asking questions about the goals of the person you are working with. These could include:
  - o Why do you think we are meeting?
  - o How important is it to you that we meet up?
  - o What goals would you like to focus on?
  - o Do you feel that the school's priorities are different from yours?
  - o What would be the best outcome, from your point of view?
  - o What would you identify as your ultimate objective?
  - o What would make your working life better?
  - o What three things would you change, if you could?
- In the second stage of coaching and mentoring, it is important to try and make sure that you have evaluated the situation in which you find yourself; the 'Reality' of the GROW model. The following questions may help work on this:
  - o Tell me about a time when you previously worked successfully towards a target.
  - o On a scale of one to ten, where do you feel you are in relation to this target?
  - o What have you already done to work towards this target?
  - o What worked well for you previously? Can you explain how that went?
  - o What do you think is the one thing that has been in your way up to now?
  - o What is working well for you now? Why do you think that is?
  - o What is causing you difficulties at the moment?
  - o What is the minimum that you think you need to do?
  - o What one thing could I do right now to help with this?
  - o Who in school do you think is good at _____ ?
  - o What strategies have you already tried? Why did you pick them?
- Finally, you need the person you are working with to come up with their own solutions and ways forward – moving if you like from directive to non-directive discussion. Questions that help to promote this stage include the following:
  - o Tell me how you will know when you have been successful.
  - o What is the penalty for not being successful? What will happen?
  - o Tell me how you are going to start. What is the first action you will need to take?
  - o On a scale of one to ten, how likely do you think it is that you will be successful?
  - o How can you increase your self-belief? What stops you from being certain?
  - o What is the one habit you can develop /the one thing that you can do that will help next week?
  - o Tell me what difference success would make to the way you feel.

Have you given opportunities to mirror appropriate skills?

- It is extremely important that coaching or mentoring does not become a dry, paper exercise. Whatever you are working on, your goals should of course be closely related to professional practice, so it should be relatively easy to get opportunities to practise the skills that you are working on. This may be more of a problem with mentoring, where you may be trying to develop your mentee's skills and experience in an area to which they aspire rather than area in which they are already working.

How can you check what is working well in this area?

- Timetable opportunities for skills at each session, so that you know that you are going to reflect on a piece of active practice in each meeting.
- Be realistic about what can be done in a particular time-frame – plan practice time during your session so that both of you know when it is expected to take place. There is no point in planning to mark exam papers if the students with whom you are working have not taken any practice tests for you to mark!
- Every time that you meet with the person with whom you are working, check that you evaluate whether they have had an opportunity to practise one specific skillset. Make sure that you rotate, so as to check a range of skills.
- Adjust lesson plans or timetables if necessary so as to ensure that the person with whom you are working is able to focus on a particular skill. For instance, if someone is trying to focus on their KS3 teaching, and they have limited opportunities to teach a KS3 group, see if they can do a lesson swap with a colleague to try out their new ideas.
- Make sure that you take into account whole-school issues that may interfere with your plans, and be realistic – it is not going to be popular if you demand that the person with whom you are working teaches an active lesson when everyone else is doing a mock exam.

Have you shown examples of excellence?

Modelling is a really important part of coaching and mentoring, as it allows the person with whom you are working to become more self-starting. It is especially important in coaching, as you will probably be focusing on very specific skills. It is essential that the person being coached can see these skills working before they practise them themselves. This is exactly as good practice in the classroom should be – you would not expect a student to write an essay without ever having read one (I hope) or perform an experiment without having seen a demonstration. In the same way, clear models are an important part of coaching and mentoring.

Whatever you do whenever you work with your coachee or mentee is going to be modelling good practice to them to some extent, so be conscious of this – they will inevitably look to you as an example of professional conduct. Don't fall into the trap of 'do as I say, not as I do' – one incident where you are seen to shout at a challenging student, after weeks of calmly explaining conflict resolution techniques will probably make all your hard work meaningless.

How can you check what is working well in this area?

- Have you arranged to team-teach at least once with your mentee? This is the best way to model your own practice. Make sure that you give space and time for reflection and honest discussion of the lesson.
- Ensure that you have sufficient models of excellence in the area that you are working on. This may mean, for instance, collating examples of what you consider to be exemplary marking or presentation to share more widely.
- Make your behaviour consistent in and out of a mentoring or coaching situation. Don't just 'talk the talk', but 'walk the walk'. If you are working on something with your coachee or mentee, offer to accompany them when they try it out – be there when they are next on duty, for instance, or ask them to accompany you on a learning walk around the school.
- Especially if you are mentoring, ask the person with whom you are working to accompany you to a high-level meeting or discussion that they would not normally get an opportunity to attend. Afterwards, ask them about their thoughts on the conduct of those at the meeting, so as to pick up tips about professional behaviour at that level.

How are there opportunities to practise skills?

It is extremely important that coaching or mentoring does not become a dry, paper exercise. Whatever you are working on, your goals should of course be closely related to professional practice, so it should be relatively easy to get opportunities to practise the skills that you are working on This may be more of a problem with mentoring, where you may be trying to develop your mentee's skills and experience in an area to which they aspire rather than an area in which they are already working.

5. Dealing with problems

Have you considered setting interim goals?

Interim goals are important to ensure that the person with whom you are working doesn't try to bite off more than they can chew. Breaking tasks down into smaller sections is something that both you and they must learn to do if they are to find themselves able to make meaningful progress. Considering the stages that take place before a goal can be achieved is a vital part of any mentoring or coaching conversation.

How can you check what is working well in this area?

- Ask the 'so what conditions must be met?' question when you are talking about long-term goals. For instance, if someone is hoping to achieve a post at senior leadership level as a result of your mentoring, and has a goal to be more successful in interviews, you need to talk them through how that would happen, asking the question 'so what conditions must be met by the successful candidate?'. Going backwards, you might come up with a plan that looks like this:
  o Being appointed.
  o Successful interview (skills needed evaluated from mock interview).
  o Successful completion of interview tasks (skills needed evaluated from mock interview tasks).
  o Ability to complete range of tasks/practise tasks related to areas of weakness.
  o Knowledge of possible range of interview questions/tasks (research).
  o Get interview – consolidate and contact referees.
  o Complete application form – practice and feedback.
  o Research school/find details of post (make contacts and use networking).
  o Knowledge of job market locally/nationally – are you prepared to move?
  o Decide on posts that would be accessible given skills and experience.
  o Evaluate current skills and experience against leadership post criteria.
- From this it is clear that a long time before you get to the stage of practising interviews you will need to have interim goals. Go through a similar process to set interim goals for any final goal – always ask questions to break down the stages.

Have you detected any recurrent patterns?

As you work with your coachee or mentee, you are likely to find that there are certain themes that recur again and again. These may relate to previous attempts to change practice, to a bad experience with a particular class, or to some mismanagement by a line manager. Depending on the stage of their career, you may also find that the person with whom you are working may have 'initiative overload' and be failing precisely because they feel that they have had to deal with too many new things in the past. In these circumstances, it can be felt, why bother? Everything will simply change soon enough again.

How can you check what is working well in this area?

- Questions which talk about feelings are very helpful in unpacking why certain patterns recur. If the person with whom you are working tells you something which you feel is showing a pattern, ask 'and how did that make you feel?' as a first step towards helping them to recognise the pattern.
- Other questions and comments which are useful in moving on a conversation in this context include:
  - o You seem upset.
  - o Can you remember when something similar happened?
  - o Has this ever happened in another context?
  - o What does this situation remind you of?
  - o If you had to compare this situation to a situation in a non-work context, what would it be?

What barriers to progress have you detected?

Recognising what is stopping the person with whom you are working making progress is really important. As you move on in coaching and mentoring, you will want to have discussed the potential barriers between the person you are working with and their goals. Some of these may be barriers that are outside their control, and others will be within their control, and they need to work out which is which if they are to make progress.

How can you check what is working well in this area?

Questions that may help here include:

- What barriers do you foresee to your success?
- What choices do you think you have here?
- How much control do you think you have in this situation?
- How much control would you like to have?
- What is the worst/best thing that could happen as a result of that choice?
- Who in the department could help with that?
- Who in the school could help with that?
- If you could remove one barrier, which would you choose and why?
- Explain how each barrier can be removed. Do you need help?
- Tell me what your department can do to help remove those barriers.
- What can the rest of the school do to help you move the barriers?
- Do you know anyone who has dealt with/is dealing with a similar situation?
- What would happen if you didn't change anything?
- If you could choose one thing to change about the situation, what would it be?
- Where have you already been successful? What did you learn from that?
- What could you do differently here?

- If there were no limits to what you could do, where would you start?
- What is the single thing that you could do that you think would have most impact?

6. Recognising success

How do you feed back about success or failure?

Thinking about the pace of coaching or mentoring is especially important in a school context, where the person with whom you are working may have many conflicting demands on their time. It is therefore helpful to ensure that they are not overwhelmed with feedback, so that the feedback they do have they are able to work on and absorb, and that they have a specific amount of time to work on that feedback before you give them more on the same point. This, again, is rather like working with students – there is no point in demanding a piece of work on the same topic from a student where you have not given them feedback. In the same way, if they have not had time to take the feedback on board, they will not be able to move on.

Although it is important to celebrate success, being allowed to make mistakes is a crucial part of mentoring and coaching. It is only through repeated attempts and trials that you will succeed, and if failure is seen as a negative thing, then it will be very hard to practise and improve. When talking to the person with whom you are working, make sure that you repeat this lesson again and again. Constantly reiterate the principle 'you have not succeeded YET' rather than 'you have failed'. Use other examples and inspirational quotations to help support the discussion, as below.

How can you check what is working well in this area?

- Ask the person with whom you are working to let you know what was the best piece of feedback you have given them so far. Spend a session discussing why it was useful, and what it taught them about how to move forward.
- Ask specific questions about the helpfulness of feedback, such as:
  o How did you feel about that?
  o What did you learn from that?
  o Could I have put that point in a more helpful way?
  o What did my feedback do to help you see how to move forward – or did it just leave you in the same place?
- Ask the person with whom you are working which pieces of feedback they have found helpful, and tie these to particular progress goals. If you can identify feedback that is successful then you can go back and look at this at any points where you get stuck.

- Make sure that in your sessions you identify when they will be able to work on the feedback. What are you expecting to see as a result of the feedback? What are their next steps? Have you made this clear, and how will you know that these steps have been taken?
- Instead of asking the person with whom you are working 'What has worked well this week' try asking 'What has failed this week? What has it taught you?'
- If the person with whom you are working is impatient about their own achievement rate, ask them how they would talk to a student in their position. Would they consider them a failure if they did not succeed immediately? How long would they wait for them to succeed?
- Share your own experiences of failure with the person with whom you are working. Discuss how you used failure in the past to succeed in targets later.
- Ask the person with whom you are working to select their favourite quotations from the list below. Which do they find most inspirational, and which do they find closest to their current situation? Discuss what each one implies, and which they agree with.
  - 'Whether you believe you can or you can't, you're right.' (Henry Ford)
  - 'Ever tried. Ever failed. No matter. Try again. Fail again. Fail better.' (Samuel Beckett)
  - 'I have not failed. I've just found 10,000 ways that won't work.' (Thomas Edison)
  - 'It is hard to fail, but it is worse never to have tried to succeed.' (Theodore Roosevelt)
  - 'Never confuse a single defeat with a final defeat.' (F. Scott Fitzgerald)
  - 'Only those who dare to fail greatly can ever achieve greatly.' (Robert Kennedy)
  - 'Success is most often achieved by those who don't know that failure is inevitable.' (Coco Chanel)
  - 'Success is not final, failure is not fatal: it is the courage to continue that counts.' (Winston Churchill)
  - 'There is only one thing that makes a dream impossible to achieve: the fear of failure.' (Paulo Coelho)
  - 'We are all failures – at least the best of us are.' (J. M. Barrie)
  - 'Develop success from failures. Discouragement and failure are two of the surest stepping stones to success.' (Dale Carnegie)
  - 'One who fears failure limits his activities. Failure is only the opportunity to more intelligently begin again.' (Henry Ford)
  - 'The greatest glory in living lies not in never falling, but in rising every time we fall.' (Ralph Waldo Emerson)
  - 'When we give ourselves permission to fail, we, at the same time, give ourselves permission to excel.' (Eloise Ristad)

Remember that humans are evaluative creatures

People sometimes resist evaluation because it seems remote from their everyday practice, and they think of it as being very data driven. In fact, it is natural to evaluate, so when you are considering evaluation, make sure that you try and take as rounded and creative an approach as you can so that people can see its value. Teachers, in particular, often evaluate all they do, but see this as simply reflection or thinking about what works. To make evaluation effective, you need to help the people that you are working with to see that it does not contrast with, but rather complements, their everyday practice. For example, look at this series of evaluative moves:

- You try out using picture-cards in class, and it works well because it engages your disengaged student who normally stares out the window.
- You try it again, and it works just as well the second and third time you use it.
- You have now evaluated that this strategy is consistently successful in attracting a student who prefers visual stimulus – which sounds much more professional, but is an equally valid way of describing your informal testing.
- If you then suggest to a colleague that they try it out with that student, you would be seeking to evaluate if it worked in different circumstances. Your discovery of whether it worked for them or not, would be something you would feed back into your knowledge data-set.
- You might then move on to try it with a student with a similar learning need, and you would naturally be curious about the effect. This would simply be an example of sharing good practice, and widening the scope of your evaluation.
- If you could evaluate that the strategy worked with all students with this need, it would be enormously helpful to those who worked with those students. On the other hand, if you work out that it only works with that particular student, that is equally useful data – though it might take you in a different direction.

When trying to decide on which interventions are worth their money, I insist on evaluation. I remember trying to do this for a series of GCSE interventions, and finding people initially resistant to this, saying things like 'Well' I know that it's good for year 11 students to have that one-to-one time even if it has no impact on their grades'. The answer to this, I found, was to broaden the base of what we were evaluating. Rather than ignore the perceptions of experienced staff, consider what it is you are valuing. The feedback in this instance suggested that the one-to-one interventions were felt to be valuable, so what was it that was noticed if it was not directly improved grades? I found that we started talking about things such as improved personal relationships, greater maturity, aspiration – all things that I was happy to invest in (and which would ultimately support attainment and achievement as well). Proper evaluative practice simply here broadens the base of what you are evaluating, so that we can share and reproduce what works well, and most teachers can agree to that.

Chapter 6 Takeaway

Reflection

Think about the nature of the data that you are using for evaluation, and how well you are using it. Are you simply sticking with what you know? Do you need to consider cutting the data another way to examine your impact (e.g. looking at particular groups)? Have you found a way to evaluate the 'soft' data that people so often want to discuss?

Pass it on

Sharing your ideas with colleagues outside your school setting
Try and get in touch with senior leaders from other schools in your area, and ask them to share some of their strategies and targets for staff development. If you are lucky they might share their SIPs, but even to have a discussion about your key priorities can lead you towards working together for the good of your wider community. Our local group of schools has a yearly 'Hot Topics' event where senior staff share projects and ideas about common issues, such as raising attainment and achievement for disadvantaged students. Sharing practice has improved outcomes for all.

Sharing with staff in your school
Following up from your discussion about SMART targets, ask staff to create a SMART target bank of really focused short-, medium- and long-term targets, so that they can be used as examples for other people. This could include personal performance management targets, and become a helpful template for future years.

Share and tweet
Search for 'evaluation' on Twitter and choose one of the tweets that interests you and retweet it to start a conversation using: #BloomsCPD. Don't feel you have to stick to coaching and mentoring, but broaden out your initial ideas.

CPD book club recommendation

Leadership for Teacher Learning: Creating a Culture Where All Teachers Improve So That All Students Succeed by Dylan Wiliam (Learning Sciences International, 2016)
(See Bibliography and further reading)

Blogger's corner

Look at Failure: the blog. It's an interesting read, linked to a book, which discusses how perceived failure can lead to success. Some great ideas and inspirational stories. http://www.failurethebook.com/blog/

TO DO LIST:

- ❑ Contact local schools to ask them if they would be prepared to start a sharing good practice group, or a yearly event like 'Hot Topics'
- ❑ Start to create a staff 'target bank' by sharing some of your own targets, past and present, during staff briefing
- ❑ Tweet and re-tweet 'evaluation' ideas using #BloomsCPD
- ❑ Read Dylan Wiliam: *Leadership for Teacher Learning*
- ❑ Read Failure: the blog at http://www.failurethebook.com/blog/

7 Self-evaluation and reflection

Ideally, what you have read so far will have encouraged you to reflect on and develop your own practice in coaching or mentoring. At this point, you need to think about what you have done so far, and where you are planning to go from here on in—what steps would you like to take in the future, both short term and longer term?

If you don't feel that what you do has really changed at all, then you may need to go back and consider taking on some of the suggested tasks in earlier chapters. Trying out some of the suggestions in the 'To-Do' lists, for instance, especially when it comes to further reading, is an important part of developing your own practice. If you have not taken these important steps, then the questionnaire is not likely to show you have developed. So pause here to consider before you move forwards.

How and why to complete the questionnaire

To make sure that you continue to progress in your coaching or mentoring practice, it is crucial to reflect on it. In a busy working life, it can be tough to find time for reflection, and it is tempting to think that you already know your own strengths and weaknesses. I can't recommend too strongly that you take a measured space to think about what you are doing and why you are doing it. Time spent thinking through what you do, as so many writers on coaching and mentoring say, is never time wasted. You know yourself how valuable it is for the people you work with. Just as though you were coaching or mentoring yourself, make time to muse over your own progress, and write down your perceptions and ideas, so as to come up with a plan of action going forward.

You will remember the questionnaire process from Chapter 2 (page 20), but here is a reminder.

Quick response approach

If your preference for the self-evaluation is to go with your gut feeling, then simply fill in the quick response section after each question with the first thing that comes into your mind when you ask yourself the question. Do not mull over the question too long, simply read carefully and answer quickly. This approach will give you an overview of your current coaching or mentoring practice and will take relatively little time. Just make sure you are uninterrupted, in a quiet place and able to complete the questionnaire in one sitting with no distractions so that you get focused and honest answers.

Considered response approach

If you choose to take a more reflective and detailed approach, then you can leave the quick response section blank and go straight onto reading the further guidance section under each question. This guidance provides prompt questions and ideas to get you thinking in detail about the question being answered and is designed to open up a wider scope in your answer. It will also enable you to look at your experience and pull examples into your answer to back up your statements. You may want to complete it a few questions at a time and take breaks, or you may be prepared to simply sit and work through the questions all in one sitting to ensure you remain focused. This approach does take longer, but it can lead to a more in-depth understanding of your current practice, and you will gain much more from the process than the quick response alone.

Combined approach

A thorough approach, and one I recommend, would be to use both approaches together regardless of personal preference. There is clear value in both approaches being used together. This would involve you firstly answering the self-evaluation quick response questions by briefly noting down your instinctual answers for all questions. The next step would be to return to the start of the self-evaluation, read

• I have done this self-assessment before. • I only want a surface level overview of my current understanding and practice. • I work better when I work at speed. • I don't have much time.	**Quick**
• I have never done this self-assessment before. • I want a deeper understanding of my current understanding and practice. • I work better when I take my time and really think things over. • I have some time to do this self-assessment.	**Considered**
• I have never done this self-assessment before. • I have done this self-assessment before. • I want a comprehensive and full understanding of my current understanding and practice and want to compare that to what I thought before taking the self-assessment. • I have a decent amount of time to dedicate to completing this self-assessment.	**Combined**

Fig. 10 How should I approach the self-evaluation questionnaire?

the further guidance and then answer the questions once more, slowly and in detail forming more of a narrative around each question and pulling in examples from your own experience. Following this you would need to read over both responses and form a comprehensive and honest summary in your mind of your answers and a final view of where you feel you stand right now in your coaching or mentoring practice.

This is the longest of the three approaches to this questionnaire but will give you a comprehensive and full understanding of your current practice. You will be surprised at the difference you see between the quick response and the considered response answers to the same questions; it can be very illuminating.

Rate yourself

The final part of the self-evaluation is to rate yourself. This section will ask you to rate your confidence and happiness in each area that has been covered in the questionnaire, with a view to working on these areas for improvement throughout the course of the book. The table below shows how the scale works: the higher the number you allocate yourself, the better you feel you are performing in that area.

Rating	Definition
1	Not at all. I don't. None at all. Not happy. Not confident at all.
2	Rarely. Barely. Very little. Very unconfident.
3	Not often at all. Not much. Quite unconfident.
4	Not particularly. Not really. Not a lot. Mildly unconfident.
5	Neutral. Unsure. Don't know. Indifferent.
6	Sometimes. At times. Moderately. A little bit. Mildly confident.
7	Quite often. A fair bit. Some. A little confident.
8	Most of the time. More often than not. Quite a lot. Quite confident.
9	The majority of the time. A lot. Very confident.
10	Completely. Very much so. A huge amount. Extremely happy. Extremely confident.

Fig. 11 Rate yourself definitions

Mentoring and coaching self-assessment questionnaire

QUESTION 1: What new things have you considered or tried that you have particularly liked in terms of mentoring or coaching?

Quick response:

_____

_____

_____

_____

Questions for consideration

- Have you tried any new strategies in mentoring or coaching that you have especially enjoyed?
- Have you changed the ways in which you planned or organised mentoring or coaching?
- How have the people you have worked with responded to what you have tried?

Considered response:

_____

_____

_____

_____

_____

_____

Rate yourself

QUESTION 1: How satisfied are you that you have tried all that you wanted to try out in mentoring and coaching so far?

1   2   3   4   5   6   7   8   9   10

QUESTION 2: What changes have you made that you feel have made the most difference to those with whom you work?

Quick response:

_____

_____

_____

_____

Questions for consideration

- What signs have you seen of the impact of these changes?
- What have people done differently as a result of your work?
- What did you try that went well, that you did not expect to work?
- What did you try, that you expected to work, that did not work well?

Considered response:

_____

_____

_____

_____

_____

_____

_____

_____

_____

Rate yourself

QUESTION 2: How much impact on other people's practice do you think that you have made following the changes to your own practice?

| 1 | 2 | 3 | 4 | 5 | 6 | 7 | 8 | 9 | 10 |

QUESTION 3: How would you describe your general approach to mentoring or coaching? Has it changed?

Quick response:

_____

_____

_____

_____

Questions for consideration

- Have you made changes to the way you plan?
- Have you made changes to the way your sessions are organised?
- Do you feel that you have established better routines?
- Have you found your changed practice taking up more or less time than before?

Considered response:

_____

_____

_____

_____

_____

_____

_____

_____

_____

Rate yourself

QUESTION 3: How happy do you feel with your approach to coaching or mentoring at the moment?

1	2	3	4	5	6	7	8	9	10

QUESTION 4: What theories, research, case studies or new ideas do you now find interesting, and how do they inform or influence your practice?

Quick response:

_____

_____

_____

_____

Questions for consideration

- Which one piece of research did you find most interesting and why?
- Which new technique caught your attention and why?
- Do you now feel more or less inclined to find out more about coaching and mentoring practice from other professionals?
- Have you shared any of the ideas with colleagues?
- Have you started any research of your own around coaching and mentoring?

Considered response:

_____

_____

_____

_____

_____

_____

_____

_____

Rate yourself

QUESTION 4: How confident are you about your knowledge of new research and thinking about coaching and mentoring?

| 1 | 2 | 3 | 4 | 5 | 6 | 7 | 8 | 9 | 10 |

QUESTION 5: What have you shared or discussed about coaching and mentoring with other colleagues in school?

Quick response:

_____
_____
_____
_____

Questions for consideration

- Have you shared any of your experiences with staff across the whole school?
- Have you shared experiences with colleagues outside your own department?
- Have you sought to make coaching or mentoring an agenda item in meetings?
- Have you had informal discussions about coaching or mentoring?

Considered response:

_____
_____
_____
_____
_____
_____
_____
_____
_____
_____

Rate yourself

QUESTION 5: How confident are you about sharing your ideas on a whole-school level?

| 1 | 2 | 3 | 4 | 5 | 6 | 7 | 8 | 9 | 10 |

QUESTION 6: What have you shared or discussed about coaching and mentoring with others in your department?

Quick response:

_____

_____

_____

_____

Questions for consideration

- Who else in your department works on coaching and mentoring?
- Have you worked as a coach or mentor with someone in your own department?
- Do you feel that departmental practice has changed as a result of your work?
- Have you shared any of your ideas in department meetings?
- Have you shared experiences or ideas with individual colleagues in your own department?

Considered response:

_____

_____

_____

_____

_____

_____

_____

_____

_____

Rate yourself

QUESTION 6: How confident are you about sharing your ideas at a departmental level?

1   2   3   4   5   6   7   8   9   10

QUESTION 7: Where do you feel your greatest strengths lie as a coach or mentor?

Quick response:

_____

_____

_____

_____

Questions for consideration

- What are your strongest skills as a coach or mentor?
- Do you think that these have changed or developed since the last self-assessment?
- Are there any areas that you have particularly focused on or been working to improve?
- Are there any areas where you have received very positive feedback from colleagues about your skills?

Considered response:

_____

_____

_____

_____

_____

_____

_____

_____

_____

Rate yourself

QUESTION 7: How confident are you about your coaching and mentoring practice?

| 1 | 2 | 3 | 4 | 5 | 6 | 7 | 8 | 9 | 10 |

QUESTION 8: Where do you feel that you are weakest in coaching or mentoring?

Quick response:

_____

_____

_____

_____

Questions for consideration

- What do you think are your areas for improvement?
- Have these changed since the last self-evaluation?
- Are these weaknesses that you have recently recognised, or new areas of weakness?
- Have you done anything to improve these areas recently, as a considered strategy?
- Have you read or researched anything that relates to these weak areas?

Considered response:

_____

_____

_____

_____

_____

_____

_____

_____

_____

Rate yourself

QUESTION 8: How serious do you think your weaknesses are in coaching and mentoring?

| 1 | 2 | 3 | 4 | 5 | 6 | 7 | 8 | 9 | 10 |

QUESTION 9: What would you like to try out in coaching or mentoring that you have not already tried?

Quick response:

_____

_____

_____

_____

Questions for consideration

- Is there an approach that you have read or heard about that you would like to try out?
- What has stopped you trying this in the past?
- Is there a method that you have discovered that you are afraid to try out? Why?
- Do you think that you have an area of weakness that a new strategy could help with?

Considered response:

_____

_____

_____

_____

_____

_____

_____

_____

_____

_____

Rate yourself

QUESTION 9: How confident do you feel when it comes to trying out new ideas in coaching or mentoring?

| 1 | 2 | 3 | 4 | 5 | 6 | 7 | 8 | 9 | 10 |

QUESTION 10: Is there anything else that you can think of that is holding you back in developing your coaching and mentoring practice?

Quick response:

_____

_____

_____

_____

Questions for consideration

- Is the barrier something new or something that has been present for some time?
- Have you tried to overcome this before?
- What training do you think would be helpful?
- What support do you think might help you?

Considered response:

_____

_____

_____

_____

_____

_____

_____

_____

_____

_____

Rate yourself

QUESTION 10: How much do you think you are being held back in coaching or mentoring practice?

1	2	3	4	5	6	7	8	9	10

QUESTION 11: Is there anything that you have tried in your coaching or mentoring as a result of reading this book so far?

Quick response:

_____

_____

_____

_____

Questions for consideration

- Have you discussed any theories or ideas with colleagues?
- How carefully did you try out the self-evaluation at the start of the book? Was it helpful?
- Did you try out any of the quick strategies listed in the book? Which were helpful?
- Have you got an overview or strategy for your coaching or mentoring that you did not have before?

Considered response:

_____

_____

_____

_____

_____

_____

_____

_____

_____

Rate yourself

QUESTION 11: How confident do you feel about trying out new ideas in coaching and mentoring?

| 1 | 2 | 3 | 4 | 5 | 6 | 7 | 8 | 9 | 10 |

QUESTION 12: Is there an aspect of mentoring or coaching that you have tried recently which does not work for you?

Quick response:

_____

_____

_____

_____

Questions for consideration

- What approaches have you tried that have not worked?
- What made you want to try them?
- What were the challenges?
- How long did you persist with the strategy?
- What did you find difficult about it?
- Would you be prepared to try it again? Why/why not?

Considered response:

_____

_____

_____

_____

_____

_____

_____

_____

_____

_____

Rate yourself

QUESTION 12: How confident are you about persisting with new approaches?

| 1 | 2 | 3 | 4 | 5 | 6 | 7 | 8 | 9 | 10 |

QUESTION 13: How do you know that the people you mentor or coach are making progress?

Quick response:

_____

_____

_____

_____

Questions for consideration

- How often do you pause to evaluate or measure progress?
- What do you think constitutes a successful session?
- Do you and the people you mentor or coach share the same view of what constitutes progress?
- Who do you think takes responsibility for progress being made in a session?
- Do you compare what you do with other mentors or coaches?

Considered response:

_____

_____

_____

_____

_____

_____

_____

_____

_____

_____

Rate yourself

QUESTION 13: How confident are you that the people you mentor or coach make progress?

1	2	3	4	5	6	7	8	9	10

QUESTION 14: Do you employ a wide range of coaching and mentoring strategies?

Quick response:

_____

_____

_____

_____

Questions for consideration

- Where do you get your strategies? From books and research? From conversations with other mentors? From formal training?
- How do you decide which strategy to use in which situation?
- How often do you use new strategies?
- Do you have favourite strategies that you use more than others?
- How often do you review your range of strategies?

Considered response:

_____

_____

_____

_____

_____

_____

_____

_____

_____

_____

Rate yourself

QUESTION 14: How confident are you that you habitually use a good range of coaching and mentoring strategies?

1	2	3	4	5	6	7	8	9	10

The results

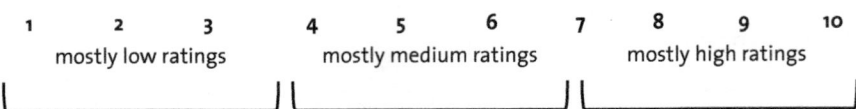

Fig. 12 How did you rate yourself?

Mostly low ratings

You surely know yourself that you have some way to go when it comes to developing and improving your own coaching and mentoring practice, but you have given an honest self-assessment, and that in itself is a huge strength. You have not yet taken full advantage of the strategies and ideas in this book, and so the impact of what you have done is limited at the moment. Remember that to be a good coach or mentor you have to take care of your own professional development, or you will not have enough to give to someone else.

Mostly medium ratings

You have tried out some new strategies, and are starting to see their impact— this should encourage you to go even further. You know yourself that there is still a long way that you could go, and that there is a lot to try out that you have not yet considered. Now is the time to give yourself that serious investment of time and attention that will make you a really expert and confident coach or mentor. You have made a really good start—don't lose heart, but press on with determination.

Mostly high ratings

You may feel confident, and with good reason, but don't stop where you are because you have got a high rating. There is no-one so good that they cannot improve, and as a coach or mentor you should be especially aware of this. Try and think about ways in which you can challenge yourself and spread your own good practice. Do you know people who struggle with their coaching and mentoring workload, while you find it manageable? Are there ways that you could support them? Is there a danger that you are complacent in your own self-assessment? What evidence do you have that your work is really successful at more than a surface level?

Now what?

It is important that you give yourself time to plan going forward for the short-term, medium-term and long-term development of your coaching and mentoring practice. A good way to start is by reflecting on what you currently see as your strengths and areas for development. Where do you feel most confident? Where are you less sure of your skills?

Once you have done this, reflect on how you have been trying to develop your practice recently. It is always important to keep track of how we develop in teaching and learning, and the same is true when it comes to coaching and mentoring. What you tried once should not necessarily be what you try always, but on the other hand, there is no point in change for the sake of change – you need to check that you are not just bewitched by novelty, but are really thinking through what you choose to change.

What are your favourite strategies, and why do you use them? What have you recently tried that is new? Have you stayed in your own comfort zone? Are you happier to use tried and tested methods than to explore the development of your own skills? Do a thorough analysis of your own practice to refresh and renew it.

When you do decide to make changes, take it slowly. Try out one or two things at a time, and take care to embed them so that you feel comfortable using them, and blending them with what you already do. There is no point in throwing the baby out with the bathwater, and getting rid of all the things that your previous experience tells you already work. New is not always better, but nor is old always valuable.

Reflecting carefully and analytically on your current practice is the best foundation for the improvements you wish to make, and the very best basis for making successful changes to what you do every day.

Chapter 7 takeaway

Reflection

Compare the tools for evaluating your coaching and mentoring with the ones that you use for marking and feedback. The processes are not so dissimilar. Do you use as rigorous practice for coaching and mentoring as you do when working with students? If not, why not? What would a 'book drop' or an observation of your mentoring or coaching practice look like?

Pass it on

Sharing your ideas with colleagues outside your school setting
Try starting a 'coaching and mentoring' group with colleagues at nearby schools. If you work with a university or teaching school to train new teachers, you will have a head start on this, as they will have mentor groups and groups for those working with NQTs. Try asking the organisation with whom you work if they would be interested in facilitating a similar group for the more experienced mentoring and coaching staff within schools.

Share with staff in your school
Meet for tea after school in the staffroom with a group of the coaches or mentors in the school or department, and bring your notes for a 'book drop'. Ask for feedback the following week. Are there any whole-school issues that can be identified?

Share and tweet
Share your thoughts on how to evaluate coaching or mentoring on Twitter using: #BloomsCPD. This might link helpfully to the discussions you started from the last chapter's tweets.

CPD book club recommendation

High Challenge, Low Threat: How the Best Leaders Find the Balance by Mary Myatt
(see Bibliography and further reading)

Bloggers' corner

This blog focuses on coaching questions, and will certainly give you food for thought if you get stuck; helpful in making you think carefully about what you actually want questions to achieve. http://www.schoolofcoachingmastery.com/coaching-blog/bid/54576/101-Incredible-Coaching-Questions

To do list:

- ☐ Ask your local University of Teaching school cluster if they are interested in starting up a group for experienced coaches or mentors to share ideas and experiences
- ☐ Try and arrange a 'coaching or mentoring book drop' by sharing notes and ideas with those in your own school, being careful to establish confidentiality guidelines and protocols before you do so
- ☐ Complete the questionnaire, and ask a colleague to try it out as well
- ☐ Use one of the questions from the questionnaire as a discussion point in the staffroom or in a department meeting
- ☐ Pursue your twitter conversation about evaluating and focus it on coaching and mentoring
- ☐ Read Mary Myatt's *High Challenge Low Threat* and consider how you can relate the ideas to your own coaching or mentoring practice
- ☐ Look at the questions on schoolofcoachingmastery.com and decide which you use already and which you should try out in the future

8

Embedding and sharing good practice

What does it mean to embed practice?

The phrase 'embedded practice' is often used by educational experts as an expression of approval, but what does it really mean? For a leader or manager, embedded practice means that they do not have to keep monitoring or watching what goes on – the practice is something taken as given, something that has become part of the way that the school runs.

You will see lots of examples of embedded practice in different areas of a school's daily life, depending on the nature of the school. For instance, uniform is a good example of a piece of embedded practice in most schools – students don't argue about wearing it, challenges are rare, they simply accept that it is a part of the unseen (or visible) contract of being at school. In the same way, in some schools there is an unspoken agreement that students will hold the doors open for teachers, allow them to precede them into a room, and so on – this kind of good behavioural practice is seen as embedded in the culture of a school with good or outstanding behaviour.

In other contexts, you might see that there are efforts going on in school that are not embedded. For instance, a school working on their behavioural policy might have to deal with incidents where teachers are inconsistent in their responses to student behaviour – either because staff do not completely agree with the ways in which the system works, or are not familiar with it – the practice is therefore not embedded. As a result, there is no consistency, and the policy does not work as effectively as it might. The gaps between policy and practice make the difference between a practice that is embedded and one that is not.

In order to embed good practice for mentoring and coaching, there needs to be certain things that are agreed as good practice, and this agreement needs to be a wholehearted one, so that people are content to follow its principles. Achieving this is harder than you might think. One of the delights of colleagues in teaching is that they are often independent-minded people – teaching is still largely a profession where you are able to work very independently within guidelines – and so sometimes there will be inevitable inconsistencies.

I would go as far as to say that it is extremely bad practice to think that you can iron out people's individuality in the name of consistency. Again, behaviour management is a good example of this. There will always be that charismatic teacher with a huge amount of experience who feels that they do not need to use the school's system of behaviour management because what they do works, and of course what they do does work – for them. Forcing them to comply with the letter of the law will simply diminish their power and authority, and reduce their confidence and pleasure in their own competence.

On the other hand, not going through the same process as someone in the classroom next door will lead to invidious comparisons, and disempower that less experienced teacher. Some would go so far as to say that a teacher who does not support school policy in this case is guilty of professional misconduct – something that they are unlikely to feel is fair. In this case, rather than being confrontational, you will find that it is more productive to open out the discussion with the teacher concerned so that they can see where their practice may actually be actively affecting others. Often this kind of behaviour is more thoughtlessness and forgetfulness (of what it is like to be a new teacher) than it is a real rejection of school policy. One really good way forward, and a way to break bad habits, is to ask them to take an active part in mentoring new staff, and explaining to them how the behaviour management system works. This can engender a new appreciation of why the rules are the rules and how they can be supportive rather than restrictive.

In a situation like this, you need to tread a fine line between your desire (and the valid need for) consistency, and what actually works in practice. This is the secret of embedding practice. If you do not accommodate people's individuality and get them to move along with you, you will never achieve that holy grail of consistent practice. One way forward is to involve that independent mind in your first discussions. Use their experience and their competence – and their incipient rebelliousness – to help you formulate your non-negotiables, the things that are most important, and then really stick to those. With other elements of practice, help them to see where you are doing the same thing under different names, or where they are actually going through routines that are really similar to the ones you want to embed. If you simply order compliance, you will spend far too much time trying to ensure obedience, and that takes you a long way away from good practice.

Mentoring and coaching non-negotiables for schools

So what are the non-negotiables for mentoring and coaching? The things that you want to ensure become as much of a part of the school routine as the wearing of uniform or the time of a lesson change? Pick carefully, because whatever you choose you will need to support and enforce. You will find that generally, less is more; selecting a few key areas to focus on will generally be more effective than trying to bring in a whole raft of ideas. Open out the non-negotiables for discussion among staff involved in mentoring and coaching. Some helpful suggestions might include the following:

- protected time for mentoring and coaching sessions
- protected locations for mentoring and coaching sessions

- a commitment to allowing others into your lessons to observe and share practice
- 'amnesty' while undergoing mentoring and coaching
- a commitment to openness and honesty in sessions
- a commitment to working on skills between sessions.

Protected time for mentoring and coaching sessions

Protecting mentoring and coaching sessions is expensive for schools; generally, an hour a week would translate into about £1000 on the salary bill, so it is understandable that many senior leaders are reluctant to give protected time unless they must. However, if mentoring and coaching is to be taken seriously, then it must be given the time necessary, and that time must not be pressured by other commitments. This is why when teachers are in training their mentor sessions are protected in their time allowance, and why universities and teaching schools that operate with trainees will insist that mentors have protected time.

In the same way, sessions must not be missed or rearranged if at all possible. It should be a given that the coach or mentor does not cancel or rearrange for anything less than illness or absence from school. Likewise, for the person you are working with, establish a clear procedure whereby there are acceptable and unacceptable reasons for cancelling or missing a session, and establish the principle that time missed should be paid back at the coach's or mentor's convenience.

A school's commitment to coaching and mentoring can be measured by its willingness to allow this time. You may need to present this idea to SLT and show them some of the evidence that demonstrates coaching and mentoring is effective – for instance the NFER research highlighted in strategies 2 and 4 which demonstrates increased effectiveness with increased buy-in from senior leaders. If finance is a problem (which it almost always will be) then encourage creative ways of dealing with this. For instance, staff who are slightly under-allocated can be used as coaches or mentors instead of being taken for cover; if the school has a surplus of tutors, then tutor time can be 'repaid' to a coach or mentor who uses one of their non-contact times; already planned directed time after school can be used for mentoring and coaching sessions instead of for meetings.

Ultimately, though, mentoring and coaching, like any form of CPD, will have a cost – explain to senior leaders that this kind of predictable, inbuilt and budgeted cost is actually more helpful to budgeting going forward than occasional external sessions which demand not only the expense of the training but also cover for a day. Mentoring and coaching in school is something where it is relatively easy to measure impact, and again this makes it good value for money.

Protected locations for mentoring and coaching sessions

The location of your mentoring and coaching is one of the things that will give it dignity and seriousness. If you are constantly having to move on or being pushed out of your usual room for a session, this degrades its importance in the minds of all involved, and sessions will not be as productive as they should be.

If you can use an office where you will be undisturbed, this is ideal. A classroom, as long as you can guarantee that there will be no room changes, is also good. Some schools have dedicated training or meeting rooms which can be booked out for this kind of purpose; if you plan to use such a room, book it out for the whole series of sessions in advance rather than working from week to week, so as to ensure continuity.

Whatever you do, do not be tempted to meet outside school for sessions, as previously mentioned, this will tend to 'de-professionalise' the process and can lead to a harmful blurring of boundaries.

A commitment to allowing others into your lessons to observe and share practice

It is almost impossible to establish good mentoring and coaching practice if people are shy and anxious about lesson observation. A 'top down' culture in schools can lead to excessive anxiety about observations, so you will need to establish firm ground rules here to make people feel protected. Set the tone by ensuring that all SLT and middle leaders are able and willing to have their lessons observed by other teachers – this is a transformational process in schools, which will immediately relax those who observe. You may find that you will not be overwhelmed by SLT volunteers; one way to get the ball rolling is to use SLT feedback from lesson observations as a starting point for 'feedback observations'. For instance, if a member of SLT observes someone and mentions that they could improve differentiation, they can be invited to ask that teacher to come and see a lesson, or part of a lesson, where they will demonstrate good differentiation themselves. As generally people comment on areas where they feel confident about their own practice, this is one way for them to open out their classrooms.

Observations that take up only a short amount of time can be extremely effective, so plan ten-minute observations as an initial strategy. Other ideas that encourage an open classroom, such as learning walks, or the 'plenary swap' or 'starter swap' (where two teachers go into each other's classes for a short time to talk to students about what they are learning, or about feedback from their homework) can also be extremely effective in shifting a prevailing culture that militates against observation.

Opening up your own classroom and leading by example is possibly the single most effective strategy for instilling confidence into other staff. Wherever possible, encourage observations. Try holding a 'golden lesson' where you invite in a number of observers for discussion of a particular point of practice, or setting up coaching trios where three or more people share lesson planning and observations between themselves.

'Amnesty' while undergoing mentoring and coaching

One reason why people are sometimes wary of mentoring or coaching, and thus fail to commit is that they see it as a process that is associated with underperformance. Don't ever underestimate how nervous staff can be at the thought that the apparently supportive process they are undergoing could turn sour. As part of appraisal policy, every school will have a capability policy designed to deal with underperformance. In many schools, this means that informal support can lead to a formalised six-week support plan and, should that fail, formal 'capability' proceedings where if they do not improve, they can be dismissed. This is something about which many teachers are worried, especially given media attention to this aspect of school improvement. Being sensitive to this anxiety is especially important if the school in which you are working has previously had a culture where staff are 'moved on' through such processes – a regrettable but surprisingly frequent feature of management in underperforming schools.

If you are committed to mentoring and coaching, then it is probably safe to say, that like Professor Dylan Wiliam, you do not believe that there are queues of outstanding teachers just waiting to come to your school, and that you would be better working to improve the teachers that you already have. You have to make sure that this vision and this belief is firmly put across to staff. You are working with them so that they will improve their practice and become even more skilled; you are not working with them as a thin mask for unfair dismissal (if you are, I have no idea why you would be reading this book).

Establishing 'safety' from capability processes while mentoring and coaching is ongoing is a helpful step in these conditions. Make it clear that while the person concerned is working and actively contributing to sessions, there is no danger to them, and they should not feel anxious about formal procedures, no matter what the situation has been before that point. Creating this kind of 'amnesty' will help to ensure commitment from staff and proper investment in the process.

A commitment to openness and honesty in sessions

If mentoring and coaching is to be effective, it has to be based on honesty. This can be difficult, especially in mentoring, when the mentor is senior to the mentee, and the mentee may wish to impress them, and not want to be wholly honest about their fears and failures. This is why working with mentors outside your own subject area, or even outside your school can be so effective.

In the same spirit, it really helps if both parties are open to honest 'critical friend' input. Establish a 'what happens in Vegas stays in Vegas' principle. What is spoken of in sessions of mentoring will be confidential unless permission is given to share it (as for instance if you are planning to go and observe someone else together because of a particular issue in the practice of the person with whom you are working), or unless it breaches safeguarding guidelines.

Do not forget safeguarding when it comes to this commitment to honesty! You may think that the guidelines you would use while working with students do not apply to teachers, but it is really important to establish that you will not keep confidential something that relates to the safety of students or staff. For instance, if the person with whom you are working reveals that they self-harm, you would need to be sure that you had not given a promise of utter confidentiality so as to make sure that they have appropriate support. That is not a burden that you should face alone.

Some ways to establish this environment in school might be as follows:

- When presenting to senior leaders about moving coaching and mentoring forward, ask them for their suggestions as to how to encourage openness and honesty – this foregrounds the idea in their minds, and will make it a priority.
- Emphasise that modelling in this respect is as important as in any other, and ask senior staff to contribute to a 'what I wish I'd said to my mentor' board in the staffroom.
- Suggest that senior staff contribute to a helpsheet of FAQs about coaching and mentoring.
- Ask staff anonymously for their suggestions about who they would like to be mentored by and why in school – the answers may surprise you. Feed back to whole staff if appropriate.
- As part of a whole-school training session, ask staff for their chosen celebrity mentors or coaches, with reasons for their choice.

A commitment to working on skills between sessions

Just as you should be firm about time commitment to the mentoring and coaching process, there should be a firm commitment to spending time between sessions working on skills, and following through the targets that have been discussed. This may seem obvious, but unfortunately teachers are very busy people, and it is all too easy to find that the focus on mentoring or coaching skips once they are away from the session and back in the hurly-burly of the everyday.

The solution to this is to not only establish the protocol and habit of gently touching on how the targets are going between sessions – even a passing comment in the staffroom over coffee can be helpful here – but also in building in the work to daily routines. It should be part of the session that you plan when exactly the person you are working with will be able to practise the skills you are working on. There is absolutely no point in saying that they will work on moderating coursework if there is not an opportunity to do this before the next session – it will simply make them feel frustrated and more likely to come up with excuses rather than reasons or better plans the next time that they are unable to do something.

Remember also to emphasise to the person that you are working with that recording their own progress, and evaluating their growing skills is an important part of their own professional and personal development. Get them to spend a little time reflecting on how they have previously made progress in a certain area, and how useful it would be to have had a more concrete record of this. Aligning this to how we develop skills in students, and record their progress, can be a really helpful thing to do. Think about discussing 'flightpaths' in skills as one way of working towards targets.

Transforming a culture

When you are trying to embed good practice, you will find that what you are actually talking about is a cultural change within school, and this may be something that is difficult to achieve. To fully embed mentoring and coaching in school you will need the unequivocal support of the SLT, and their belief in the benefits of the process. To achieve this, you will need more than an informal agreement, you may need to present to SLT and get their wholehearted, minuted consent to making this a priority.

Make sure that mentoring and coaching is not only in the budget (for the time allowances) but also in the School Improvement or Development Plan (SIP or SDP). This will mean that it is given the importance that it deserves. Ensure also that members of staff are aware that it is a part of the larger plan, and that this is reflected in the Departmental Improvement or Development Plan (DIP or DDP) for each department.

Once you have managed these initial stages, you will need also to publicise and make manifest a more 'open' culture in school. This can be as simple as having an 'open door' policy or one where doors have 'open for learning' signs that invite in observers. Similarly, you might encourage a regular 'teaching tip' in staff briefings or a 'drip feed' just before subject or year group team meetings.

Use those people in the school who are working as coaches or mentors as the basis for a TLC or Teacher Learning Community (one step on from a Professional learning Community or PLC). You can share evidence and data to ensure that you are tracking progress effectively and picking up on school-wide issues.

Establishing active rather than diagnostic listening skills

A characteristic of schools that have an active mentoring and coaching culture is the use and understanding of active listening skills as opposed to diagnostic listening skills, right across the school. One way of embedding good practice is to familiarise all members of staff with this concept, and make it accepted practice across the school. A good side effect of this is that it is a principle that is also helpful when dealing with students.

The difference between diagnostic listening and active listening has been expressed sometimes in terms of the 'Mars and Venus' visualisation that suggests an opposition of male and female ways of thought; though this is far too crude an expression for this idea, it can be helpful in quickly establishing the main characteristics. In this description, a woman shares a problem with a man, who immediately suggests things that she could do to deal with it (diagnostic). A man shares a problem with a woman, who immediately asks him how he feels about it (active).

Diagnostic listening, as the name suggests, is the kind of listening a doctor might do in order to diagnose an illness. It often happens when people are trying to deal with the repercussions of a complex situation, and someone is telling them all about it. What it means, in effect, is that they try to analyse what they are hearing as though they need to diagnose and solve the problem. In many ways it is similar to puzzle-based thinking. The impetus is towards fixing or making better the problem described, and as a result the person listening will tend to only hear properly certain key aspects of the problem, which they will sift out of the conversation. This may mean that their responses unconsciously direct the person that they are working with towards certain ways of behaving that are seen as acceptable. Responses are aimed at dealing with the perceived problem, and there is a danger that they will tend to be mechanistic and formulaic, turning the coach or mentor into an advisor with perceived authority to 'fix' problems. Questions which arise from diagnostic listening will typically be closed, able to be answered simply by 'yes' or 'no' responses, or else be suggested courses of action disguised as questions, which prompt responses that only repeat information already known to both parties.

Active listening, on the other hand, relies less on trying to locate patterns and check facts, and more on the overall picture. Its intention is to help support the person speaking, so that they become able to find their own way through a problem. It will typically listen to both what is said and what is unsaid – in other words, it will pick up emotional patterns and feelings as well as facts. Active listening, importantly, takes seriously all that is said, because all that is said is important to the speaker. It does not judge or discriminate while listening, but will typically reflect back to the speaker an overview or understanding of the emotions that are expressed. It will pick up on the details of language because how things are said are as important as what is said, and the dialogue that arises from it will typically involve open questions, inviting lengthier responses, or invitations to elaborate or explain.

For example, look at these two different responses to a comment made in a coaching session:

'At the moment I just feel overwhelmed with work, as though I've been buried under it. After the CPD session last week I felt that there are so many initiatives to work on that it just seems impossible to ever get through them.'

Response A:

- How many initiatives are we talking about?
- Are these the ones in the school plan?
- Which initiatives did you find especially challenging?
- Have you talked to your line manager?
- How do you manage your time?
- Have you tried dealing with them one by one?

Response B:

- So, it seems that you feel as though work is really suffocating you at the moment.
- Can you tell me more about the CPD session?
- What could have been done to make that CPD more supportive and less of an added pressure?
- It sounds as though things at work have changed for you recently.
- Is there anything else that you can think of which has changed that might be having an impact on how you feel?

It is immediately evident how the active response B opens out the discussion more than the diagnostic comments in response A. This is not to say that diagnostic comments don't have their place; there will be times when you may need to ask those kind of questions – or more realistically a mixture of diagnostic and active questions – but a school whose staff are taught about active listening feels like a very different place.

Running a student-led project

Embedding any excellent practice in schools ultimately means getting students to completely understand that practice. The mindset that allows a teaching and learning-led culture in schools and encourages mentoring and coaching for the staff body will inevitably lead to work with students which mimics this kind of interest in improvement.

If you think about the ideal conditions for mentoring and coaching in terms of frequency and commitment, then many of these are met by normal teaching. Whenever we work with students, we have the opportunity to use coaching methods in order to help them improve their performance. There are some subjects that naturally use these strategies – sport and performing arts being the most obvious – but best practice in many subject areas relies on what are effectively coaching strategies, and schools that are dedicated to school improvement typically use peer mentors to encourage high aspirations for all. Working with students is therefore a natural next step for those who have themselves been coached or mentored.

Student coaching

Working with a group of students in class, aiming to improve their specific skills, means that you already have the outline of a coaching session in every lesson. One way of making this very evident to the students themselves is to teach them about the GROW model of coaching (page 69), and encourage them to come up with their own goals for a module of work. Going carefully through the possible ways in which they could achieve a desired goal, the reality of the situation they are in, and the potential difficulties they may face will often engage students in a particularly powerful way. If you simply give students an outline of what you want to achieve and then ask them how they think they can best achieve it, it is surprising how rigorous their suggestions are.

When coaching students, try sharing planning with them. I remember once teaching a challenging group of Year 10 students a Shakespeare play in preparation for a controlled assessment, as part of a trial of coaching strategies. Having finished the basic course, I opened out the lesson planning to them for the last few weeks before they took the test, asking them how they wanted to consolidate their work and revise, and how they would advise me to teach them to achieve the best results. I said that they could choose any methodology they wished, but that it would need to be focused on their ultimate goals, and take account of the learning of everyone in the class.

I anticipated I would simply get requests to watch films, but instead I found that the students became very focused on the variety of means that I might use to help them, ranging from close textual analysis to drawings, rote learning, and acting out sections of the play. Giving them autonomy over their work led to them making some powerful choices, which they then seriously invested in, meaning that the work in those weeks was especially productive. One of the most interesting things was how they relished looking at where each lesson fit into our overall plan, marking out where we had got to, and how the lesson that day related to their initial suggestions.

This strategy is now one that I use regularly, particularly coming up to an exam or test. Giving students the chance to reflect on their own learning before a test, and to plan what help they need to consolidate it, is a statement of your confidence in them and in their judgement. Allowing them the autonomy to pick their own 'route map' means that they are inevitably more invested in the results.

Another way to do this kind of coaching is to share with students at the start of a module the test that they will have to take at the end of it. Looking at the test, and learning the answers to it, is far more inviting than traditional lesson objectives, and has the unmistakable illicit lure of 'cheating' by looking ahead. It is interesting when we think how as adults we prepare for any kind of test – being very careful to know exactly what it will involve before we start our learning – that this is a routine we often deny children. Dylan Wiliam (in *Inside the Black Box* and in many other speeches and articles) has well documented how effective it is to ask students to create questions on a topic as a way of revising. As the creation of a question involves finding out its answer, this strengthens their knowledge in a much more engaging way than a traditional test. In the same way, giving students a test and asking them what they think they will need to know to pass it allows them to help to plan their own lessons.

In the same way, effective differentiation for students is really a form of coaching. Identifying where students with particular needs require more help when working on a particular skill is exactly what a good coach does, and devising ways in which to help that students practise that skill is simply good differentiation. Thinking of learning in this way is often engaging for students, because from sport and music they are familiar with the idea of how repetition and practice can improve performance.

Quick ideas for student coaching strategies in lessons:

- Students who lack literacy skills, for instance, who will resist the idea of being helped by a TA, will often respond more positively to the idea that someone already in the class can coach them in a skill such as effective punctuation.
- Ask students to select an effective coach for themselves – you may be surprised at who they pick, and how alert they are to others' skills.
- Create a system of 'coaching trios' where students who are coached in one skill become the coaches for another.
- Plan special 'coaching sessions' with experts on a particular skill located on a particular table, and other students free to move around the room for one half of the lesson, then reverse the system for the second half so that those who were coached become the coaches.
- Ask students to peer-mark work in groups, selecting specific criteria, before selecting a coach based on the skills that they have seen that match the skills they need to enhance.
- When working on handwriting and presentation, give students a range of books and get them to analyse what features make writing legible and clear as a way to setting up goals for themselves.
- Allow students to pick a task from a variety that you have devised to reinforce a particular skill – give them a choice of between four or five tasks to select.
- Use coaching metaphors such as 'match fit', 'building stamina', 'reliable aim' to make connections between sport and the methodology of curriculum work.

Student mentoring

Peer-to-peer mentoring using students is one of the most popular school improvement strategies, because it works. Mentors do not necessarily have to be much older or a great deal more competent than those with whom they work; you will be amazed by how effective mentors even within a year group will be. What they do have to be is to some extent aspirational. This can be a Year 4 student helping a Year 2 student with times tables, or with a sixth-former talking to a Year 9 student about options choices; in whatever context you use mentors, like adult mentors, they will be asking the people they work with to think about their next steps and how they can improve their life chances by what they choose to do.

What is most important in peer-to peer mentoring is that the mentors are trained; they need to be aware of the professional and safeguarding boundaries around working with other children, and this is true even if the mentors themselves are of primary school age. Especially if they are older, they will need to be careful to be age-appropriate in their conversations, and able to resist the temptation to become out-of-school friends where that is not a part of the planned interventions (sometimes you can have mentors working out of school with children, but it is rarely a good idea to do this with student mentors – it works with adult mentors only in carefully-controlled circumstances). They will need to be warned, for instance, not to become Facebook friends with their mentees, or exchange mobile numbers with them, while they are working on the project.

Even when you are doing fairly small-scale mentoring, such as the mentoring of Year 10 maths students by Year 11 in a breakfast club, you will need to provide this kind of initial training. Whatever you do, do not neglect this. It is really important that students are aware that they are to some extent role models for their mentees, and so their behaviour and their approach to their mentoring work has to be as professional as possible.

Quick ideas for student mentoring strategies in schools:

- Train sixth-formers to be mentors to Year 7 students. In sixth form, students will be able to deal with quite a range of behaviours, and if you are selective about who you choose, then it will become a prestigious activity – and one that is great for UCAS forms or CVs. Students can work with form tutors or even TAs in classes in their free lessons.
- Use successful applicants for university from your own school to return and talk to your sixth-formers and Year 11 students, and tell them about university life and the application process.
- If students in a KS3 class are showing challenging behaviour and need to be removed from class, get them to work in a sixth-form lesson.
- Ask students who lack reading confidence in Year 10 or 11 to work with Year 7 students who have not managed to achieve expected levels. Their reading skills may not be stellar, but they will be way ahead of the Year 7 students, and confidence will be created in both parties as a result. Very able readers may intimidate those who struggle.
- Get Year 8 students to welcome new Year 7 students and 'buddy' them at break time and lunchtime. Carefully choose students to support the most vulnerable, and train them before September so that they have a clear sense of the school's expectations for the new Year 7. Year 8 tend to be much stricter than teachers, but much more listened to!
- If you have an isolation room, create a peaceful area to one side, nicely decorated, where staff or sixth-formers can work quietly. This makes an immediate difference to the restlessness that you can get in such rooms, and gives a terrific model of what serious silent work looks like.

- Use sixth-formers to mentor students in Year 10 or 11 for reading for pleasure. Encourage them to set up a 'book club' or 'reading tree' to share online written reviews of books, and link it to the books in the library.
- Get sixth-formers who have had to retake maths or English to work with lower sets in both subjects. It is a big confidence boost for them, and they will be sharp on exam strategies for other students.

Chapter 8 takeaway

Reflection

Write an imaginary OFSTED report for your school, which focuses on its use of mentoring and coaching. How might they comment on what you now do? How would you like them to comment? How does it involve student mentoring and coaching?

Pass it on

Sharing with colleagues outside your school setting

Try linking with other schools that use peer-mentoring or coaching and asking them to share strategies or training. You could share the ideas you come up with using: #BloomsCPD.

Sharing with staff in your school

Work with your student council to discuss the potential for student mentoring. Ask the students to think about the context in which it might be useful and the ways in which it could be used to advance existing strategies for student voice.

Share and tweet

Share your thoughts on the ideas explored in this Chapter using: #BloomsCPD.

CPD book club recommendation

Peter J. Collier, *Developing Effective Student Peer Mentoring Programs* or Teresa Bliss et al., *Transition: A Peer Mentoring System* (see Bibliography and further reading)

Blogger's corner

Check out Peter Collier's blog on peer mentoring and coaching for older students; he gives some interesting advice – mainly aimed at programmes involving older students. It is well worth a read. Visit: drpeterjcollier.com/blog.

TO DO LIST:

❏ Create a survey monkey survey for staff to see how far good practice is embedded in your school, and help with your 'OFSTED' reflection. What would they agree are the 'non-negotiables' in current school practice?

❏ Use one of your 'golden lessons' to publicise the idea of student coaching in lessons as a strategy

❏ Meet with your school council to canvass their ideas about peer mentoring

❏ Go to Twitter and search for 'peer coaching' or 'peer mentoring'. Choose one of the tweets that interests you and retweet it to start a conversation

❏ Tweet your own ideas and experiences of peer coaching and mentoring using: #BloomsCPD

❏ Have a read of Peter Collier's blog: drpeterjcollier.com/blog

❏ Read Teresa Bliss et al., *Transition: A Peer Mentoring System*

Part 2

Train others

1

Planning and preparing for your training

Having read the first part of this book, you will perhaps already have been thinking about ways in which you can develop a mentoring and coaching mindset in your school. Mentoring and coaching are both such powerful tools for school improvement that it is rare to read about a transformational school that has not used them both as a key element in enhancing performance.

Developing this way of thinking, as a whole-school priority, is not something that you can do by yourself – you will need to have a focused and well-planned process of CPD to drive the change. You may already know, or suspect you know, some of the key players going forward amongst your staff; really effective CPD will allow you not only to use these existing experts to drive change, but to release the untapped resources that exist among the rest of your staff.

'That is the best INSET I've had in twenty years of teaching.'
(Comment by subject leader after teacher-led in-house training)

To have a whole-school mentoring and coaching environment to support your mentors and coaches and really develop staff in a positive way will immeasurably increase the effectiveness of what individuals can do. In the resources that follow, you will be able to choose from a range of possible ways of introducing this – from whole-school training to twilight sessions for small groups. Whichever you choose, planning carefully and reflecting on your CPD needs are your route to success. Whether you are in charge of organising whole-school training, responsible for an element of it, or only looking for a way to develop yourself as a more expert trainer, what follows should help you to establish your plans more confidently.

The need for CPD

'I've never been on an external course that genuinely taught me something I wanted to know or didn't already know – I think that's really sad, and a waste of school money.' (Science teacher)

The quality and effectiveness of CPD is a much-vexed question among educationalists, and before you start you should be confident about your vision for training and where you want it to take you. In John Hattie's synthesis *Visible Learning*, he tried to analyse which of the practices routinely performed in schools actually contributed most to student progress. CPD essentially came out well from this study, with a large effect size of 0.62 on pupil achievements, putting it in the top 20 of analysed methods for improving schools. However, although every school has an obligation to provide its staff with CPD, it is largely left up to the school itself to decide what form this takes. This, of course, can lead to problems and huge variations in quality. On the plus side, it is therefore one of the areas where it is easiest to make a rapid and effective impact on existing practice.

A vast number of companies compete to provide CPD to teachers and this is a profitable market, with some long-term courses for senior leaders coming in at nearly £5,000 per participant. Even attendance at a conference on questioning, for instance, can cost participants over £300 for a day, and this is before you factor in the expense for schools of cover and travel. In a time of tightening budgets, staff rightly look carefully at which sessions to choose and the advertising for CPD is full of the buzz words that aim to draw schools in, sometimes explicitly promising to 'dramatically improve student outcomes' with courses described as 'essential' for particular categories of staff.

Despite this, evaluation of external CPD in schools rarely questions the value and impact of the CPD in any objective way. On returning to schools, participants are asked to fill in a CPD feedback form, but this relies heavily on the teacher's opinion of the provision, which can sometimes hinge on something as simple as the venue, the other people who went, or the entertainment value of the speaker. To evaluate seriously the impact of CPD, you would really need to have a follow-up survey some time later, which allowed the participant to discuss how the lessons learned in the CPD had been used in the classroom.

> *'Often the best thing about INSET is just getting out of school for the day— and a decent lunch! Teachers always say over lunch that they never normally get time to eat.' (Year group leader)*

Of course, firms that provide CPD also do surveys at the end of courses to see how successful the provision has been, surveys which can often form the basis of their future advertising. But again, the most common form of analysis is to do with 'customer satisfaction', where providers are able to cite grades for a number of elements, only one of which may be the quality of the speaker, and rarely is there a grade which asks for an evaluation of the impact on future practice. I have never known a conference or INSET provider ask for a follow-up evaluation of how the practice learned was taken forward – this is more the province of consultants. High grades for INSET training can therefore sometimes be based on the excellence of the food and drink provided, or the charm of the venue and speakers, rather than the impact on student learning.

In Janet Goodall et al.'s study 'Evaluating the impact of CPD', a definition of CPD is quoted which describes it as '...all natural learning experiences and those conscious and planned activities which are intended to be of direct or indirect benefit to the individual, group or school, which contribute, through these, to the quality of education in the classroom.' Quite apart from the awkward syntax, the definition seems flawed, not only in that it covers a truly vast scope of activities, but also because it embraces the idea of CPD as being all about good intentions, not results. The main gap in that definition, it seems to me is the phrase 'intended to be'. CPD, all too often, is *intended to be* of benefit, but isn't. Before you start planning a programme of CPD for your teachers, you need, I believe, to be quite clear about what does and doesn't work; it's too important not to consider this. As a result, you will need to start by considering what provision you currently have.

What does CPD look like at your school?

CPD can take many forms; there is no one-size-fits-all design that is agreed on as being best, and it varies to a quite remarkable extent between schools. Some have a carefully tailored programme, others buy into a multi-academy trust model that provides certain sessions, whereas others seem to leave it almost to chance, with responsibility for arranging whole-school CPD rotating uneasily around the members of SLT. Many members of staff, if you ask them, will define CPD as simply INSET days plus after school sessions and the odd day out at a conference. However, in schools nowadays CPD is likely to be a far richer mixture of different types of activity, only some of which involve external providers. Typically, in schools, you might see the following types of CPD:

- **INSET days** – obligatory, whole-school sessions, usually at the start of term. Generally teachers complain about the whole-school talks that typically start off an INSET because what they really want is more time to get to grips with their new classes, or deal with organizational issues at the start of term.
- **Twilight INSET sessions** – sometimes INSET days are 'disaggregated' to get more holiday and turned into twilight sessions which are not always as well-monitored or useful as they might be. They can sometimes be used for moderation or devising new schemes of work rather than for CPD. Additionally, teachers often forget that these sessions would otherwise be a whole INSET day at the end of term, and resent having to deal with a later evening after a tiring day in school.
- **After-school sessions** – generally these are whole-school sessions that are not always as focused on individual need as would be useful. If you are not careful, these can turn into information-giving meetings, hijacked by different people who want five minutes for an important announcement that could as easily have gone through briefing or been sent by e-mail.
- **CPD after school with an outside provider** – these are similar to INSET sessions and can be a lot cheaper for schools than sending several people on a conference.

- **Conferences** – schools may pay to send individual members of staff to attend conferences and the like. These can be expensive, as the school has to pay for cover as well as paying for the cost of travel and the conference itself.
- **Sessions by exam boards** – these are sometimes required by exam boards, e.g. for moderation, or may be provided at a small cost when new specifications are being delivered.
- **Coaching trios or PLCs** – these forms of CPD are increasingly popular, as they have been demonstrated to be effective in creating long-term change in practice. Staff work together on a project, observing each other and working on agreed goals.
- **Drip feeding or good practice sessions** – these are often placed at the start of briefings once a week, or perhaps before departmental meetings. Different members of staff will take turns to deliver good practice tips.
- **Small-group twilight sessions** – a series of sessions run over a number of weeks aimed at a particular group of staff, e.g. middle leaders or NQTs, so as to develop a specific area or areas of practice.
- **Shared CPD with other schools** – increasingly multi-academy trusts and clusters of schools are getting together to share CPD, perhaps buying in a notable speaker to share the costs. Speakers are catching on to this trend, and starting to charge different (and higher!) prices depending on audience size, which makes it slightly less of a bargain.
- **School or teacher-funded further study** – many schools now offer support – both financial and in terms of time – to members of staff who wish to study for an MA or other professional qualification. Indeed, in some schools these are offered as ways of retaining top quality members of staff who might otherwise wish to move on.
- **External sessions by specialist organisations** – organisations such as National Association for the Teaching of English (NATE) or The Historical Association often provide talks and discussions which members of staff may attend whether as part of a formal INSET or as part of their own professional development. Tracking which of your members of staff are doing this is very important.
- **TeachMeet sessions** – the idea of a TeachMeet, in which teachers and other educators present briefly on an area of shared interest, is gaining ground as a popular method of CPD. Some are arranged by organisations such as ASCL, others by groups of schools. TeachMeets are often events that do not feature in the school's CPD calendar, but are seen as something that teachers go to in their own time.
- **Mentoring and coaching sessions** – the topic of this book, and an essential part of any CPD programme, mentoring and coaching sessions are a way of individualising provision and thus maximising its effectiveness.

Connections between these different elements of CPD are not always as clear as they might be, and a first step in evaluating how CPD at school works is to establish how useful staff find the different sessions and what is your current range of CPD practice. Look at the list above, and tick off those that you have experienced over the past year. What kind of pattern or system is there in arranging CPD sessions? What kinds of CPD does your school not seem to have explored? You may find the first quiz in Part 2, Chapter 4 on 'staff evaluation of INSET' helpful for this exercise (pages 261–262) as it will help you to establish a baseline from which you can start to evaluate what is your best practice.

Clarify the purpose of CPD with staff

'It is not enough to be industrious; so are the ants. What are you industrious about?' (Henry David Thoreau, *Letters to Various Persons*)

You will still find some people who are cynical about the whole idea of CPD. They will tell you that it is simply an industry set up to make money out of schools. Teachers, goes the argument, are already trained in their subject. Further work for CPD should focus on very practical 'top-ups' of knowledge (for instance when specifications for exams change) or on statutory requirements such as safeguarding training rather than on helping teachers to do better at what they already do every day.

There is a good argument, in fact, for saying that all training should be subject-specific, but this is not quite the same thing. This kind of argument can often come from those keen to save money, as well as from the grumpy person in the corner of the staffroom, and if you are not careful you can end up with a very disconnected pattern of training as a result. CPD seems an easy target for budget cuts as its impact is not immediately visible and its cost is very visible. I've seen this argument work persuasively, especially in schools that are under financial pressure and as a result staff engagement with and understanding of the school improvement plans seems to be lost. The CPD that is out of house seems disconnected from the school, and as a result the whole CPD budget suffers.

The problem with this way of thinking is that it assumes that teacher training is a finite process, and that once a teacher gains QTS they will have little further need for professional development. It also disconnects CPD from performance management, and now they are tied together more tightly than ever before. When staff pay progression depends on their effectiveness and their impact, not to use CPD to develop staff according to their needs as well as the school's, is madness. In any case, staff needs and school needs shouldn't and won't differ far; what is good for individual teachers is what is needed by an 'improving' school.

> ## Top Tip
> ### Make it work
> To create effective in-house CPD you may have to start from the very beginning – which, as *The Sound of Music* says, 'is a very good place to start'. Try talking to your interns or NQTs about what they learned at their university sessions and you may be surprised by what they were and were not taught. Has anyone ever formally taught them about marking and feedback, for instance? Have they had the opportunity to compare different ways of planning? What preparation have they had for behaviour management or conflict resolution?

Part of any vision for a self-improving school should be developing a school which is 'outward facing'; a school actively interested in planning and delivering its own training.

Often, NQTs or teachers new to a school, find themselves thrown into a full timetable with little opportunity to reflect on the way that they are doing things. After the first INSET day when they learn how to call for help, and how the behaviour system works, they are given their timetable and the staff handbook and left to get on with it. A busy department can mean that although people will be friendly, they will not have the time or space to offer a break for really focused discussion about teaching and learning. Strategically planned CPD sessions are an invaluable opportunity to stop the work merry-go-round for a while and have a chance to discuss and reflect with other teachers.

Strategic planning of CPD

'Make your work to be in keeping with your purpose.' (Leonardo da Vinci)

I firmly believe that somewhere, somehow, there exists schools where CPD is managed seamlessly, every piece of it integrated into the overall plan of development for the school. I dream about schools like that. I bet that they also have their photocopying done before term starts. However, in most schools, there is a lot of time wasted in CPD. It is not that what is done is not useful, it is that what is done is not always planned in such a way as to ensure that it is the most useful way to spend time *at that moment*. CPD that is not carefully planned – and this may mean planned up to a year ahead – is potentially CPD which is wasted, because it is not going to get the benefit of the momentum of the school development plan, and the direction of travel of the school as a whole.

> **Top Tip**
>
> **Great minds: Ross McGill**
>
> Ross McGill writes about how you can plan your training days better when you are working in-house in his Teacher Toolkit blog: 'Training days pitfalls: What to Avoid and how to Put it Right' (www.teachertoolkit.me/2012/10/15/ badcpd).

A school which had fully integrated CPD planned well in advance would be a really outstanding school. How much of what actually takes place in INSET or CPD sessions realistically comes under the umbrella of proper professional development? There is a need to be ruthless about what you include if you are to actually have an effect on what teachers do in the classroom. Unfortunately, what we all too often see is CPD that is cobbled together from a variety of sources.

INSET days in particular, are often left to the final meetings of SLT at the end of the summer term, when planning gets subsumed into the rush towards the end of the school year. I can remember incidents of such 'planning' from personal experiences, and the discussion typically opens out something like this:

> 'Let's see now... what do we have? There is the presentation from the local authority person which is statutory – or maybe not – but certainly important for INSET we think... then there is the session that the literacy coordinator begged us for that we really need to fit in this time because you forgot it last term... then there is the reminder which is really important that the KS4 coordinator asked if they could fit in before the main session. Then subject leaders always ask for more time for meetings. Then we were going to put in that bit about how to be a good tutor – where should that go?'

Rarely have I heard a discussion that starts: 'Well, we already know what the plans are for INSET day. From the development plan, we know...' By the time you have dealt with the statutory elements, the starting of new staff, the pressure to give staff time for planning, then considering how it relates to your school improvement plan can seem academic, to say the least.

The same problem comes up when it is time to assign the sessions of outside CPD. There's the new specification conference that the head of history has to go on – not fun, but necessary; he'll feed it back to his department you feel sure. Then there is the conference that the mathematics department is absolutely adamant that they all have to go on, because last year's was so good. Do they really all need to be out at the same time? Then there's the one that the music department are obliged to attend because their moderation last year wasn't quite up to scratch... you have to let them go to that. Then there's the CPD promised in performance management to the middle leaders about preparing for leadership, etc. Before you know where you are your budget has vanished, and you're not entirely sure it was all spent on quite what you intended. Effective planning is the reverse of this 'reactive' behaviour. Take control of your CPD needs, and lead on them with courage and conviction.

A 'top ten' template for effective planning of a year's CPD

1. Work out a timescale for your planning. You will need a **final deadline** (e.g. the SLT meeting where plans are agreed before being published to staff) and **three interim deadlines** to ensure that this final one really is just a matter of confirming plans and sending them on their way.
2. Set out the timescale and deadlines and publicise them to everyone involved in planning. This should include all senior and middle leaders, and subject leaders.
3. Have an initial meeting where SLT look closely at the school development plan, and ask them to suggest CPD which is necessary to achieve the key aims before a **first interim deadline**. These suggestions can be marked roughly into the plan, and should be thoughtfully placed so as to have maximum impact in terms of timing.
4. Ask all senior and middle leaders to submit specific CPD needs of those departments and individuals whom they line manage by the **second interim deadline**. These should not be suggestions, they should be needs based on departmental improvement plans or on the individual needs of their department. If subjects will need CPD in a subject area for a new exam specification in the coming year it MUST be proposed by the second interim deadline, with a rationale and a reasoned projection of impact.
5. Following the second interim deadline, have an interim meeting where the departmental requests are discussed and ranked in order of importance. Those that already match with whole-school needs should be prioritised. Those which link together with other departmental or individual needs should be accommodated on the draft plans wherever possible.
6. As the plan grows, mark in who will be leading each area of CPD, and who will be responsible for monitoring its effectiveness. It is worth dividing up this responsibility to create a more positive dynamic in your senior team – CPD left in the hands of one person can become one-dimensional and lacklustre.

7. On the plan, sketch in where evaluations are going to take place and have a **third interim deadline** by which you decide these, e.g. if you need to observe lessons or have a marking drop as a follow-up to CPD, this should be on the school calendar well in advance, so that all staff know about it. If your plan involves individuals going on courses, make sure that you also have space on the calendar for those individuals to feed back to departments or link areas about the sessions that they have attended.

8. At this point you should be working with a copy of the whole school calendar so as to be sure not to clash with parents' evenings and the like as you start to firm up the CPD plans. They should fit in with performance management interim deadlines so as to be as useful as possible to all staff.

9. As you finalise the plans, make space to answer all subject and middle leaders with regard to their CPD requests, explaining how the final plans relate to their requests. If you have disregarded a request, be sure to be extremely clear about why this is, and what is in place for that department or person as a substitute. Any comments they have following this should be returned by the **final deadline**.

10. Following the final deadline, meet to confirm all CPD plans and ensure that all senior and middle leaders are happy with the timings and choices going forward. Publish your timetable.

Delivering CPD in-house

Moving towards delivering your CPD in-house may seem like a bold step, but there are many reasons that support such a move. Firstly, you need to remember that your CPD needs form a substantial and important part of your budget. Like any other part of your budget it needs to be value for money. It is worth revisiting your staff evaluations (if you have them) of external INSET training, and finding out what were their likes and dislikes.

This process in one school revealed the following perceptions and comments:

Out-of-house CPD pros:

- it's seen as prestigious – the school is investing in your training
- you get to hear experts, which is inspiring
- the training can be highly personalised to your needs
- you are perceived as more expert by your peers when you return
- it is a day out and a break
- you get to meet staff from other schools
- you come back with useful resources.

Out-of-house CPD cons:

- a day out of school is not always convenient
- you have to travel to get there which can be inconvenient
- it's expensive to pay for travel; even if you claim back costs it's a hassle
- some of the trainers are not good teachers
- sometimes a whole day can only produce one useful piece of input
- there is often little time to report back to the rest of your department
- as no one else has shared the CPD it is hard to implement change when back at school.

The conclusions from this piece of analysis were that staff primarily valued out-of-house CPD for its perceived prestige, the opportunities to hear experts, and the comfort. On the other hand, these advantages were substantially reduced by the perceived inconveniences. Making in-house CPD more prestigious, more expertly organised and more relaxing was the first step towards changing attitudes. When they realised that for the cost of sending one person to a conference, the school could buy in an expert to deliver a session, in-house CPD immediately started to seem better value for money.

A similar evaluation and analysis of your own CPD feedback could be shared with staff as a first step towards opening out a discussion about how to get better value for CPD, and a lead-in to considering more in-house training.

The National Teacher Enquiry Network (NTEN)'s round table discussion identified five steps for effective CPD, which are worth bearing in mind:

1. Ensure that you embed your work in the culture of the school, so as to fully involve staff. This will mean that all members of staff are concerned in how to develop the school's priorities for professional development. It gives them choice and will increase 'buy-in' from them if they feel that CPD is relevant to their own needs and the needs of their students.
2. Give CPD the right priority in terms of time and budget. You will always be dealing with competing priorities, but if you are committed to school improvement, CPD is one of your key tools. Good practice shows that initiatives need to be sustained over at least two terms so that new ideas learned have time to be embedded in practice.
3. Make sure that your CPD demand is not led by the external pressure of OFSTED or other priorities, but focused on the needs of students. Members of staff need to feel that they are free to experiment with different strategies if they are to teach innovatively and excitingly.
4. Don't forget to evaluate what you do, keeping student outcomes in mind. If you evaluate carefully then you will be able to sustain CPD that properly meets the needs of students.

5. Give teachers the power and authority to lead CPD and work together on plans going forwards. Collaboration is the key to successful professional learning such as lesson study.

How to empower good in-house CPD

When you take on the responsibility for training people in-house, it is of crucial importance that your training is well organised – and this is not just because teachers are the most critical audience, as many trainers say! Doing things professionally will make sure that teachers respond professionally, and it is likely to make them more enthusiastic about taking part themselves in the future as presenters or workshop leaders.

Before you organise any sessions, you should make sure that you look carefully at the following checklist. These principles apply to any in-house CPD:

- **Is the training necessary?** Ideally the strategic planning should take care of this, but be sure that the message is communicated to staff. People who are not convinced of the usefulness of the training will not attend with enthusiasm.
- **Do you know your audience?** Planning should include whether the session is whole school, or directed at a particular group such as NQTs or middle leaders. How sure are you of their starting point, and of what they already know about the topic? Do they know what you mean when you say 'growth mindset' for instance?
- **Have you planned the session carefully?** Planning training should be like planning a lesson: you should be clear about timings, purpose, tasks, activities, and so on. Every detail should be organised in advance in so far as possible so that on the day you can just concentrate on delivery.
- **Do you have appropriate support?** You need to have someone – preferably more than one person – to help you when it comes to organising. Doing everything yourself will just make you exhausted, inefficient and resentful. Make sure that you have people helping on the day with handouts, and someone to catch up any last-minute problems for you when you can't be in two places at once.
- **Have you publicised the session sufficiently?** This should not just be a shout-out in a staff briefing, but a properly organised campaign. Not only should it be on the school calendar, but you want teachers to be looking forward to it; no-one should have an unexpected appointment that they really can't avoid.
- **Is the person delivering the CPD an expert?** You don't have to buy in Dylan Wiliams, but you need to make sure that you have thought carefully about the expertise of the person delivering the training. Have they read up on the

topic, been to training themselves? Are they an acknowledged expert? Do your members of staff know their credentials?

- **Is the presentation appropriate?** Death by PowerPoint can be easily avoided, yet it remains a valuable tool if not misused. Check that the presenter is not planning on simply reading out their slides. Pictures, cartoons and so on are often better prompts, and more interesting for the audience to look at. What about music as they arrive?
- **Is the IT organised?** It is easy to get this wrong. Have you had a rehearsal? Is the sound working properly? If you are planning to use a video, have you got the IT department to download it, so that you won't be annoyed by adverts, or waiting for it to buffer? Does the speaker need a microphone? Does the remote control for slides work?
- **Is the room comfortable?** Check that the room is not too warm or too cold, that it is not draughty or noisy, and that you won't be disturbed during the training. If there is a creaky door, for instance, and latecomers come in, people will be distracted – prop it open if you anticipate this will be a problem.
- **Is the room arranged appropriately?** One of the pet hates of many teachers is when they have to sit in rows, with no facility to take notes or lean on a table. If possible, arrange cabaret-style seating. Ideally you will want people to work together in any case – a lecture-style CPD gets the worst evaluations.
- **Have you planned to welcome people properly?** Make sure that you have a colleague working with you whose only job is to welcome in people and show them where to sit/where refreshments are/where handouts are. This will be invaluable, as they can then stay at the back and welcome in latecomers, if there are any, with minimum fuss.
- **Are members of staff going to be actively involved?** No CPD session should involve people sitting and listening for an hour. Are the activities planned suitable and not patronising? Have you considered how people are going to sit, e.g. in subject groups or friendship groups? Will the groupings help staff to get involved?
- **What will staff take away from the session?** Ideally, any session should mean that members of staff go away with something that they can use the next day in a lesson, and try out straightaway. What will their takeaways be? How will you know?
- **Are all the handouts ready?** Check and double-check that the handouts are printed clearly, and that there are enough for everyone. Giving a conference-style pack looks professional and means you can number sheets and refer to them during the CPD. Having different colours also works well for this.
- **Have you considered SEND?** Just because you're not dealing with students doesn't mean you should forget your members of staff's needs. In effect this is a lesson, so prepare it as well as you would a lesson. Are chairs comfortable to sit in for those who have any disability? Does the speaker need to use a radio

aid for anyone with a hearing impairment? Have you checked the print is clear on handouts and presentation for any partially sighted members of staff?

- **Are the refreshments appealing?** Home-made cake is a good way of attracting members of staff to come to training – and tea and cakes is a good way to bring people together before the presentation starts. Have warm drinks available in cold weather, cool drinks in warm weather. Provide some fruit nibbles for those who don't fancy cake. Bear in mind any dietary requirements and have plates clearly labeled gluten-free, or vegan, or vegetarian, as necessary.

- **Have you prepared an evaluation?** Make sure that you have prepared an evaluation form for staff to complete. Survey monkey is a good way of doing this easily – though paper forms are more likely to be filled in! Don't just ask them about the refreshments...

- **How will you check impact?** What are you plans for checking impact over time? Make sure that staff know what you are going to do, e.g. if everyone is supposed to use a strategy over the next fortnight, and if you are going to use student voice to check, it is only fair to let them know that immediately.

- **Is your timing right?** No matter how good your session, you will lose your audience the moment that you go over time. Make sure that you keep to your timings, and plan to finish early so as to give time for any questions – or for any problems or emergencies. Your audience will be grateful!

- **Where will you go from here?** Any training session should have a clear sense of the follow-through – not just what you will do for evaluation, but also what the next piece of training will be, and how this prepares for it, or follows through to it.

- **Have you got succession planning in place?** Who will do this training if you are ill? Who will deliver the next piece of training, and why? Are you planning to do everything yourself (not a good idea) or have you thought seriously about how you are going to grow your experts? Developing teacher expertise is what effective CPD is all about, and one day – not too far away – the people you train should be leading training themselves.

Chapter 1 takeaway

Reflection

What was the most effective CPD session you ever attended? Identify what made it so successful. How can you reproduce some of its essential elements in your own planning for CPD?

Pass it on

Sharing with colleagues outside your school setting

Invite other schools to join you in a TeachMeet. Choose a focus for each meeting (e.g. subject; middle/senior leader CPD) and share speakers. Share ideas through #BloomsCPD. Work out your annual cost of CPD in each area. Have you had good value for money? How else could you have spent it on staff CPD?

Sharing with staff and students in your school

Prompt staff in CPD evaluations to list their top three likes and dislikes about the sessions. Compare these with Ross McGill's 'Pitfalls for Training Days'. How can these help you to improve your next INSET day? Create a working wall in the staffroom: 'the best idea I ever got from CPD', and ask members of staff to offer their suggestions for improvement.

Discuss with your student council how student mentoring could be used to advance existing strategies for student voice.

Share and tweet

Share your staff's thoughts on the best value CPD using the hashtag #BloomsCPD.

CPD book club recommendation

Visible Learning by John Hattie

Geoff Petty – interview with John Hattie, 'The first and only commandment is "know thy impact"' (See Bibliography and further reading)

Blogger's corner

Tom Sherrington's blog 'Developing Our In-house System for Improving Teaching' explores a new system for in-house CPD Visit his blog at headguruteacher.com.

Read Joe Kirby's blog 'What makes effective CPD?' at pragmaticreform. wordpress.com/2013/06/01/cpd.

TO DO LIST:

☐ Make contact with other schools to investigate hosting a TeachMeet

☐ Look at your CPD costs for the past year. Start to plan your CPD calendar for next year. What do you need to include? Where will you get your CPD from?

☐ Go through staff evaluations from CPD and see what lines of enquiry you can start to investigate to improve your practice – use them to start off your working wall in the staffroom

☐ Set a time to talk to student council about mentoring

☐ Tweet your staff's ideas about CPD using the hashtag #BloomsCPD

☐ Read John Hattie's *Visible Learning*

☐ Read Joe Kirby's blog entry 'What makes effective CPD?'

2 Training plans – Mentoring

Creating in-house CPD for mentoring

Mentoring is in essence a one-to-one activity, and as a result many mentors do not communicate effectively with each other. Often, mentoring can be informal, or slightly hit and miss, and this means that the experience and the knowledge gained through working with someone else can be lost.

One of the important things that you can do in terms of in-house CPD, therefore, is to ensure that your mentors are confident and knowledgeable about who else in school is working as a mentor. You will also want to make links with student mentors, if you use them, as the same skills are necessary for working with them as for working with other members of staff.

Mentoring training is part of creating a whole-school culture that is effectively concerned with driving forward professional development. Both for staff and students, the principles of mentoring are principles that emphasise the importance of developing and growing as a professional person.

A good way to start can be through a whole-school session about working with student mentors, emphasising the basic principles of mentoring, and demonstrating how useful the practice can be in an immediately accessible way. From this session, you should find some people who want to work with other teachers, as well as working with students, to develop their skills. You can then hold a series of twilight sessions to support student mentoring, and other after-school sessions that would work to support those moving into leadership positions, who need to think about the wider aspects of leadership and mentoring.

Whole-school session

Mentoring as a means to school improvement

When organising mentoring CPD for your staff, you will find that some will know more about it than others. However, if you are serious about creating a really vibrant teaching and learning culture for your school, you will need at least one whole-school session to support what you are doing so that staff understand why mentoring is an important part of whole-school development. A whole-school session will also signal its importance, allowing members of staff to reflect on their own ideas about development.

> 'If you cannot see where you are going, ask someone who has been there before.' (J. Loren Norris)

Thinking about audience

You will want to consider your audience before you start any whole-school session, and find out what they already know about the subject. In particular, you want to make sure that what you say is pitched at the right level so that you are not going too fast or too slow for those to whom you are speaking. When introducing something such as student mentoring, it is likely that you will already know if any members of staff have expertise in this, but just in case, it is worth publicising the session in advance, and asking those who are going to attend if they already have experience in this area. You can then ask these people to lead a part of the session, or take part in it in a more interactive way, so as to ensure that they feel valued, and feel that they are being developed as experts – very much in tune with the idea of mentoring!

The advantage of this strategy is that you will get people thinking about mentoring very early on, and engaging their minds with the issues in a lively discussion before you even open your mouth. You can then further this interest and engagement through your opening activities, encouraging discussion and sharing of information.

Most teachers will certainly have had direct experience of mentoring in their own training, and will be able to make connections between this experience – whether good or bad – and your plans for the school. Do bear this in mind and assume a certain level of expertise. Be happy to refer to what you know is shared experience. Remember that teachers always tend to be impatient with exactly the kinds of presentation that they are told not to do themselves in the classroom, e.g. talking from the front, information giving without time for reflection and so on. You will often hear teachers at a conference complaining about information read from a slide, or about information that could have been given in written form to save time.

Be aware of this, and be careful that you treat your teachers as the experts that they are. Teach them as you would wish to be taught, and give them time and space to reflect at each stage. Ensure that you also build into your session opportunities for questions and for information sharing, and that you offer opportunities where they can be the expert.

Thinking about purpose

For your whole-school session, your primary purpose will be to encourage and enthuse staff about the project that you wish to develop. You want to inform people about the benefits of mentoring, and also give them some hints as to how it might be developed, while letting them contribute themselves to the planning.

Think about it in terms of a lesson, and what you want to achieve. You will need to ensure that people understand what mentoring is, and perhaps distinguish it from coaching, or from other kinds of related activity. You will also need to discuss the parameters that will enable it to take place.

Remember that you want to try and get people moving along with you, and actively supporting your ideas, so make the session as interactive and interesting as you can.

Thinking about content

Always remember that you are introducing ideas, and that not every person you are speaking to will become a mentor or work with a mentor, even a student mentor. Nonetheless, you want to ensure that they are on board with the ideas and the rationale for them. It would be a good idea if your session were to contain the following elements:

1. an initial activity that allows people to reflect upon their own experience of mentoring
2. a section which allows people to share expertise
3. an explanation of why student mentoring is effective, with some research input that backs up the ideas
4. a discussion of the practicalities of implementing this
5. some examples of successful strategies in different contexts
6. an opportunity for staff to discuss possible strategies and how they would fit into the existing culture of the school
7. opportunities for staff to offer feedback and work with different groups moving forwards.

Thinking about structure

When structuring your session, you should be careful to vary activities and tasks; be aware of the need to give people breaks. Evaluations are consistently better in sessions where participants are allowed to discuss and suggest ideas.

It also makes sense to indicate to people that there will be opportunities to talk and ask questions throughout the sessions. If participants know that there will shortly be an opportunity to clarify ideas and question, then they are more likely to focus for the time you wish.

Make sure that you have an outline plan for the session that you can fiddle about with as you add in further thoughts and ideas. Below is the outline for a one-hour session that you can use immediately to introduce and generate the idea of a mentoring culture. You may wish to adapt this slightly so as to personalise it for your school. In this session, participants will consider what mentoring means, reflect on their own experiences, explore the features of a good mentor, speculate about how mentoring can help particular individuals at different career stages, consider the effect of mentoring young adults and look at some research on peer mentoring, and decide if they wish to commit to developing the school as a mentoring school.

Resources required

You can download the resources required for this training session from the online resources. They include:

- PowerPoint presentation: 1 Whole-school mentoring
- 1A Mentoring sort cards
- 1B Worksheet: How could mentoring help these people?

One-hour session: overview plan

Timeline of session	Resources needed	Description of activity
Before start	• Chairs and tables set up for 'cabaret-style' seating: groups of 5–8 per table • Large display board • Projector and PowerPoint presentation	• Arrange tables for 'cabaret-style' seating with PowerPoint display easily visible to all.
5 mins	• Slides 1–2	**Brief introduction** • Why are we here? • What are the objectives of the session?
10 mins	• Slides 3–8 • Writing implements and sticky notes or small squares of paper • Display board	**What is a mentor?** • Explain the origin of the term 'mentor' and show Denzel Washington quotation found on the PowerPoint slide for this session. • Participants reflect on who acted as a mentor to them; then, on a sticky note. Each write the name of someone who has helped them to move forward personally and emotionally. • Groups discuss their experiences and each person explains what their named person did for them. • Each person writes down on a sticky note an example of what their mentor did to help them develop, to be shared on the display board. • It is important to clarify at this point that a mentor can be anyone that you respect, who is able to show you a good example of how to move forward.
10 mins	• Slides 9–12 • Mentoring sort cards	**What do mentors do?** • Introduce the idea of how mentors behave by discussing the Joe Jonas quotation, found on the PowerPoint slide for this session. • Reminder of how official mentoring works for teachers themselves.

Timeline of session	Resources needed	Description of activity
		• Look at the statement from the headteacher about a good mentor – a reminder about how unofficial mentoring sometimes works. • The four key points on the slide should be noted as typical features of a good mentor. • 'My mentor was like this' activity – card sort and prioritisation exercise to get groups considering how mentoring works. Groups should consider each of the statements about mentoring, and then consider which they prefer. • Groups to arrange the statements about mentoring in order of priority.
10 mins	• Slide 13 • How could mentors help these people? worksheet	**How could mentors help these people?** • Groups discuss the possible clients for mentoring on the worksheet. They make notes about how a mentor could help each person. • Individuals should be encouraged to reflect on the difference between a mentor and other forms of support, e.g. what can a mentor do that a staff handbook cannot? • Feedback and whole-staff discussion. • At this stage, ideas coming forward should include the sense of a mentor as a role model who can help people move past a particular point in their lives through their own experience.
15 mins	• Slides 14–25 • Writing implements and sticky notes • Display board	**Research evidence?** • Go through the slides that discuss the research evidence supporting the value of mentoring for young adults. • Open out the discussion of the issue of peer mentoring in schools, as an alternative to external mentoring by adults, and move through the research evidence that supports its effectiveness. • Ask participants to predict the effect of mentoring in Budmouth before you reveal the statistics. • Ask individual groups to briefly discuss why they think peer mentoring is effective, and then give feedback to the whole group either verbally or via sticky notes on the display board. • After feedback share slide 25 and discuss.
5 mins	• Voting card or sticky notes • Display board	**Put it to the vote** • Revisit the session objectives, and agree they have been covered. • Ask participants to make a commitment to the idea of participating in peer mentoring – this is one way to get your participants to attend the twilight session that will follow.
5 mins		**Question time** • Time for questions and discussion around feedback and the display board.

Whole-school session: PowerPoint presentation

Brief introduction *(Slides 1–2)*

Display slide 1 when participants enter. It includes the statements: 'Mentoring as a means to school improvement: How can we use mentors to develop a culture of excellence and aspiration?' It will help to prompt participants for their first activity. Then, discuss the session objectives to give participants an idea of the structure of the session.

Session objectives

- To reflect on our own experience of mentoring, and assess some of the qualities of a successful mentor.

- To explore the ways in which mentoring could be used as a tool for school improvement.

- To evaluate some of the evidence that supports student mentoring as an effective form of mentoring.

What is a mentor? *(Slides 3–8)*

What is a mentor?

- The word 'mentor' comes from ancient Greek!
- When Odysseus went off to the Trojan war, he left his friend Mentor to look after and advise his son Telemachus.
- So a mentor is someone who guides and helps you to grow up successfully.

Use slide 3 to introduce the origin of the term 'mentor'. Ensure that there is clarity about the role of a mentor. You could add in the story of how the Goddess Athena disguised herself as Mentor to give Telemachus good advice.

Display slide 4 with the Denzel Washington quotation. This should help participants think about their own ideas about mentoring.

Display slide 6 and get participants to write about their best mentor on one of their post-it notes. Not discussing at this point allows participants to reflect on private experience. Having thought about what mentoring means, participants should now be ready to reflect on their own experiences.

Who was your best mentor?

- Think for a moment about the person (not including your parents, but not excluding other members of your family) who has had the most impact on you and your career and personal progression.

- Who were they, and what did they do that helped you move forwards? This does not have to mean literal promotion – it could be simply increased confidence or increased happiness at work.

- Write their name on the sticky note to celebrate them and what they have done for you.

Discussion time

- In your groups, share your experiences of this personal development, and of the person that you have chosen.

- What did this person actually do that helped you move forwards?

- Think of an example and write it on the second sticky note in front of you.

This may take some time as people share their experiences. Don't let momentum slip, but you will find that the discussion is productive in getting everyone focused on mentoring and its significance.

Display slide 8 encouraging participants to stick their post-it notes on the board. The physical cue of movement will help to end the discussion neatly.

In education...

- Mentoring is considered so important in education that all teachers are trained with the help of a mentor who works closely with them to help them develop their skills; additionally all NQTs are assigned a mentor.

- But your official mentor may not always be the most effective one for you. Often, people have found that someone senior acts as an unofficial mentor for them in their career.

- You may have experienced these informal mentoring relationships with members of your own or another organisation.

What do mentors do? *(Slides 9–12)*

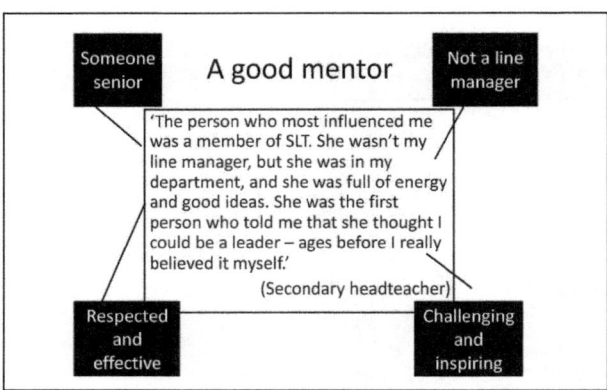

Display the Joe Jonas quote on slide 9. Ask participants to consider how far they agree with this definition of what a mentor does.

Open out the idea of informal mentoring. Who helped you once you had qualified? Was your official mentor always the most effective person?

Encourage participants to discuss what about this description is typical of a good mentor and what features are likely to recur? Then reveal the answers. Ask participants: What would it be like if everyone had someone like this to support them? Would it provide a more productive and personalised learning environment for staff and students?

Give groups the mentoring sort cards (available on the online resources: 1A Mentoring sort cards), which contain a variety of statements from different people about how mentors have helped them. Groups should arrange the statements in order of agreed priority, from the statement that they think is most true and reflects their experiences as a group, to the one which they think is least true to their experience.

How could mentoring help these people? *(Slides 13)*

Ask groups to work through the list of people on slide 13 (also available in the worksheet on the online resources: 1B How could mentoring help?) and consider how mentoring could support each of the suggested clients. What kind of mentor would each one need? They should make notes about how a mentor could support each person named. What can a mentor do that a staff handbook cannot do? Encourage feedback, growing to a whole-staff discussion. At this stage ideas coming forward should include the sense of a mentor as a role model who can help people to move past a particular point in their lives through sharing their own experience.

Research evidence? *(Slides 14–16)*

Run through the research results from MENTOR (a US organisation) on slide 14 and discuss the idea of adult mentors for young people. Your school may already work with a similar programme.

Display the facts about the positive effect mentoring has on attendance and behaviour on slide 15. Ask participants to consider why it might be that mentoring shows these positive effects. Can they add to them from their own experience?

Use this prompt question to discuss why we might move towards peer mentoring.

Peer mentoring *(Slides 17–25)*

Display the quote on slide 17. Discuss the extent to which your school uses similar support networks.

Display the quote on slide 18. Introduce the idea of the effectiveness of peer mentoring – there is good research evidence.

Display the quote on slide 19. Why might peer mentoring have had these effects?

Budmouth Technology College

- The college tracked 40 pupils throughout the year 2009-10.
- The tracked pupils represented four groups –10 peer mentors, 10 mentees, 10 year 10/11 pupils not acting as peer mentors and 10 year 7 pupils not having one-to-one support from peer mentors.
- The aim was to provide data of those involved in peer mentoring and those not involved. The focus of the measurement was on attendance and well-being.

If you want to do similar evaluation it is worth emphasising the parameters on slide 20.

Results – can you predict?

- 80% of the mentees improved their attendance compared to only 40% of those who were not mentored.
- 60% of the peer mentors improved their attendance compared to only 30% of those who were not mentoring other young people.
- 60% of the mentees improved their behaviour compared to 20% of those who were not being mentored.
- 50% of the peer mentors improved their behaviour compared to 30% of those who were not acting as peer mentors.

Ask participants to guess the results before revealing them.

Why is peer mentoring so effective?

- The results of the quantitative studies into peer mentoring were a surprise to many, who felt that its effects were primarily anecdotal and 'soft' in terms of data.

- In your groups, discuss why you think peer mentoring has such a high success rate. What is it about being mentored by another student that has a positive effect?

In groups, discuss why peer mentoring has such a significant effect on both participants.

Allow feedback and discussion.

Feedback and a vote *(Slides 25–27)*

Display the quote on slide 25. Discuss as a group how far you agree with the statement. Ideally this comment will reflect some of your discussions.

Slide 26: Session objectives

Display slide 26 repeating the session objectives. Discuss to what extent the objectives set out at the start of the session have been reached. Then, as a plenary, ask staff to consider how far they would be prepared to commit to involvement in the organisation of student peer mentoring.

Twilight CPD

For a twilight CPD session, you will typically be working with a slightly smaller grouping of staff on a particular project. Although in certain ways it will be similar to running a whole-school session, and the same, or similar priorities should be in place when it comes to ensuring a comfortable context and environment, there will be some key differences. A twilight session is likely to be aimed at a particular group of people – it may be quite a large group of staff, but it is likely that they will be defined to some extent by their willingness to participate in the project that you are proposing for developing mentoring.

This particular twilight session is designed to start staff off on a peer mentoring project. Establishing a mentoring culture in school is not always easy, especially if it has not always been a feature of how the school has worked in the past. Working with peer mentoring to start with is an easy way to introduce the benefits of mentoring, as research on its benefits is very well-established. Through working on peer mentoring, staff start to understand many of the principles of mentoring, and thus tend to become more receptive to using coaching and mentoring for their own professional development. Peer mentoring is also highly inclusive, as it can involve all staff, not only teaching staff, and this is important in creating a positive whole-school culture around coaching and mentoring.

Thinking about audience

One really effective way to select staff for a twilight session such as this, is to allow them to self-select through a process similar to the final exercise in the whole-school CPD session above. You may wish to include non-teaching members of staff in the training; especially if you have non-teaching pastoral leads such as year group leaders or deputy year leaders. You may also wish to include TAs, school receptionists or counsellors, learning mentors, the librarian and so on – in short, anyone who may be of assistance in starting up the mentoring culture in the school.

Thinking about purpose

Your main purpose in this session will be to build skills and expertise and create a shared culture of expectation. In other words, all those who participate need to be convinced of the value of peer mentoring, and by the end of the session should be very familiar with the basic principles that you will need to inculcate. This is the reason why this session should use real data and real groups of students. Thinking about how specific people may react is genuinely helpful when it comes to reinforcing certain principles.

Thinking about content

Bear in mind that a twilight session will by its very nature be more pressured. Staff may have had (probably *will* have had) a busy day, and the last thing that they want is to attend a session that will not be immediately useful. As a result, you will need to consider how to make the session as practical and effective as possible. Working with groups in the school should help them to feel purposeful and also encourage them to apply the principles in a real world situation. Ideally they should come away from the session with a sense of how they are going to progress next.

Thinking about structure

Again, avoid too much 'from the front' activity. Make sure that you have 'hands on' activities that will be used later on. Be prepared to copy the SWOC (Strengths, Weaknesses, Opportunities and Challenges) analysis sheets for instance so as to share them more widely. Writing up ideas on sticky notes for feedback is another valuable exercise which ensures that nothing is lost.

For these twilight sessions, you may be working with a group of staff on an ongoing project. It is a good idea therefore, to have shorter sessions that you can fit in after school, each focusing on one important element of mentoring training and planning.

Here are the plans for three short (45 min) sessions of twilight training on student mentoring. This training will equip staff to commence a student mentoring project, focusing on a particular group of students, and give them the knowledge and understanding that they need in order to train student mentors to work with other students.

Resources required

You can download the resources required for this training session from the online resources. They include:

- PowerPoint presentation: 2 Working with student mentors
- 2A Objectives sort cards
- 2B Group record sheet
- 2C Good mentor cards
- 2D Asking better questions sheet
- 2E Barriers to listening worksheet

Three short twilight sessions: overview plan

Timeline of session	Resources needed	Description of activity
Before start **FOR ALL SESSIONS**	• Chairs and tables set up for 'cabaret-style' seating: groups of 5–8 per table • Large display board • Projector and PowerPoint presentation	• Arrange tables for 'cabaret-style' seating with PowerPoint display easily visible to all. • Divide participants into groups, with each group assigned to a different group of students. (You could use year groups, and divide with tutors, or you could use particular groups of students you wish to monitor, e.g. those with attendance or behavioural issues.) It is important that participants are aware that they are going to be constructing the principles by which they will be working, and that they are working with particular groups in mind.
SESSION 1 Developing a culture of excellence		
10 mins	• Slides 1–3 • *Yellow* sticky notes	**Brief introduction** • Why are we here? • What is the objective of the session? • Using yellow sticky notes, ask participants to write down problems that they think we might encounter in establishing student mentoring in school.
10 mins	• Slides 4–6 • 'Objectives' sort cards	**Objectives of peer mentoring** • Each group should work on a different group of students for this exercise (e.g. year group, research group). • They should use the sort cards to discuss the priorities for their group of students, choosing and arranging them to indicate which are the key priorities for that group.
10 mins	• Slide 7 • Group record sheet	**How to measure improvement** • On the record sheet they should record their agreed priorities, and then start to consider what measurements they can use to evaluate their priorities. • The use of attendance data, for instance, might seem relatively straightforward as a measure, but they will still need to decide what kind of improvement in attendance indicates success.

Timeline of session	Resources needed	Description of activity
10 mins	• Slides 8–9 • A3 paper for each group for SWOC analysis	**SWOC analysis** • Following this, groups should work on a SWOC analysis of the strengths, weaknesses, opportunities and challenges that the student group offers when it comes to peer mentoring. • This should be recorded on the A3 sheet, and placed on the display board.
5 mins	• Slides 10–12 • Display board for feedback • Yellow sticky notes from the introduction and green sticky notes to write on	**Discussion and feedback** • Reflection on solutions that have been thought of for problems – on display board. • Brief evaluation.
SESSION 2 Key principles for mentoring		
10 mins	• Slides 13–14 • Yellow sticky notes	**Brief introduction** • Why are we here? • What are the objectives of the session? • Ask participants to write down their most important principle for a mentoring programme on a yellow sticky note.
15 mins	• Slide 15 • Writing implements and sticky notes • Display board	**How do we create effective mentoring programmes?** • Look at the four opening 'rules' about peer mentoring programmes. • Ask staff to discuss in their groups what should be the other non-negotiable features when establishing a student mentoring programme. • Answers on sticky notes should be shared on the display board.
15 mins	• Slides 16–17 • 'Good mentor' cards • Diamond nine framework if necessary	**Matching mentors and mentees** • Ask groups to look at the 'good mentor' cards about the qualities of mentors and consider what factors should be taken into account when matching mentors and mentees. • Be aware that in the feedback and discussion it should be emphasised that a desire to be friends with younger children may be a child protection warning sign, and that blurring of the boundaries between friends and mentors is also something about which organisers need to be wary.
5 mins	• Slides 18–20	**Discussion and feedback** • Reflection on solutions that have been thought of for problems – on display board. • Brief evaluation.

Timeline of session	Resources needed	Description of activity
SESSION 3 Key mentoring skills		
10 mins	• Slides 21–22 • Sticky notes	**Brief introduction** • Why are we here? • What are the objectives of the session? • Using sticky notes, ask participants to write down one thing that they think that students will need to know about being a successful mentor.
5 mins	• Slide 23	**Feedback and discussion** • What do young people need to know about – what are they aiming at? • Discussion of principles and skills of mentoring. • Discussion of limitations of the student role.
5 mins	• Slide 24	**Visualisation exercise** • Introduce visualisation exercise. • How does this work for students? • What kind of responses might you get from this? • How does it work to raise aspirations?
10 mins	• Slide 25 • Barriers to listening worksheet • Sticky notes and display board for feedback	**What makes a good listener?** • Open out the David Hockney quotation for discussion. How hard is it to teach students to really listen to other students? • Ask participants in their groups to suggest four barriers to listening, and share feedback with the whole group. • Have the group come up with all the barriers on the Barriers to listening worksheet? • In groups, use the worksheet as a basis for discussion to suggest ways in which students may circumvent this tendency, e.g. you might counteract a tendency to ride over people's feelings by asking them 'How did that make you feel?' as a deliberate strategy. • Try and encourage groups to share solutions and formulas to help with listening skills.
10 mins	• Slide 25 • 'Asking better questions' sheet	**What are the most useful questions?** • Look at the 'Asking better questions' sheet which is aimed at adult mentors. • Which questions are useful for student mentoring? • How will we need to change them, and alter phrasing to make them useable for student mentors? • Groups work on rephrasing and share ideas in feedback.

Timeline of session	Resources needed	Description of activity
5 mins	• Slides 26–28	**Assessment of objectives and discussion around feedback** • Review and reflect on the objectives set out at the start of the training. • Ask participants to look at the sticky notes they wrote at the start, and reflect on what they wrote, then write on a different coloured sticky note another important priority that they have worked on in the session. • Share priorities on display board.

Twilight session 1: PowerPoint presentation

Brief introduction *(Slides 1–3)*

Display slide 1 when participants enter. It includes the statements: Working with student mentors: How can we develop a culture of excellence and aspiration. It will help to prompt them for their first activity. Then, discuss the session objective to give participants an idea of the structure of the session.

Ask groups to come up with ideas about the barriers that exist to fostering mentoring in school. By doing this you will allow them to have these issues in mind during the training, and this will help them to use solution-focused thinking throughout.

Objectives of peer mentoring *(Slides 4–6)*

How can we develop peer mentoring in our school?

- In your groups, you have been assigned to a particular group of students.

- Your task is to consider how peer mentoring might work for that group.

- You need to consider how it will work both for students who are mentored and for students who act as mentors.

Groups should be assigned to work on the issues of a particular student group – perhaps a year group or a sub-group within that group, such as Pupil Premium students. You might have tutors working with the issues for their tutees, for instance.

What are the objectives of introducing peer mentoring?

To improve attendance?	To improve relationships?
To improve behaviour?	To improve punctuality?
To improve attainment?	To improve aspiration?
To improve participation?	To improve confidence?
To improve social skills?	To improve transitions?

Ask participants to suggest the objectives before showing these in turn on the slide. Note down any they suggest which are not on the agreed priorities. This would be the time to link them with the SIP.

Discuss school priorities

- First in pairs, and then as a whole group, use the sort cards to decide the priorities for using peer mentoring in your given group.

Use the 'Objectives' sort cards to allow participants freedom to discuss priorities without preconceptions (these can be found on the online resources: 2A Objectives sort cards). Remember they may be different for different groups; emphasise that there is no right answer. How does this link to the school's improvement priorities?

How to measure improvement *(Slide 7)*

Staff should record their agreed priorities on the record sheet (see online resources 2B Group record sheet) and then start to consider what measurements they can use to evaluate their priorities. The use of attendance data, for instance, might seem relatively straightforward as a measure, but they will still need to decide what kind of improvement in attendance actually indicates success.

SWOC analysis *(Slides 8–9)*

I prefer using SWOC analysis (strengths, weaknesses, opportunities and challenges), rather than the slightly more aggressive SWOT analysis (strengths, weaknesses, opportunities and threats). The word 'challenges' is the language educators are more likely to use in any case.

Ask groups to record their thoughts on using peer mentoring for their specific student group on A3 paper.

Display slide 9 and encourage participants to share their SWOC analyses. This will allow for comparison and perhaps some small changes in response to others' ideas. Allow time for discussion over the display board.

Discussion and feedback *(Slides 10–12)*

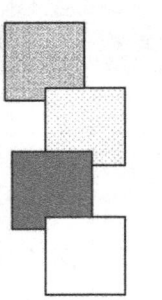

Where have we got to?

- In your group, look at the yellow sticky notes you created at the start of the session with examples of problems that you thought we might encounter in establishing student mentoring.
- Then use the green sticky notes to come up with solutions to these problems.

Asking people at the end of training to come up with solutions to match the problems they thought of at first should encourage them to think of the solutions in terms of what they have done during the training.

Twilight session 2: PowerPoint presentation

Brief introduction *(Slides 13–14)*

Share the objective – this keeps the short session focused. Then revise the key principles of mentoring. Focusing participants on key principles again reinforces objectives and encourages self-reflection.

Session objective

To decide on the key principles of our mentoring programme.

How do we create effective mentoring programmes? *(Slide 15)*

Some mentoring non-negotiables

✓ Ensure that all participants have parental consent for the project.
✓ Make sure that all student mentors have training in safeguarding as appropriate.
✓ Have clear criteria for establishing who participates in the programme.
✓ Ensure that you are in regular contact with all participants.

What should be the other non-negotiables when establishing student mentoring?

It is really important to ensure that in this discussion the essential elements such as safeguarding are mooted and fully understood, which is why these are prioritised as non-negotiable.

Answers to the question posed at the bottom of the slide might include the following, though any relevant answers should be sensibly considered and appropriately responded to, especially if they raise concerns about participants' understanding of the nature of mentoring:

- Enough time for preparing mentors and mentees.
- Ensuring that students understand the purpose and aims of the project.
- Making sure that participation is not seen as a sign that you are failing in school.
- Ensuring positive commitment from both parties.
- Explaining what mentoring does and does not involve.
- Training with a non-judgmental and unprejudiced approach.
- Careful screening of mentors.
- A careful matching process between mentors and mentees.
- Training for mentors in listening and questioning skills.
- Training in establishing appropriate boundaries for mentors.
- Sensitive attitude towards cultural issues in terms of matching mentors and mentees.

- Dedicated timetabled time for mentoring.
- Support from all in school for the mentoring project so that teachers are aware of the benefits of any missed lesson time.
- Careful monitoring of meetings.
- Consideration of time implications of mentoring itself and effect on other subjects.

Ensure that your discussions are covering all the important issues.

Matching mentors and mentees *(Slides 16–17)*

> # What makes a good mentor?
>
> Using the 'good mentor' cards as prompts, discuss in your groups what you think should be taken into account when matching mentors with mentees.
>
> Can you decide on the most important elements?

It is important that groups look through the 'good mentor' cards (see online resources: 2C Good mentor cards) and use their critical intelligence and their knowledge from previous sessions here. You want to establish the ground rules about selecting mentors, and how many of the skills can be taught, rather than being 'innate'. Paradoxically, sometimes students eager to think of themselves as natural mentors can be doing it for the wrong reasons.

Display slide 17 instructing participants to make a diamond nine demonstrating their priorities

Discussion and feedback *(Slides 18–20)*

> # Where have we got to?
>
> • In your group, look at the yellow sticky notes you created at the start of the session with examples of your most important principle.
>
> • Have you changed your ideas, or is this still the most important principle for you?
>
> • On the green sticky notes write down either your new priority, or note down that you have not changed.

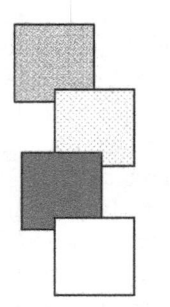

Asking people at the end of training to come up with solutions to match the problems they thought of at first should encourage them to think of the solutions in terms of what they have done during the training.

Twilight session 3: PowerPoint presentation

Brief introduction *(Slides 21–22)*

Session objective

To explore some of the methods we may need to teach our mentors when starting off student mentoring.

Share the objective – this keeps the short session focused. Then revise the key principles of mentoring. Focusing participants on key principles again reinforces objectives and encourages self-reflection. Participants write one key thing that they think students will need to learn to become successful mentors on a post-it.

Feedback and discussion *(Slide 23)*

What are our mentors aiming at?

- We are trying to encourage a positive relationship.
- The principles should be aspirational.
- Students need to know key ways of envisioning change.
- Students need to be trained in listening.
- They also need to be trained in questioning strategies.

Encourage discussion to clarify the difference between student and staff mentoring, especially if you have used staff mentoring of students before.

Visualisation exercise *(Slide 24)*

How do you envision change?

- Imagine that you have achieved your life's ambition. You are being celebrated for your success. Your family and friends are so proud of you! So are your teachers.
- Looking back, how did you change so as to get to where you are now?
- Give your younger self some good advice.

To enliven this exercise you can show an interview from a sports personality, for instance, talking about their journey to success – it is a trope most students will be familiar with.

What makes a good listener? *(Slide 25)*

Remind participants how challenging it can be to listen (even to you!) and how it is a learned skill to be attentive – and one that student mentors may not have. What might be the barriers? Discuss the question 'What stops people listening effectively? Then use the 'Barriers to listening' worksheet (see online resources 2D Barriers to Listening) to consider how to overcome those first barriers, for instance using scripted comments such as 'how does that make you feel?' to overcome a tendency not to consider other people's feelings.

What are the most useful questions? *(Slide 26)*

> What are the most useful questions?
>
> - In your pairs, look at the questioning sheet.
> - For each question, grade it 1–3 in terms of usefulness to a student mentor, where 3 is the most useful.
> - Share your ideas in your group – do you agree on the most useful questions? What are your criteria?

Use the 'Questioning' sheet (see online resources 2E Asking better questions) to focus participants on language. It will be no good student mentors using most of the questions in their current form – how can they be made student-relevant and student-friendly?

Assessment of objectives and discussion around feedback
(Slides 27–29)

Ask participants to look back at and reflect on the post-its that they wrote on at the start of the session, and then write down another priority that they have learned about that they did not anticipate. This should demonstrate the progress that they have made, and be a foundation for productive discussion when it comes to assessing if they have achieved the session objective.

After-school leadership training

If you have a group of middle leaders who, for instance, wish to work as mentors – or who need some further mentoring themselves – it is often a good idea to lay on some specific in-house training for them. This is the kind of training that can be offered by teaching schools in your area, and although this training can be excellent in quality, the danger is that it is both costly and time-consuming.

The beauty of running after-school sessions in your own school is that you build capacity for developing leadership, and also know how people are progressing. Although visits to other schools are part of the charm of external sessions – and an important part of leadership development – it is quite possible to arrange reciprocal visits for members of staff as part of the development following their training.

Indeed, in a recent set of sessions that I ran in my school, I invited participants from neighbouring schools at no cost; this meant that they were in return very welcoming to visitors, and offered to generate swaps and shared learning in a really constructive way. If you have the capacity to make this kind of offer, it is a really good idea to try and share expertise in this way.

Thinking about audience

For this kind of training, it is likely that your audience will be middle leaders, or those who aspire to middle leadership. In my school, the training was provoked by the fact that we had had a lot of staffing change, and some people were having to take on responsibilities with relatively little preparation.

Being a new leader means that you have to make crucial decisions about your area of responsibility. SLT will rely on your subject expertise and knowledge of your specialism to support them, and this can mean that you can sometimes feel as though you are left too much alone in the early stages of leading your team. Add to this the vulnerabilities of new or existing staff who desire strong and clear leadership, and you can find that there are many responsibilities that leaders have not had time to think through.

Leading a subject area, or a whole-school area of responsibility, is something for which teachers rarely get specific training. Therefore, even as a former second in a department or acting subject leader there is a danger that there are unfamiliar areas for which leaders will be expected to take responsibility, or issues that they may not have encountered before.

In this kind of training, you will need to be responsive to your audience and their needs, and be prepared to change what you are doing if their needs reflect that necessity.

Thinking about purpose

The purpose of the training must be at least in part, determined by your participants. You know yourself how frustrating it can be to be 'trained' when you are already competent – leadership training needs a particularly gentle touch in this respect. Always be aware that those you are working with are highly competent professionals, and make sure that you allow for discussion and feedback in every session so that the sharing that is the mark of good training is clearly enabled.

The training plan that follows is designed to ensure that there are no gaps in basic leadership knowledge, and perhaps most importantly, establish where participants can ask for help and support as they set off on their leadership journey. Ideally it will also give them a model as to how to train those they work with, and build leadership capacity in their team through really effective work with TLR postholders.

One of your purposes should be to bond together your group of would-be mentors and trainers. You want people to feel that they can work with others to find out more, and perhaps to watch and coach each other as well. Building an atmosphere of trust is extremely important – they should feel able to share and discuss issues with no fear of comeback.

Thinking about content

Again, your audience will define your content in part. You will know that there are certain things that you absolutely want to cover, but the depth and detail in which you cover them will depend in part on the reactions of your participants, and their self-awareness. Using quizzes and reflection will allow them to demonstrate to you their areas of competence and also let them ask questions and show vulnerability.

Don't be afraid, though, to have your own non-negotiables. In my case, I thought about what I would have wanted to know as a new leader, and included all those things in the training, being aware that some of it might be content that some participants felt expert in already, but also wanting them to show that expertise before I moved on. I found that most people were extremely happy to go through the 'must do's', even if they already knew them, as this in itself was reassuring and made them feel that they were working on the right lines.

Thinking about structure

After-school sessions for middle leaders are tough, as all the participants have responsibilities. Where possible, make the sessions include elements of their daily work so that they feel that the time is usefully spent. You might move sessions around to reflect this, working on evaluating marking for instance, just before a whole-school marking drop.

Be aware that timings should be approximate, and variable depending on your audience response. When you are dealing with a small group like this, it is important to reflect their needs and interest, and be prepared to cut a session short, or spend longer on one aspect than you had planned, so that they remain enthused participants.

Here is the outline plan for four short after-school sessions of mentoring training for people in a position of middle leadership (or aspiring to be in that position).

It discusses how they can see themselves as leaders (referring back to how we establish credibility as mentors), how they strategise the curriculum challenges, raising aspirations (for both staff and students) and how to have difficult conversations:

- Session 1: Setting the climate
- Session 2: Facing curriculum challenges
- Session 3: Raising aspirations
- Session 4: Difficult conversations

Resources required

You can download the resources required for this training session from the online resources. They include:

- PowerPoint presentation: 3 Leadership mentoring training slides 1-11
- 3A Leadership sort cards
- 3B What makes a good leader
- 3C Changing the weather worksheet
- 3D Priorities worksheet
- 3E Display worksheet

After-school leadership sessions: Session 1 overview plan

Session 1: Setting the climate		
Timeline of session	Resources needed	Description of activity
5 mins	• Slides 1–2	**Introduction and objectives** • Opening question to set the scene. • Objectives for the session.
15 mins	• Slides 3–5 • 'Leadership' card sort • Sticky notes and display board • 'What makes a good leader?' worksheet	**What makes a good leader?** • Open out the question on the purpose of leaders, and use answers on slide as a starting point. • 'Leadership' card sort activity to prompt group discussion. • Reflect on leaders. Think about good leaders they have known and write down their qualities on sticky notes – one idea per sticky note. • Use the display board to present the feedback, and display sticky notes that list identical or similar characteristics on top of or next to each other to demonstrate similarities. • Reflect on whether the teams led would make similar choices – and why/why not. • Make notes on the 'What makes a good leader?' worksheet.

Session 1: Setting the climate		
Timeline of session	**Resources needed**	**Description of activity**
10 mins	• Slides 6–7 • 'Changing the weather' worksheet	**Changing the weather** • Discuss the idea of the 'weather' in school – most people should appreciate this metaphor. You can talk about how people feel in different weather as well, as a way of starting it off. • Tim Brighouse talks about how each leader creates their own 'climate'. How far do the group feel that the climate is their responsibility? • Discuss ways of making a department or area feel more 'sunny'. How do we deal with 'storms'? • Make notes on the 'Changing the weather' worksheet
10 mins	• Slides 8–9 • 'Priorities' worksheet	**Departmental priorities** • Discuss departmental plans, and how they are shared. How transparent are they, and how clearly do they link to the SIP (they should!)? • Discuss keeping a departmental folder to make priorities clear. What should this include (there will be some obvious elements such as data, interventions, records of meetings and so on, but also allow the leaders to share what they think would be useful to include)? For each element the focus should be on 'how does this make things clearer?' • One way to focus people on this is to ask them to consider how someone else can know what they were doing or planned to do I f they were taken ill or had to be away. • Make it clear that good leadership consists of being able to delegate effectively, not on doing it all by yourself.
20 mins (or as long as you are prepared to give)	• Slides 10–11 • 'Display' worksheet	**The importance of display** • Discuss how display is a key way of setting the climate in an area or department. • Discuss key display rules (e.g. displays to show off good completed work go outside the classroom; displays that aid the formation of work go inside – although of course good completed work can also be used to help develop student work). • Using the 'Display' worksheet, take staff on a tour of the school, asking some to imagine they are parents, some to be children, some to be OFSTED inspectors or other visitors. What do they notice? What do they like or think could be done better? • This is a really good opportunity to get people looking outside their own departments for modelling purposes. • The group should make notes and be ready to come to the next session with their reflections.

After-school leadership training session 1: PowerPoint presentation

Introduction and objectives *(Slides 1–2)*

Open with a question about what it means to 'set the climate'. Participants should contribute ideas about responsibility and mood-setting. Then discuss the objectives for the session using slide 2. Using the assertive 'we will', will encourage leaders to feel more determination about what they are trying to achieve. It is a good opportunity to adjust the objectives where necessary, or even replace some of them with 'we can' where people are already confident to share.

We shall be...

- Reflecting on leadership.
- Improving the climate in school.
- Keeping an eye on the bigger picture.
- Seeing through others' eyes.

What makes a good leader? *(Slides 3–5)*

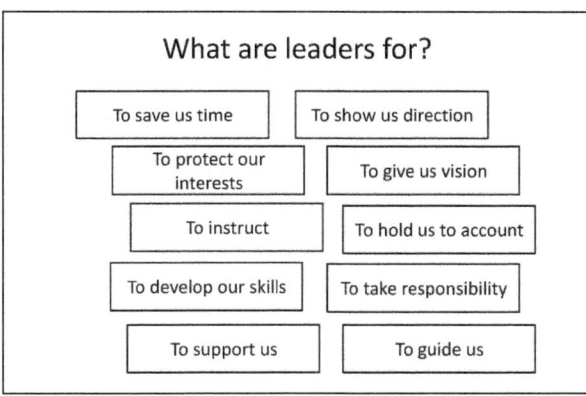

Open out debate and discussion, and then use the 'Leadership' card sort activity (see online resources 3A Leadership sort cards) to reinforce discussion.

Encourage discussion and reflection on the qualities of a good leader, getting participants to write their ideas on post-it notes, and then for feedback make clear where there is agreement and disagreement. Encourage participants to fill in the What makes a good leader worksheet (see online resources 3B What makes a good leader).

Changing the weather *(Slides 6–7)*

Using the metaphor of weather as displayed in slides 6-7, discuss the current mood in school – this can be for the day, the week, the term or the year! Then develop this to a discussion about the department or area led by each leader. Discuss how leaders are able to set the tone for their own area, and improve the weather for staff and students. What ideas do the group have for ways to improve 'bad days'? They should note their ideas on the 'Changing the weather' worksheet (see online resources 3C Changing the weather worksheet).

Departmental priorities *(Slides 8–9)*

> ## What are your top priorities for your department next year?
>
> - How visible are your plans for your department or area of responsibility to your team?
> - How visible are they to your line manager?
> - How do they link to the School Improvement Plan?
> - How can you make them completely visible and clear to everybody?

Discuss sharing departmental priorities. They should link together, as they should all be linked to school priorities. Give leaders a chance to see how they will fit together, and how they can make them clearer to each other and their teams.

Department folders are a helpful way of clarifying priorities, and can be an agreed system within school, making line management easier as well. Discuss with the group what they could contain (use examples if you have good ones existing). Encourage participants to fill in the 'Priorities' worksheet (see online resources 3D Priorities worksheet).

The importance of display *(Slides 10–11)*

> ## Display and room organisation
>
> - What is display for?
> - What difference does it make to the climate of the school?
> - What are the 'display rules'?
> - How can you prevent displays being damaged?

Discuss display; use the display in the room you are meeting in as an indication of expectations. Get participants to look at the room from the back – from the perspective of a student or an observer – and note what you can see. Often displays look better from a teacher perspective! Many leaders never get a real look at classrooms outside their own area. Get them to tour the school with you to pick up ideas and suggest improvements, filling in the 'Display' worksheet (see online resources 3D Priorities worksheet).

Resources required

You can download the resources required for this training session from the online resources. They include:

- PowerPoint presentation: 3 Leadership mentoring training slides 12-25
- 3F Competition cards

After-school leadership sessions: Session 2 overview plan

Session 2: Facing curriculum challenges		
Timeline of session	Resources needed	Description of activity
5 mins	• Slides 12–13	**Introduction and objectives** • Opening question to set the scene. • Objectives for the session. • Feedback from impressions of the tour of the school at the end of last session.
15 mins	• Slides 14–17 • 'Competition' cards • Sticky notes and display board	**What is the point of a curriculum?** • Open out a question on the purpose of a curriculum, encouraging participants to write answers on sticky notes. • Using the idea of the hare and the tortoise as a starting point, discuss the nature of the 'race' of the curriculum. What is the place of competition – is it legitimate aspiration? • Complete the 'Competition' card sort activity to prompt group discussion on the nature of competition. Is it a way of increasing aspiration, or something that leaves out the most vulnerable? • Share and reflect on the story of Daniel Boyers. This is a heart-warming story – is it how we should arrange our curriculum? • Consolidate the discussion by looking at the key questions on Slide 17. How carefully do we need to consider these questions before we can really develop our department or area of responsibility?
10 mins	• Slide 18 • Sticky notes and display board	**What are the key skills for starting school?** • Ask the group to individually write down the eight skills that they think a child should have before they start school using eight sticky notes. • As you reveal the eight skills on Slide 18 (voted for by primary teachers) get participants to come up and stick their sticky notes on the display board to show where they have come up with the same skills.

Session 2: Facing curriculum challenges		
Timeline of session	**Resources needed**	**Description of activity**
		• What skills have they come up with which have not been named?
		• What is it that distinguishes these skills?
15 mins	• Slides 19–20 • Sticky notes and display board	**What are the skills for secondary school?** • Ask participants to come up with eight skills for secondary school in the same kind of format. • Sticky notes for eight individual skills can then be shared with the group by way of feedback to see whether the whole group can agree on eight key skills.

		• Appropriate skills might include:
		  o To be able to read fluently at an age appropriate level
		  o To be able to write fluently at an age appropriate level
		  o To be able to get themselves to and from school by themselves when necessary
		  o To be able to understand how to have a debate or discussion without losing their temper.
		• Feedback and share ideas, looking particularly at different emphases in different curriculum areas.
		• Discuss how much participants think their teams would agree. Why/why not?
		• This kind of exercise increases empathy as well as encouraging deeper thought about differentiation.

10 mins	• Slides 21–22 • Sticky notes and display board	**The importance of transition** • Transition – whether from KS2 to KS3, KS3 to KS4 or KS4 to KS5 – is a key time at secondary school. • Ask participants to discuss how curriculum plans can become problematic in transition. • Look in particular at the case of a child who has failed to hit their KS2 targets. • What about a child who is out of line in the other direction – a child for whom the curriculum is too easy? • Open out the discussion to consider the alternative curriculum. What about students who are not likely to achieve the GCSE grades you would expect from someone of their age; students who are frequently absent; students who have SEND; students with behavioural problems. • How far should we create alternatives to ordinary school days for such students? Is the aim to get them back into the GCSE course, or to provide an alternative mode of progression? • Look at the profile of 'Sam'. What else would you want to know?

Session 2: Facing curriculum challenges		
Timeline of session	Resources needed	Description of activity
		• As a group, devise a curriculum for 'Sam' that you feel you could support through your department. • The group should make notes and be ready to put their reflections on the feedback board.
5 mins	• Slide 23 • Sticky notes	**Assessment of objectives and discussion around feedback** • Look at the objectives slide again and reflect on it.

After-school leadership training session 2: PowerPoint presentation

Introduction and objectives *(Slides 12–13)*

Display the opening question: 'How do we face curriculum challenges?'. What kind of challenges do we mean? Encourage discussion. Ask for feedback from last week's tour of the school. Then discuss the objectives for the session using slide 13. Often leaders will not have considered these kinds of large issues – they tend to think instead of the curriculum as a thing set in stone. This kind of lateral thinking is all the more valuable for self-reflection and strategic growth.

We shall be…

- Considering the nature of the curriculum.
- Planning for transition issues.
- Reflecting on the alternative curriculum.

What is the point of a curriculum? *(Slides 14–17)*

Discuss the question: 'What is the point of the curriculum?' Emphasise the model of the hare and the tortoise – is a race all it is? At this point you can discuss how aspiration fits into the sense of the curriculum. How do we decide what is appropriate? How about the national curriculum?

What kind of race should it be?

Daniel Boyers story

Students at St. Oswald's Catholic Primary School in Ashton-in-Makerfield, Wigan, slowed down in their sports' day race so that their classmate with cerebral palsy could win a race for the first time ever.

10-year-old Daniel Boyers did not want to take part in the race, and had told his mother he felt awkward coming to sports' day, after having surgery on his leg. She persuaded him to join in, and his kind-hearted classmates all ran slower and slower until he crossed the line first.

Point out that some ungenerous commentators protested at this story as it took away from the proper competition of a sports day. Use the 'Competition' card sort activity (see online resources 3F Competition cards) to help facilitate discussion of how we regard competition.

How restricted are we when it comes to the curriculum?

- What dictates what we teach?
- What are we trying to achieve?
- What controls the order in which students learn skills?
- How do we ensure that children have learned skills?
- What about those who don't? How do they catch up?
- What about those who already know the skills?
- How do we think about the stage before and the stage after the student is with us?

Especially in an Academy context, discuss the freedom of setting your curriculum. If we were absolutely free, what would we want students to learn?

What are the key skills for starting school? *(Slide 18)*

What are the eight skills a child should ideally have before they start school?

1. Be able to go to the toilet independently.
2. Be able to get changed for P.E.
3. Eat their lunch without fuss.
4. Not be afraid to speak up.
5. Read or recognise their name.
6. Know that rules exist.
7. Be able to listen and focus.
8. Know how to wipe their noses (more important than knowing the alphabet).

Discuss the eight skills you would want children to have for school. Slowly reveal those voted for by early years teachers, listed on slide 18. Discuss and agree; share other ideas.

What are the skills for secondary school? *(Slides 19–20)*

Display slide 19 with the question: 'If you could dictate eight skills for secondary school what would they be?' After participants have discussed in groups, feedback to compare similarities and differences.

Appropriate skills might include:

- To be able to read fluently at an age-appropriate level.
- To be able to write fluently at an age-appropriate level.
- To be able to get themselves to and from school by themselves when necessary.
- To be able to understand how to have a debate or discussion without losing their temper.

This could also move into a discussion of 'skills for life', i.e. the skills you need when you leave school. It is interesting to talk about skills that are useful outside school and skills of emotional maturity, as well as those which are useful inside school.

The importance of transition *(Slides 21–24)*

Display slide 21 with the question: Why is transition an important time? Remember here to include transition from all key stages, not just from primary to secondary school! Look at the particular case of a child who has failed to hit their KS2 targets. This is a very live issue, with those students not making expected progress being allocated extra support. How will this affect the rest of their curriculum?

What about an alternative curriculum? This will probably always be necessary for certain children. What should it include?

Consider 'Sam'. What are the detectable needs, and how can a curriculum serve these? Watch for those who assume Sam is a boy, and ask them why they do so.

Creating a curriculum for Sam

- Sam is a student in Year 9.
- Sam's attendance is below 85%.
- Sam exhibits challenging behaviour and has anger issues.
- Sam's parents are involved, but at their wit's end about his behaviour both at home and at school. Sam stays at Gran and Grandad's at weekends to help his mum and dad get a break.
- Sam likes gardening, enjoys the outside, is fond of bike riding and wants to be an engineer.
- Sam has few friends at school, and some teachers have refused to have Sam in their classes because of violent incidents.
- Sam has severe literacy difficulties.

Assessment of objectives and discussion around feedback *(Slides 25–26)*

Discuss how well the session objectives have been achieved, and get pointers for future work.

Resources required

You can download the resources required for this training session from the online resources. They include:

- PowerPoint presentation: 3 Leadership mentoring training slides 26-41

After-school leadership sessions: Session 3 overview plan

Session 3: Raising aspirations		
Timeline of session	Resources needed	Description of activity
5 mins	• Slides 26–27	**Introduction and objectives** • Opening question to set the scene. • Objectives for the session. • Make sure that you link here to the idea of mentoring – when we are trying to raise aspirations, we are also trying to move people forwards.
15 mins	• Slides 28–30 • Sticky notes and display board	**What is outstanding and aspirational teaching and learning?** • Focus on the idea of the distinction between 'outstanding' and 'good' in lesson judgements. Though these are no longer used by OFSTED, they will still ask about the quality of teaching overall. How can we identify this without grading individual lessons? How do we know what it looks like when we see it? • Ask participants to write on sticky notes what they would consider as the identifiers of outstanding, aspirational teaching, and then share this with the whole group to see areas of disagreement and areas of commonality. You should expect to see: o Outstanding progress by all students o No one left behind o Progress for groups such as Pupil Premium or EAL students outstanding o SEND provision excellent o Differentiation thoughtful and thorough o No wasted time o A sense of energy and purpose o No students waiting with their hands up o TA working in harmony with teacher – but not doing the work for the students o All students engaged o Students responsive to teacher cues.

Session 3: Raising aspirations		
Timeline of session	**Resources needed**	**Description of activity**
		• Consolidate the discussion by looking at the key questions on Slide 30. How carefully do we need to consider these questions before we can really develop aspirations in our department or area of responsibility?
10 mins	• Slides 31–33 • Copy of the *Teachers' Standards* downloaded from www.gov.uk	**What are the key elements of aspirational teaching?** • Ask the participants to discuss the seven 'true or false' statements on Slide 31. • Look carefully at the *Teacher's Standards*, and emphasise how aspirational they are by asking participants to highlight the aspirational elements (e.g. to set goals that stretch and challenge pupils; to promote a love of learning and intellectual curiosity). • Reflect on the points on Slide 33: what principles should we establish to maintain high aspirations?
15 mins	• Slides 34–37 • Copy of the *Teachers' Standards*	**Scenario 1** • Look at Slide 34, and establish the four principles of how to intervene and support someone you are going to mentor. • Ask participants to look through scenario 1, and discuss the situation. What would they consider to be the problem here? (A classroom management issue to some extent) • What questions would they want to ask Anna to move this situation forward? • What action would they take? • What support would they put in place? • What non-negotiables apply? • Point out (using Slide 36) that behavioural issues are almost always a sign of failed differentiation. • Discussion and feedback. • This kind of exercise increases empathy as well as encouraging deeper thought about differentiation.
10 mins	• Slides 38–40 • Copy of the *Teachers' Standards*	**Scenario 2** • Revise the four principles set out on Slide 34. • Ask participants to look through scenario 2, and discuss the situation. What would they consider to be the problem here? (Issues with regard to teamwork and collegiality) • What questions would they want to ask Penny to move this situation forward? • What action would they take?

Session 3: Raising aspirations		
Timeline of session	**Resources needed**	**Description of activity**
		• What support would they put in place? • What non-negotiables apply? • The group should make notes and be ready to put their reflections on the feedback display board. • Some suggestions might include that Penny starts to watch other people as a first step – clearly it is not appropriate that she should refuse to allow people in her classroom, no matter how good a teacher she is, and this also needs to be addressed. Emphasise that the 'We Are Learning To' and 'What I'm Looking For' principles of WALT and WILF can be used as team statements to emphasise why it is important to share good practice.
5 mins	• Slide 25	**Assessment of objectives and discussion around feedback** • Look at the objectives slide and reflect on it.

After-school leadership training session 3: PowerPoint presentation

Introduction and objectives *(Slides 26–27)*

Display the opening question to allow focus at the start of the session: 'How do we raise aspirations for staff and students?'. Then discuss the objectives for the session using slide 27. Sharing and discussing objectives helps to clarify the 'shape' of the session. Remember the focus is on mentoring here.

We shall be...

- Deciding what we are aiming for.
- Exploring how to raise aspirations.
- Establishing our non-negotiables.

What is outstanding and aspirational teaching and learning?
(Slides 28–30)

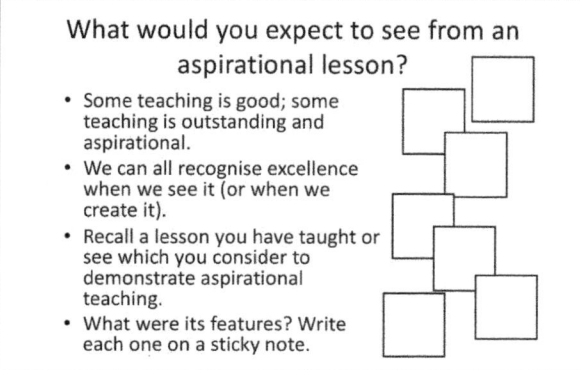

What would you expect to see from an aspirational lesson?

- Some teaching is good; some teaching is outstanding and aspirational.
- We can all recognise excellence when we see it (or when we create it).
- Recall a lesson you have taught or see which you consider to demonstrate aspirational teaching.
- What were its features? Write each one on a sticky note.

Make the connection here between aspirational and outstanding – most teachers will be more familiar with the idea of 'outstanding' but this is less useful. Participants write down on sticky notes identifiers of outstanding and aspirational teaching; share these as a group. Discussion on the nature of lessons across subjects will be especially useful here. You should expect to see:

- outstanding progress by all students
- no one left behind
- outstanding progress for groups such as Pupil Premium or EAL students
- excellent SEND provision
- thoughtful and thorough differentiation
- no wasted time
- a sense of energy and purpose
- no students waiting with their hands up
- TA working in harmony with teacher – but not doing the work for the students
- all students engaged
- students responsive to teacher cues.

Consolidate the discussion by taking the time to go through each of the questions on Slide 30 and allow for discussion.

What are the key elements of aspirational teaching? *(Slides 31–33)*

It is worth examining participants' preconceptions here – many may have insufficiently aspirational aims. The features of 'inadequate' teaching are not always recognised. Check the *Teachers' Standards* for support in this discussion. Highlighting the aspirational elements of the *Teachers' Standards* is an important reminder. Discuss the idea of 'non-negotiables' – high standards of practice and collegiality that you hold to across the team.

True or false?

1. A lesson is not good if students have to wait with their hands up.
2. If some students find the task too easy this makes the lesson inadequate.
3. If some students find the task too hard this makes the lesson inadequate.
4. Low level disruption means a lesson cannot be good.
5. Teacher-led questioning is found in good lessons.
6. Progress needs to be at or above national average to be good.
7. If the TA ensures SEN students make progress this means the lesson is good.

Ask: What standards are we aiming for (slide 32)?

How do you encourage your team to raise aspirations?

- There will be some non-negotiables – establish them first.
- Look again at the *Teachers' Standards*.
- Model best practice and welcome in watchers.
- Establish who is good and use them as exemplars – across subjects if necessary.

Scenario 1 *(Slides 34–37)*

Four useful principles:

- **Questions** – clarify the situation; make sure that you have all relevant information.
- **Action** – what needs to happen immediately to improve this situation?
- **Support** – what longer term support would you put in place?
- **Non-negotiables** – what here is infringing or may be infringing your non-negotiables?

Talk through the reasons for the four principles in terms of mentoring and support.

Then look at Scenario 1 and allow free discussion of the dilemma. Explain the ways in which differentiation can help to

Scenario 1

Anna is a teacher with ten years' experience. Students in her class are not making progress. When you have spoken to her in the course of monitoring, she complains about the behaviour of certain students in her class, and says that it is impossible for her to teach the others while these students remain in her lessons.

How do you start to mentor Anna?

Differentiation

- Behavioural issues are almost always a sign of problems with differentiation.

- Students will often kick off because the work is either insufficiently challenging or not engaging enough – or because they are embarrassed at not being able to access it.

Scenario 2 *(Slides 38–40)*

Scenario 2

Penny is a teacher who has been at the school for 15 years. She always gets excellent results, and students speak fondly of her. However, she is extremely reluctant to be observed, and will refuse to have an observer in her classroom, to the extent that she will only accept one person to do her performance management and refuses all others. You are concerned about this, and would also like her to share her good practice.

How would you start to mentor Penny?

support behaviour management. Changing the way she teaches can help with Anna's perceived behaviour issues. She might want to talk to the students in the class about their experience of being taught, from another perspective.

Allow free discussion of the dilemma. One way of helping people become more prepared to share what goes on in their classrooms is to help them think of it in terms of teamwork – like a class, you need to see what goes on in each part of a team.

Be clear...

- WALT and WILF work for a team as well as a lesson.
- How will you know students have learned?
- How will you be able to show progress?
- Work backwards from what you want to achieve, and share this with your team.

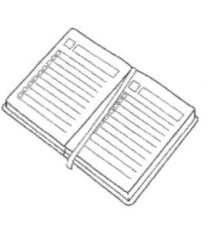

Assessment of objectives and discussion around feedback *(Slide 41)*

Discuss how well the session objectives have been achieved, and get pointers for future work.

Resources required

You can download the resources required for this training session from the online resources. They include:

- PowerPoint presentation: 3 Leadership mentoring training slides 42-58

After-school leadership sessions: Session 4 overview plan

Session 4: Difficult conversations and positive relationships		
Timeline of session	**Resources needed**	**Description of activity**
5 mins	• Slides 42–43	**Introduction and objectives** • Opening question to set the scene. • Objectives for the session. • Make sure that you link here to the idea of well-being and its importance in running a team as well as mentoring individuals.
15 mins	• Slides 44–46 • A4 paper, two colours of sticky notes and display board	**What do we mean by the 'well-being' of our staff?** • Ask groups to define the idea of well-being, and discuss until they have a clear definition that they are happy to share. • Write the definition on a piece of A4 and place it on the display board. • Discuss the signs of well-being – both positive and negative. How can they tell if someone is not doing well? What might be the warning signs?

Session 4: Difficult conversations and positive relationships		
Timeline of session	**Resources needed**	**Description of activity**
		• They should write their ideas on sticky notes, using a different colour for positive indicators, and negative indicators, and share them on the display board, placing them around their definition. • Feedback and discussion.
20 mins	• Slides 47–54 • Sticky notes and display board	**The PERFECT model of well-being** • Go through the slides that explain the PERFECT mnemonic for well-being. • For each slide, ask the group to add suggestions as to how they can add to this area of advice, and add it to the display board on sticky notes. • For the final slide, 'Teamwork', get them to share their best tips for developing a sense of shared teamwork.
15 mins	• Slides 55–57	**Scenario 1** • Look at Slide 55, and ask groups to reflect on the ways in which they should start their conversations with the teachers concerned. • Do they all start the same way? Do you need a script? • Look at Slide 56, and go through the principles. Discuss, for instance, having a clear and neutral space, and alerting the person to the topic of the conversation rather than springing it on them. • Make sure that people are clear about what they want to achieve and how to move forward. • Look again at Slide 55, and reconsider how to apply the principles to the conversations concerned. • Ask the participants to work in pairs to practise role-playing the first part of a difficult conversation. • This kind of exercise increases empathy towards the team, and encourages reflection. • Look at Slide 57. How far do we need to have scripts to support us in difficult conversations so as to move people on?

Session 4: Difficult conversations and positive relationships		
Timeline of session	**Resources needed**	**Description of activity**
5 mins	• Slide 58	**Assessment of objectives and discussion around feedback** • Look at objectives slide and reflect on it.

After-school leadership training session 4: PowerPoint presentation

Introduction and objectives *(Slides 42–43)*

Display the opening question to allow focus at the start of the session: 'How do we create positive and productive relationships in a team?'.

We shall be...

- Considering the PERFECT model for well-being.
- Practising difficult conversations with staff.

Then discuss the objectives for the session. Sharing and discussing objectives helps to clarify the 'shape' of the session. Remember the focus is on mentoring here.

What do we mean by the 'well-being of our staff'? *(Slides 44–46)*

Well-being

- How would you define 'well-being' in respect to members of staff?
- In your group, create a short definition and share it on the display board when you are ready.

What do we mean by well-being, and how can we define it? Emphasise the importance of well-being and its impact on the smooth functioning of a team.

Discuss the positive and negative signs of well-being; include indicators for positive

wellbeing such as people talking happily about what they did at the weekend.

Staff well-being

- Studies show that happiness in staff leads to increased productivity. Conversely, unhappy people do not thrive at work.
- If work is adding to unhappiness, these effects are magnified a thousandfold.
- Unhappiness can manifest in different ways, such as increased time off sick, lack of punctuality, forgetfulness and so on.
- What other evidence can you think of?

The PERFECT model of well-being *(Slides 47-54)*

Briefly go through the PERFECT mnemonic for well-being. For each slide, discuss the points on the slide and remember to ask 'what else?':

- **P**ositive emotions – e.g. think of good news items to share from other areas of school.
- **E**ngagement – e.g. ask other team members for advice in areas where they are expert.
- **R**elationships – e.g. remember birthdays if you are told them, and mention them or send a card!
- **F**airness – e.g. make decisions explicit to encourage the sense that you behave justly, or use the phrase 'I hope you agree that's fair' to give people a chance to speak their minds.
- **E**njoyment – e.g. emphasise how well they are doing against last year.
- **C**elebration – e.g. remember fairness and don't over-celebrate some people at the expense of others' feelings.
- **T**eamwork – encourage discussion. Be careful to give due weight to people's personal experiences – try asking them when they feel people haven't worked well in a team and what they think caused this.

Scenario 1 *(Slides 55–57)*

Discuss how to start these difficult conversations – allow the group to share experiences.

Discuss the principles for difficult conversations.

Establish the reasons for these principles – reflect again on the well-being principles of justice. Not rushing, and not trying to get everything done and dusted in one conversation is also important. Reflect on the principles of

---

How do you work with teachers who need improvement?

How would you start a conversation about the following problems:

- a parental complaint about favouritism in class
- a parental complaint about homophobic bullying in class
- a marking drop which picked up marking left undone for more than a month
- a high number of C4s from a particular class.

---

mentoring: the ability to listen and to think of what lies beneath what is said, and the need to challenge and move people forward as well. A focus on development and positive change can be really helpful in these conversations.

Principles for difficult conversations

- approach directly
- be clear about the problem
- know the objective you want to achieve
- listen to the story
- focus on the facts
- acknowledge emotions
- give space and silence
- reflect before acting

How can you set up a mentoring culture?

- Do we need scripts?
- Do we need an identical style?

- Do we need to be experts?

Assessment of objectives and discussion around feedback
(Slide 58)

Discuss how well the session objectives have been achieved.

3 Training plans – Coaching

Creating effective in-house CPD for coaching

The very methodology of coaching means that training for it is best delivered in-house. If you are trying to draw out someone's innate strengths and help them to share their own good practice, then by its very nature sending them to an outside provision is likely to result in little impact once they come back to school. To be effective, coaching CPD needs to be intimately integrated into the whole life of the school, so that participants do not think of it as a 'bolt-on' but rather as an integral part of their everyday practice. To do this, you will need to run in-house CPD and this chapter gives you a selection of ways in which to do this, from whole-school sessions, through twilight input, to regular 'coach the coach' sessions to support those who wish to work as coaches.

Whole-school session

Creating a coaching culture for staff

When organising coaching CPD for your staff you will find that different kinds of session will help at different times. However, if you are serious about creating a coaching culture for your school, you will need at least one whole-school session to support what you are doing so that your staff understands the rationale for your ambitions. Giving coaching that proper time and space will also signal its importance and allow staff to consider and plan the ways in which they might contribute towards developing a coaching culture throughout school.

'The art of teaching is the art of assisting discovery.' (Mark Van Doren)

Thinking about audience

Before you start any whole-school session, you will want to consider your audience, and what they will already know about the subject. It is, of course, difficult when you are working with a diverse staff body to be sure that your presentation is going to hit the spot. It's all too easy to find that you are going too fast for some people while making others feel that they are being talked down to. To avoid this, it is key that you find out something about your audience's level of expertise before you start.

Assuming that you are not totally new to your school, this should not be as difficult as it sounds. One way of finding this out is to plan a short survey before the session and use it to help you pitch your presentation (you could use the self-evaluation questionnaire in part 1, chapter 2); another way is to ask line managers and middle leaders to give you an overall sense of where their teams are on the issue; another is to ask departments or year group teams to gather before the session starts and do an exercise which puts together their ideas about coaching.

Although all the strategies can be effective at finding out information, the advantage of this last strategy is that you will get people thinking about coaching very early on and engaging their minds with the issues in a lively discussion before you even open your mouth. Like Mark Van Doren advocates, you want to assist discovery, not force ideas upon people.

When thinking about planning a whole-school CPD session it makes sense to be aware of previous feedback about CPD. Ideally, of course, this feedback would be from previous sessions and so particular to your school, enabling you to tailor your session to existing expertise and existing understanding, but even if you do not have access to this kind of data there will be certain principles that will almost always hold true and can help you to structure your session.

It has been said that teachers are the worst possible audience, and there is a reason for this. Most teachers are independent-minded self-starters who are used to knowing things – if they don't know something, for instance in preparation for a class, they are highly likely to have strategies already available to them whereby they can look it up for themselves. As a result, they tend to be impatient with exactly the kinds of presentation that they are told not to do themselves in the classroom: talking from the front, information giving without time for reflection and so on. You will often hear teachers at a conference complaining about information read from a slide, or about information that could have been given in written form to save time.

Be aware of this and be careful that you treat your teachers as the experts that they are. Teach them as you would wish to be taught and give them time and space to reflect at each stage. For one thing, if you are sincerely trying to create a coaching culture in school, it makes sense to ensure that you give each teacher room to breathe, dignity of thought, and a chance to express their own opinions.

On the other hand, you don't want to have a situation where people don't understand something and find it frustrating – but don't tell you as they don't want to slow the pace. Ensure that you build into your session opportunities for questions and for information sharing and that you also have summary factsheets that can be useful, for instance to reference an unfamiliar acronym or check the name of an expert.

Thinking about purpose

If you think about your purpose when planning, you won't go far wrong. Just as with a lesson, think about what you want to achieve. Think about it as though you were presenting to students, so that you don't miss out on important stages. For instance, when planning an English lesson, if I wanted students to learn about how to analyse language in a scene in *Macbeth*, I would have to go through some necessary stages: first, make sure that they knew the scene I wanted to discuss and understood what was happening in it; then I would want to be sure that they understood the meaning of all the words and phrases used; then I would need to ensure that they knew the parameters of analysis we were talking about and the expectations – what kind of language would I be expecting them to use? What kind of detail would I be expecting? I would need to model this before I could ask them to try it out for themselves, and then I might want them to do a short example before I set them off on the whole thing.

In the same way, when planning your whole-school coaching CPD, consider what you want to achieve at the end. What should people be able to do as a result of your session that they are not currently able to do? Notice how this connects back to knowing your audience – if you don't know where they are coming from, then how can you address their learning needs? Think about how embarrassing it would be to pontificate about coaching to someone and then discover that they are a professional life coach in their spare time.

Thinking about content

There are many ways to plan a whole-school session. Bear in mind that you are introducing the ideas, not actively trying to start people off as coaches (this can be done in smaller sessions). As a result of this, your session should probably contain the following elements:

1. a pre-survey or discussion to get people thinking about the advantages of coaching
2. a warm-up activity to clarify what you mean by coaching
3. an information section that explains how coaching connects to existing ideas about school improvement, and perhaps some research evidence for the benefits of a coaching culture in schools
4. some examples of successful strategies in different contexts
5. an opportunity for staff to discuss possible strategies and how they would fit into the existing culture of the school
6. opportunities for staff to offer feedback and work with different groups moving forwards.

Thinking about structure

When structuring your session, be aware of the need to give people breaks. This means that you should be careful to vary activities and tasks to ensure that no one has to concentrate too long on one speaker. To neglect this strategy can reduce the level of meaningful uptake from your participants. Evaluations are consistently better in sessions where participants are allowed to discuss and suggest ideas.

It also makes sense to signal to people that there will be opportunities to talk and ask questions throughout the sessions. If participants know that there will shortly be an opportunity to clarify ideas and question, then they are more likely to focus for the time you wish.

Make sure that you have an outline plan for the session that you can fiddle about with as you add in further thoughts and ideas. Below is the outline for a one-hour session, that you may wish to adapt and personalise further for your school. The session introduces the idea of coaching, and the principles of coaching, and encourages the participants to reflect on their personal experience. It gives some research background, and invites participants to consider how to build a coaching culture in school. It also explores the idea of what makes good teaching as a starting point for coaching.

Resources required

You can download the resources required for this training session from the online resources. They include:

- PowerPoint presentation: 4 Leadership mentoring training slides 42-58
- 4A Reflection sheet
- 4B Discussion cards
- 4C Good teacher sort cards

One-hour session: overview plan

Timeline of session	Resources needed	Description of activity
Before start	• Chairs and tables for 'cabaret-style' seating: groups of 5–8 per table • Large display board • Projector and PowerPoint presentation	• Arrange tables for 'cabaret-style' seating with PowerPoint display easily visible to all
5 mins	• Slides 1–2	**Brief introduction** • Why are we here? • What is the objective of the session?
15 mins	• Slides 3–8 • Writing implements and sticky notes or small squares of paper • One large piece of paper for each table • Display board • Reflection sheets	**What do you understand by coaching?** • Participants should write on one sticky note a definition of coaching, without speaking to anyone else in their group, using slide 1 as a stimulus • Once definitions are written, groups discuss them and see if they can find commonalities between individual ideas • Each group should then come up with a definition of coaching that they feel they can all agree with, to be shared on the display board • Groups discuss other groups' definitions

Timeline of session	Resources needed	Description of activity
		• Participants to record one example of a coaching experience on their second sticky note • Participants to record outcomes and opinions on their personal reflection sheet
10 mins	• Slides 9–14 • Reflection sheets	**Introduction to coaching in schools** • Introduce the principles of coaching through reflecting on personal experience • Establish how these fit with Geoff Barton's principles of effective school improvement • Discuss research evidence: there is not much at present that measures 'hard' impact for schools, but the CUREE study establishes the benefits of a coaching culture, and evidence from other areas outside education is convincing in terms of the effect of a coaching culture • Introduce, or remind participants of, the idea of 'growth mindset' and how this fits into coaching • Ask participants to note down any details that they find interesting on their reflection sheet
10 mins	• Slide 15 • Discussion cards • Sticky notes	**What does effective coaching look like?** • Ask participants to arrange the discussion cards into activities that they think describe coaching-style activities and those which do not • Most of the cards describe activities that could be described as coaching for students – the point here is not to get right and wrong answers but to facilitate discussion about which activities allow you to demonstrate the features of coaching • Participants should then write on sticky notes some activities that they think could contribute towards a coaching culture for staff • Place these sticky notes on the display board for sharing at the end of the session
15 mins	• Slides 16–19 • 'Good teacher' sort cards (including blank cards) • Writing implements and sticky notes • Display board	**What does effective teaching look like?** • Ask participants to discuss in their groups what they think makes a good teacher, using the sort cards to help them. What characteristics would they like to add to those on the printed cards? The blank cards can be written on too, so supply these • They should pick three top characteristics, and share them with the whole group • Look at the quotation from the self-confessed 'bad teacher'. Does this person really have to leave the profession? Thinking about Geoff Barton's principles, and coaching principles, what alternatives could there be, and when would you want the intervention to take place? • How can we, as colleagues, help to move someone from the habits and experiences that make them a 'bad teacher' towards being a 'good teacher'?

Timeline of session	Resources needed	Description of activity
		• Whole-group feedback: each group to nominate someone to report back their ideas to the whole staff
5 mins	• Slide 20	**Questions and discussion around feedback** • Give staff an opportunity to discuss the overall ideas thrown up from feedback from each group

Whole-school session: PowerPoint presentation

Brief introduction *(Slides 1–2)*

Display slide 1 when participants enter; the question: 'Creating a whole-school coaching culture: Why is it important, and how can we start to do it?' will help to prompt them for their first activity. Then, discuss the session objectives to give participants an idea of the structure of the session.

Outline and objectives of session

- To explore our current ideas of what coaching means and how it connects to our roles.
- To understand why coaching is seen to be an effective school improvement tool.
- To identify how coaching strategies could support our work with students.
- To consider how coaching can be used to effectively improve school development in teaching and learning.

What do you understand by coaching? *(Slides 3–8)*

You have two sticky notes before you.

Without talking to anyone else on your table, write on <u>one</u> of them the answer to the question on the following slide…

Ensure that there is clarity about the 'no talking' rule before you start, as the initial activity works better if individuals work on the idea before they share definitions. The quotations should help participants think about coaching without giving

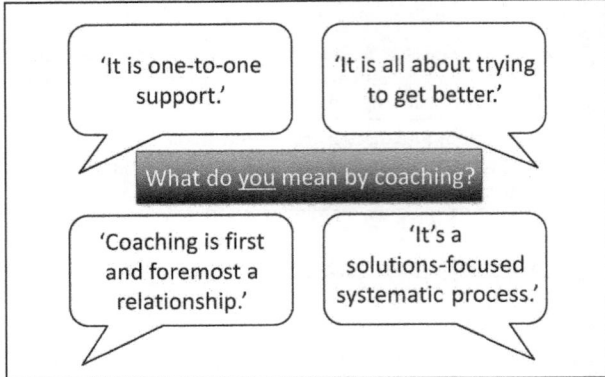

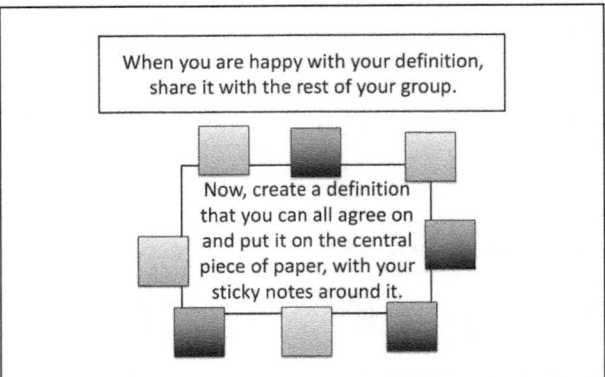

them the answers. It is important to give time for the shared discussion; don't hurry it. Move around tables to get an idea of participants' responses.

Having thought about what coaching means and discussed it, participants should then be ready to reflect on their own experiences. It may take some time for people to look at each others' definitions: again, don't let momentum slip, but you will find that the discussion is productive in getting everyone focused on coaching and its significance.

Repeat the activity, this time getting participants to write an example of a coaching situation on their second post it. Then display the quote on slide 8 entitled 'What is coaching' and see if participants agree.

Introduction to coaching in schools *(Slides 9–14)*
Ask participants to consider how others have affected their own personal experience of growth. Use the prompt question: what would happen if we did this for students? Would it provide a more productive and personalised learning environment? Encourage participants to discuss what makes a helpful coach – be aware that some of these elements may be challenging.

How do we help others to flourish?

- Think of someone who has had a profoundly positive impact on your personal development.
- Someone who has helped you to get to be the person you are now.
- It could be a colleague or a friend.
- What did they do, and what qualities did they demonstrate that helped you to flourish?

Did they...

- Listen to what you had to say?
- Give you space and time to think for yourself?
- Give you things to think about?
- Believe in your abilities?
- Challenge your ideas?
- Encourage you?
- Treat you with respect?
- Make you feel safe?
- Make you feel valued?
- Make you feel more confident?

What would happen if we did this for students?

As an expert on school improvement, Geoff Barton is influential and well respected. Go through his basic principles about school improvement on slide 12 and explain how these lead to a coaching culture. Then use CUREE's research on slide 13 as a springboard to talk about impact and effectiveness. We know that coaching has an impact outside schools, in a business context – there is lots of evidence for this. The evidence for impact in schools is often more anecdotal, but this new research from CUREE establishes that there is a measurable impact. Then use slide 14 to run through the idea of the growth mindset – that believing in predetermined talent and 'genius' is a brake to development and excellence; those students who believe that they can improve will improve, because they will persist.

What does effective coaching look like? *(Slide 15)*

Ask participants to consider which of the activities used in class are typical of coaching, and why. Can they add to them from their own experience? Which kinds of activity are necessary but not coaching in nature?

What does effective teaching look like? *(Slides 16–19)*

Use the 'Good teacher' sort cards (see online resources 4C Good teacher sort cards) to discuss what makes a good teacher, and prioritise those characteristics. Arrange the cards in a 'diamond nine' to show the most and least important qualities.

Discuss what makes a 'bad' teacher. Look at the case study and discuss what support this teacher needed, and when it should have come into place.

> ## What makes a bad teacher?
>
> 'I think I was a bad teacher. It wasn't that my results were bad, though they were not good. It was that I went into class every day dreading it.
>
> The school I worked at was not that tough, but it was challenging. I spent ages planning but lessons never went well, and I was always behind with my marking. Everyone knew I was no good – even students would make jokes about how I was a rubbish teacher.
>
> Eventually I decided I couldn't stand coming in any more and went off sick with stress.'

How could coaching help to support teaching and learning development?

> ## How could you help this teacher?
>
> - What strategies do you think could move this teacher on from being a 'bad' teacher?
> - How do you think coaching strategies could help this teacher to improve their experience at work?
> - Discuss this in your table groups, and be ready to report back – nominate a spokesperson!

Questions and discussion around feedback *(Slide 20)*

Feedback and final discussion – don't forget to ask participants to fill the evaluation sheet!

After-school training: working with a group of coaches

Thinking about audience

For this kind of session, your audience is likely to be a group of staff members with a particular interest in using coaching strategies in their daily work. This might consist of deputy middle leaders, heads or deputy heads of year, teachers in their second or subsequent year who are considering becoming learning coaches, learning mentors, etc.

The training should be organised so that although it is progressive, there are elements that they can use as soon as possible. Ideally, every session would have a 'takeaway' that they can try out, so that they can then bring feedback to the next session.

Thinking about purpose

You will need to ensure that the course makes your participants feel more confident and adept at their daily role. You are aiming to create areas of expertise, but also to reinforce the good practice that already exists. For most members of staff with whom you may be working, they will have done something like coaching, though they may not have done it formally, and they may even have made some errors. Establishing what they already do well will give them confidence moving forward or in changing practice where this is necessary.

Thinking about content

The content of the training will need to give participants the tools to coach effectively. Thinking through the coaching process will allow you to work out what is most necessary to include. For instance, you will want to make sure that you include: how to set up a coaching session, the professional parameters, how to set SMART targets, and some detailed information on effective questioning.

The sessions should involve reflection and discussion, and so you will need to make it clear that they will themselves be confidential – a 'safe space' for the participants, where no question is a bad one, and no comment is unsayable. You will also need to be aware that voluntary sessions attended after school rely on the participants being committed to the whole course. Make sure this is clear from the outset, and reinforce the sense of being in a team through group work and discussion.

For best effect, the sessions should be highly interactive and problem-solving. It should actually matter whether people attend the sessions, in other words, you should not be able to get the same effect through just reading through the notes as you get from being there!

Thinking about structure

If you want your participants to be able to use the materials as they go, then it makes sense to start with the key elements, such as safeguarding and confidentiality parameters, target setting and goals, and move onwards. The following is the outline of a training plan that you can use immediately, though if you wish you can personalise it further for your school. It consists of five after-school sessions with a small group of about six would-be coaches.

- Session 1: The qualities of a good coach
- Session 2: Setting the scene for coaching
- Session 3: Setting targets
- Session 4: Listening skills
- Session 5: Developing questioning skills

Resources required

You can download the resources required for this training session from the online resources. They include:

- PowerPoint presentation: 5 Working with a group of coaches slides 1–10
- 5A Diamond nine cards

After-school training: Session 1 overview plan

Session 1: The qualities of a good coach		
Timeline of session	**Resources needed**	**Description of activity**
5 mins	• Slides 1–2	**Introduction and objectives** • Make introductions, and set the overall parameters for the sessions (confidentiality etc.). • Introduce session objectives.
15 mins	• Slides 3–4 • Display board	**What makes a good coach?** • In pairs, discuss the qualities and demeanour of a good coach, using personal experience where relevant. • Report back ideas on the display board and open out the discussion to the whole group.
15 mins	• Slide 5 • Diamond nine cards • Diamond nine template	**Working out priorities** • Introduce the qualities of a good coach, and go through them – especially if the previous discussion has not mentioned any of them. • Use a diamond nine to arrange the qualities of a good coach in order or priority, with the most important quality at the top. • Pairs to feedback to the group and discuss an agreed set of important qualities and demeanour for a good coach.

Session 1: The qualities of a good coach		
Timeline of session	Resources needed	Description of activity
10 mins	• Slides 6–7 • Sticky notes or cards of two colours	**Self-reflection** • Individually, participants use two sticky notes or cards to write down qualities that they think will make them a good coach, and qualities that may hinder them. • Hold a group discussion – use the idea on Slide 7 to place the sticky notes on a continuum (expressing how a good quality can be negative in certain contexts and vice-versa).
10 mins	• Slides 8–9	**What have we decided?** • Mini-plenary to establish the principles on Slide 8. • Reflection on how far objectives have been achieved.
5 mins	• Slide 10	**Feedback** • Give feedback on what has been established, and share sticky notes about qualities. • Time for questions.

After-school training: Session 1 PowerPoint presentation

Introduction and objectives *(Slides 1–2)*

Display slide 1 when participants enter with the question: 'What are the qualities of a good coach?'; it will help to prepare them for the session. Then, discuss the session objectives to give participants an idea of the structure of the session.

Objectives

- To explore the qualities of a good coach.

- To determine how our own qualities can further effective coaching.

- To set up parameters for coaching sessions.

What makes a good coach? *(Slides 3–4)*

Participants should reflect on their own experience to help with this activity. Encourage discussion about both good and bad qualities in a coach, and include demeanour (tone of voice etc.) to make it clear it is not innate qualities you are discussing, but conscious (and changeable) behaviour.

Working out priorities *(Slide 5)*

What qualities would you look for above all in a coach? • Sense of humour • Empathy • Ability to create rapport • Non-judgemental • Supportive • Engaged • Honest • Enthusiastic • Optimistic • Realistic • Resilient • Determined • Passionate • Knowledgeable

With your partner use a diamond nine to explore which qualities you agree are MOST important.

Talk through the qualities, reflecting on how far these agree with the previous discussion, and ask pairs to work on a diamond nine using the sort cards (see online resources 5A diamond nine cards).

Self-reflection *(Slides 6–7)*

Encourage individuals to reflect on their own qualities and which will help and hinder them in a coaching situation. Again the emphasis is not that these are bad or good but that they are more or less appropriate. Explain how these qualities are part of a continuum. Encourage participants to see how they can place their 'bad' or 'good' qualities on a continuum, and perhaps move them in the direction that they wish.

What have we decided? *(Slides 8–9)*

Working as a coach may mean... • You have to bite your tongue at times. • You have to resist judging what other people say. • You have to remain positive and encouraging. • You have to be prepared to challenge others. • You have to be able to see other people's points of view. • You have to give others space and time to think.

Discuss how you may have to moderate your natural reactions to be an effective coach. Then reflect on the objectives for the session.

Feedback *(Slide 10)*

Resources required

You can download the resources required for this training session from the online resources. They include:

- PowerPoint presentation: 5 Working with a group of coaches slides 10-20
- 5B Messages worksheet

After-school training: Session 2 overview plan

Session 2: Setting the scene for coaching		
Timeline of session	**Resources needed**	**Description of activity**
5 mins	• Slides 11–12	**Introduction and objectives** • Establish the purpose of the session and reflect on the conclusions from the last session, reminding the group of the demeanour and qualities of a good coach. • Introduce session objectives.
10 mins	• Slides 13–14 • Display board	**What would be the best conditions for coaching?** • In pairs, discuss the best environment for coaching. What would be really unpleasant or difficult to deal with (e.g. interruptions, a room with others in it)? • Report back ideas on the display board and open out the discussion to whole group.
15 mins	• Slides 15–16	**Working out how you affect others** • Consider the statement on Slide 15 and ask the group for feedback about what they think may have produced such a negative impression.

Session 2: Setting the scene for coaching		
Timeline of session	Resources needed	Description of activity
		• Look at the statement from the coach. What do they think has gone wrong with the relationship? • As a coach, how would they react to this complaint from someone after the first session? How would they move this relationship forward in a positive way?
15 mins	• Slide 17 • 'Messages' worksheet	**Self-reflection** • What messages do the behaviours listed send? Participants should work individually, then discuss their answers in pairs. • Open out the discussion to the whole group – what are the opposite behaviours, to produce the opposite impression?
10 mins	• Slides 18–19 • Sticky notes or cards	**What are the non-negotiables?** • Individually, participants to use post-its or cards to write down what they think would be the non-negotiables for an effective coaching session. • One post-it for each rule. • Post-its should be placed on the board for feedback, and grouped to show where participants have agreed shared rules.
5 mins	• Slide 20	**Reflection and feedback** • Reflection on how far objectives have been achieved. • Time for questions.

After-school training: Session 2 PowerPoint presentation
Introduction and objectives (Slides 11-12)
Display slide 11 when participants enter, with the question: 'How can we set the scene for effective coaching?'; it will help to prepare them for the session. Then, discuss the session objectives to give participants an idea of the structure of the session.

> # Objectives
>
> • To determine the best physical conditions for coaching.
>
> • To reflect on how our behaviour and body language affects others.
>
> • To set up parameters for coaching sessions.

What would be the best conditions for coaching? *(Slides 13–14)*

Time and place

- In pairs, decide what conditions would be best for a coaching session.
- What kind of room would you need?
- What kind of time would be best?
- What would you need to have in the room?
- How would it be best arranged?

Participants work in pairs to consider the best context for coaching. You could try actually moving furniture around at this stage to explore how different arrangements make a difference to comfort in speaking!

Working out how you affect others *(Slides 15–16)*

Just as important as the room...

> In my first coaching session I felt really uncomfortable for some reason. I had the impression that the coach wasn't really very keen on working with me, and that they didn't think the problems that I brought forward were really worth bothering with. I just got the impression that I should buck up and work harder. I decided not to go back to the next session.

Discuss the feedback on a coaching session – what might have caused it?

The coach responds...

> That feedback seems really unfair to me. I did make an effort to move things on, but that was because I knew that we had a lot to do. I found her difficult to work with, to be honest. She spent a lot of time looking at her phone, which I thought was really rude.

Discuss the coach's response – how could you improve this situation?

Self-reflection *(Slide 17)*

> # What messages are you sending?
>
> - If you leave the door of the room open?
> - If you sit on a sofa?
> - If you have your phone out?
> - If you offer a cup of tea or coffee?
> - If you sit with your arms folded?
> - If you sit behind a desk?
> - If you take a phone call during a session?
> - If you don't make eye contact?
> - If you doodle while you listen?
> - If you look at your watch?

The 'Messages' worksheet (see online resources 5B Messages worksheet) should become the basis for discussion about how to change behaviours – notice not all these behaviours are bad ones!

What are the non-negotiables? *(Slides 18–19)*

> # Prioritising what is important
>
> - Using the sticky notes, decide what would be your non-negotiables for a coaching session.
> - What 'rules' would you want to set up with the person that you are coaching?
> - What 'rules' would you want to set up with others who work with them?
> - Write your ideas on the sticky notes – one for each rule.

It is important here to establish shared rules and emphasise their importance. Ask participants to put their feedback sticky notes in a way that demonstrates shared agreement and rules.

Reflection and feedback

Give participants the opportunity to reflect on the feedback from others, and decide if they feel comfortable that the objectives have been met.

Resources required

You can download the resources required for this training session from the online resources. They include:

- PowerPoint presentation: 5 Working with a group of coaches slides 21-38
- 5C Target statement cards
- 5D SMART target handout

After-school training: Session 3 overview plan

Session 3: Setting targets		
Timeline of session	**Resources needed**	**Description of activity**
5 mins	• Slides 21–22	**Introduction and objectives** • Establish the purpose of the session and reflect on the conclusions from the last session, reminding the group of our non-negotiables. • Introduce session objectives.
10 mins	• Slide 23 • Target statement cards photocopied on card and cut into strips – one set for each pair	**Why do we need targets?** • In pairs, discuss the statements about targets. • Arrange the statements in order of importance. • In fours (2x pairs) discuss which statements you agree are most important. • Reflect if anyone strongly disagrees with statements. • Report back ideas on the display board and open out the discussion to the whole group.
15 mins	• Slides 24–29 • 'SMART targets' handout	**Working out why we need SMART targets** • Consider the statements on each slide and ask the group for feedback about why each element of SMART is important. • Record reasons and make notes on the 'SMART targets' handout.
15 mins	• Slides 30–34 • 'SMART targets' handout	**Practising changing targets to make them SMARTer** • Go through the slides in order, discussing the flaws with each target. • For each example, participants should work in pairs to improve the target and make it better in the specific way focused on. • Ideas should be recorded on the 'SMART targets' handout. • Each pair should report back to the group before moving on to the next slide.
10 mins	• Slides 35–36 • Sticky notes or cards • Display board	**Creating completely SMART targets** • Individually, participants use sticky notes or cards to try to improve the targets using the other elements of SMART. • Sticky notes should be placed on the display board for feedback, and participants can discuss which are the most effectively defined.
5 mins	• Slide 37	**Reflection and feedback** • Reflect on how far the objectives have been achieved. • Time for questions.

After-school training: Session 3 PowerPoint presentation

Introduction and objectives *(Slides 21–22)*

Display slide 21 when participants enter with the question 'How do we set effective targets?'; it will help to prepare them for the session. Then, discuss the session objectives to give participants an idea of the structure of the session.

Objectives

- To understand the importance of setting targets in coaching.

- To investigate what makes targets SMART.

- To be able to construct SMART targets, and improve targets that are not SMART.

Why do we need targets? *(Slide 23)*

Participants work in pairs to agree the importance of setting targets. They read through the targets on the sort cards (see online resources 5C target sort cards) and arrange them in order of importance. Are there any statements they strongly disagree with?

Working out why we need SMART targets *(Slides 24–29)*

Open out the discussion to see whether participants understand the **SMART** principles: **S**pecific, **M**easurable, **A**chievable, **R**elevant, **T**ime-related. Discuss what goes wrong if targets are not all SMART.

Practising changing targets to make them SMARTer *(Slides 30–34)*

Slides 30-34 list different targets. Go through each slide and discuss the ways in which the targets fail. There will be some repetition here, but it is all to the good to firmly establish the principles of setting targets.

Creating completely SMART targets *(Slides 35–36)*

Some of the work will already have been done – again repetition is important, and participants should now be thinking of ways to make targets different

---

Make these into SMART targets

- Improve my results.
- Get higher grades.
- Learn 50 vocabulary words each week.
- Get a part-time job.
- Go to homework club for maths.

---

and effective. Get participants to share ideas as to how to improve targets. Get them to fill in the SMART target sheet (see online resources 5D SMART targets worksheet).

Reflection and feedback
Discuss if the objectives were achieved. This is also a time for questions.

Resources required
You can download the resources required for this training session from the online resources. They include:

- PowerPoint presentation: 5 Working with a group of coaches slides 38-55
- 5E Analysing and reflecting handout

After-school training: Session 4 overview plan

Session 4: Listening skills		
Timeline of session	Resources needed	Description of activity
5 mins	• Slides 38–40	**Introduction and objectives** • Establish the purpose of the session and reflect on the conclusions from the last session, reminding the group of SMART targets. • Introduce session objectives. • Introduce the information about positive listening skills and start by asking participants to reflect on how much time they spent listening today.
10 mins	• Slides 41–42 • Stopwatch or timer on board (you could use www.online-stopwatch.com/full-screen-stopwatch/)	**Practising listening** • In pairs, decide on who is participant A and who is B. • Time two minute sessions where A and B take turns to talk to each other about the three most important things they have listened to today.

Session 4: Listening skills		
Timeline of session	Resources needed	Description of activity
		• Participant A reports back to the group on B's day, and B on A's. • For each pair, the person reported on has to comment on the accuracy of the commentary. Open out a discussion reflecting on listening skills to the whole group.
10 mins	• Slides 43–44	**Working out what is really being said** • Explain the idea of the 'Columbo question'. You could show a clip of the TV series from YouTube – if you search for 'Columbo question' there are many examples of suitable clips. • Get participants to look at the statement and decide what are the real concerns lying behind it. • Participants should pick out that the speaker is intimidated by their friends, and doesn't feel able to express their own taste in books for fear of looking babyish.
10 mins	• Slides 45–48 • 'Analysing and reflecting' handout	**Reflecting and paraphrasing** • A key listening skill is being able to reflect what someone says. You do this through picking out key passages in the statement, and either repeating (reflecting) them or else putting them into different terms (paraphrasing). • Explain the ways in which this can be done, using the Slide 47 as an example. • Ask participants to go through the statement line by line and write down possible reflective responses, using Handout TW5. • Open out feedback to the group by moving on to Slide 48, showing some possible responses.
15 mins	• Slides 49–53 • Cards for participants to write their statements	**The power of silence** • Explain the idea of the power of silence, and listening to body language. • Go through the slides explaining how body language and words can conflict, and discuss what non-verbal cues you might look for to show that someone was happy or unhappy. • Play the 'truth or dare' game, where participants have to think of two truths and a lie about themselves. • They give one truth and one lie on a card to their partner, and their partner asks them about themselves. • They start with a truth, to 'benchmark' their response, and then their partner hands them the card showing either the truth or the lie. • They have to state the truth or lie, and the partner has to guess which it is from non-verbal cues.

Session 4: Listening skills		
Timeline of session	**Resources needed**	**Description of activity**
5 mins	• Slides 54–55 • Sticky notes and display board	**Reflection and feedback** • Reflect on how far the objectives have been achieved. • Sticky notes should be placed on the display board for feedback. • Time for questions.

After-school training: Session 4 PowerPoint presentation

Introduction and objectives *(Slides 38–40)*

Display slide 38 when participants enter with the question 'How can we become effective listeners?'; it will help to prepare them for the session. Then, discuss the session objectives to give participants an idea of the structure of the session and follow this by introducing the information about positive listening skills on slide 40 in preparation for paired work on listening.

Objectives

- To understand the importance of listening in coaching.

- To investigate what are the most positive listening skills.

- To be able to distinguish what messages lie behind what is said to us as coaches.

Practising listening *(Slides 41–42)*

Talk about your day

- In pairs, name yourselves participant A and participant B.

- Participant A should talk to participant B for two minutes about the three most important things that they listened to in their day today.

- When the bell rings, swap over so that participant B talks to participant A about their three most important things that they listened to.

Use the stopwatch to time the listening exercise. Afterwards, open out the discussion to see whether participants understand the principles of effective listening.

Working out what is really being said *(Slides 43–44)*

'Oh, one more thing doctor...'

- Doctors, GPs in particular, are always alert for the 'Columbo question'. Just like the TV detective Columbo, some patients leave it until the last minute of the consultation – even on their way out the door – before saying what is really on their mind.
- Notoriously, such patients will come to the doctor for some small reason, while they are really worried about something much more serious.
- In coaching the same holds true.

Try and show a clip of Columbo's questioning technique – easily found on YouTube, for instance at https://www.youtube.com/watch?v=eNvzRnotGsY – to give participants this idea of noticing even apparent afterthoughts. Then discuss what the student on slide 44 is really thinking, and what the participants can pick up from her clues.

What is really being said here?

'I suppose that I've never really enjoyed reading that much. I used to like it a lot at primary school, and I really liked Harry Potter, but when I came to secondary school I found out that those books are actually really for little kids and so I don't read them any more. I go to the library sometimes with my friends and they like to hang out there, but we get sent out sometimes because we're not reading. The other day there was actually a book I picked up when I was pretending to read and I thought I liked it at first but then I found out it was really lame and babyish and so I didn't get it out, though it was quite good.'

Reflecting and paraphrasing *(Slides 45–48)*

Reflecting and paraphrasing

- A key listening skill is being able to reflect what someone says.
- You do this through picking out key passages in what they say, and either repeating (reflecting) them or else putting them into different terms (paraphrasing).
- As you become more experienced, you will find that you can delve deeper with what you say, and turn neutral comments into questions.

Talk through the ideas of reflecting and paraphrasing, and why these are non-aggressive ways of encouraging people to open out their thoughts. Go through the increasing complexity of the 'For example' responses,

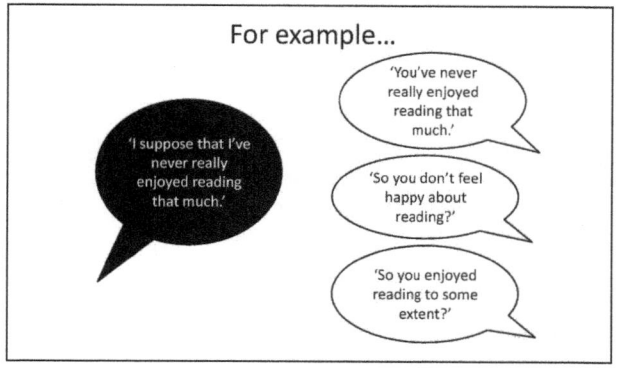

For example...

'I suppose that I've never really enjoyed reading that much.'

'You've never really enjoyed reading that much.'

'So you don't feel happy about reading?'

'So you enjoyed reading to some extent?'

and discuss the difference between them. Use the 'Analysing and reflecting' handout (see online resources 5E Analysing and reflecting handout) to support the group in really picking apart the statements – though of course you would not use every possible response in a real coaching session!

The power of silence *(Slides 49–53)*

Power of silence

- Repeating and reflection can prompt further speech, but it is not the only way to encourage people to open up.
- Being quiet is a very effective tool for encouraging people to develop their ideas.
- Using non-verbal cues such as smiling and nodding can be very encouraging, but don't be afraid of a sympathetic silence.
- Minimal verbal cues can also be helpful such as saying, 'I see', 'uh-uh', or 'I think I understand'.

Discuss non-verbal cues. Explore the group's knowledge of what non-verbal cues might consist of. This can be a good opportunity to role play or model some of the ways in which non-verbal and verbal communication can be a mismatch.

The 'truth or dare' game can be a fun way to discuss how well we are able to read non-verbal cues. Most people are actually good at telling truth if they are given a benchmark.

Reflection and feedback *(Slides 54–55)*
Get participants to share what they have learned. This can also be a time for questions.

Resources required

You can download the resources required for this training session from the online resources. They include:

- PowerPoint presentation: 5 Working with a group of coaches slides 56-73
- 5F Developing questioning

After-school training: Session 5 overview plan

Session 5: Developing questioning skills		
Timeline of session	**Resources needed**	**Description of activity**
5 mins	• Slides 56–57	**Introduction and objectives** • Establish the purpose of the session and reflect on the conclusions from the last session, reminding of listening strategies. • Introduce session objectives.
15 mins	• Slides 58–61 • Sticky notes	**Mission impossible?** • Working individually, ask participants to try and come up with ten questions on the sticky notes that will help you find out all about someone you have just met. • Share ideas in pairs, and decide on the ten best questions overall (there may be some duplicates). • All report back to the group and discuss duplicate and identical questions. • Open out the discussion and suggest possible 'deeper' questions. Did anyone think of these kind of questions? Why/why not? • Open out a discussion reflecting on questioning skills to the whole group.
10 mins	• Slides 62–68	**Different types of question** • Go through the six different types of question, and explain that they are sometimes limiting when coaching. • Discuss the differences between closed and open questions, and use sticky notes from the first exercise to illustrate examples, if you have some. • With each slide, ask participants to suggest examples of the type of question you are explaining.
15 mins	• Slide 69 • Developing questioning handout	**Trying out questioning** • Explain the idea of the example student – participants may prefer to use an example of their own in pairs. • In pairs, discuss the student and the aims of the coaching session. What goals or targets would you want to set for this student? • Imagine that it is your first meeting with this student. He has been sent to you and you want to try and create a positive first session. • Using the Developing questioning handout, try and think of at least one question in each category that you could use.

Session 5: Developing questioning skills		
Timeline of session	Resources needed	Description of activity
10 mins	• Slide 70 • Developing questioning handout	**Questioning Ryan** • Participants then swap pairs, and role-play asking questions to Ryan in turn with their new partner. • Each partner reports back and discusses how the questioning made them feel.
5 mins	• Slides 70–72 • Sticky notes and display board	**Reflection and feedback** • Reflect on how far questioning has been improved. • Place sticky notes on the display board for feedback. • Time for questions.

After-school training: Session 5 PowerPoint presentation
Introduction and objectives (Slides 56–57)

> ## Objectives
>
> • To understand the importance of questioning in coaching.
>
> • To distinguish between different types of question.
>
> • To investigate what are the most effective questioning skills for different purposes.

Display slide 56 when participants enter with the question 'How can we use questioning more effectively?'; it will help to prepare them for the session. Then, discuss the session objectives to give participants an idea of the structure of the session.

Mission impossible? (Slides 58–61)

> ## Your mission – if you choose to accept it
>
> • Imagine that you are meeting someone for the first time. It is of vital importance that you find out as much about them as you can in a short space of time.
>
> • On the sticky notes, write down ten different questions that you think will help you to discover as much as possible about this person.

This is a way of finding out the level of questioning skill participants already have. It's a harder exercise than it looks! Comparing answers participants should find that they are asking similar questions – allowing them to pick the ten best encourages discrimination. Gradually you should find that you are discovering how alike the

---

Reflection

- Share your answers with the person sitting next to you.

- How many questions did you have which were identical or almost identical?

- From the questions you have, between you, choose the best ten to report back to the group.

---

answers are. Note those who have thought outside the box for this exercise. Explore with the group how you might use such questions to draw out more profound insights. Also, note how you phrase questions (e.g. don't say 'Christian name', 'parents gave you', 'your job' etc. to avoid leading the answer).

Feedback

- Put your questions on the display board in turn, and explain why you chose them.

- If your question is identical to someone else's, then put it on top of theirs.

- Look at the questions you didn't choose to share.

- Are there any which have not been used?

Different types of question (Slides 62–68)

Discuss the different types of question:

- Closed questions – restrict answers and tend to shut down dialogue. They have their place but can be limiting.
- Open questions – tend to provoke deeper answers as they refuse 'yes' and 'no' answers.
- Questions that suggest – can be asked about reading options, e.g. 'Why do you think this character behaved in this way?' giving several choices. This often helps with those unwilling to respond to open questions.
- The two-question strategy – students get used to expecting another question quickly, and this can help to open out discussion.
- Leading questions – the questioner may not intend this, but often this kind of question unconsciously predisposes the person questioned towards a certain answer by, for instance, implying that their maths is not going well. Use with caution.

- Creative questions – practise how these questions lead to deeper thinking and more speculative ways of response.

Trying out questioning *(Slide 69)*

> ### Here is your student
>
> - For this exercise you can use a student with whom you are working, or planning to work.
>
> - For each type of question, once you understand how it is used, come up with a suggested example question you could use with this student.
>
> - If you prefer not to use a real student, use the example student, Ryan, on the sheet.

You can use either the example given, or if you prefer, genuine student examples that the group are working with. You may find that running through the example first will help in any case.

Questioning Ryan *(Slide 70)*

> ### Questioning Ryan
>
> - Work with a new partner.
>
> - Take turns practising your questions, and pretending to be Ryan.
>
> - After the questioning, give feedback to your partner about how the questioning made you feel.

This pair-based role play will help the group practise questioning skills. Use the developing questioning handout (see online resources 5F Developing questioning).

Reflection and feedback *(Slides 71–72)*

Reflection and discussion of questioning skills. Then, go through the objectives and discuss. Finally, talk about the best questions – using examples will help people come up with ideas for real life questions to ask.

Twilight session: Creating a coaching culture for students

Thinking about audience

If you are planning to run a twilight CPD session, you will need to in some ways plan it in the same way as you would an INSET session during the day. The same, or similar priorities should be in place when it comes to ensuring a comfortable context and environment. However, there will be some key differences. A twilight session is likely to be aimed at a particular group of people – it may be quite a large group of staff, but it is likely that they will be defined to some extent by role. In this instance, it is likely that you would be asking your pastoral staff and pastoral leaders to work in groups together.

If you are interested in creating a coaching culture for students, you will need to ensure that all those members of staff who work with students regularly are present. You may wish to include non-teaching members of staff for this reason; especially if you have non-teaching pastoral leads such as year group leaders or deputy year group leaders. You may also wish to include TAs, school receptionists or counsellors, learning mentors, the librarian, and so on.

Bear in mind that a twilight session will by its very nature be more pressured. Staff may have had (probably *will* have had) a busy day, and the last thing that they want is to attend a session that will not be immediately useful. As a result, you will need to consider how to make the session as practical and effective as possible.

Thinking about purpose

Twilight CPD should be a supplement to the 'big ideas' kind of CPD that you might use to open out a coaching or mentoring programme. You can assume a certain amount of knowledge in your audience as they will have attended your previous CPD, and you will know what they have already considered with regard to coaching. This means that you can be a lot more precise about your aims, and you can even use the end of the whole-school CPD to generate ideas for this future work, helping you to plan your after-school session.

Ideally, twilight sessions will generate very practical ideas that you can quite literally start to use the next day. Because of this you will need to ensure that staff have real ownership of the resources. Make sure that they have the opportunity to revisit presentations and access additional information in their own time.

Thinking about content

Again, thinking of practicality, it would be worth asking staff to 'bring their homework' – that is, bring to the session particular problems and issues that they need to work on. To connect the session directly with the issues that they are most concerned with will guarantee their engagement early on. To present the CPD as a response to their needs is not only common sense, but from the point of view of implementing strategies quickly it is likely to make it be seen as far more effective from the outset.

Thinking about structure

In the same way as whole-school CPD, you will need to intersperse opportunities for work and discussion through the session. Avoid lengthy presentations from the front. Staff will be tired and potentially not patient with information-giving that could be done by other means. It is worth considering a lively opening activity that will harness their natural desire to chat at the end of the school day.

It is of crucial importance to finish early. For a one-hour session, it is better to plan for fifty minutes so as to deal with the inevitable issues when people arrive late or there are last-minute issues with the room and so on.

Make sure that you have an outline plan for the session, which you can fiddle about with as you add in further thoughts and ideas. Below is the outline for a one-hour session, which you may wish to adapt and personalise for your school. It includes a discussion of the effect of a coach on a famous student, and asks participants to reflect on those who have inspired them. It then runs through the GROW and STRIDE models of coaching before asking participants to explore the idea of developing coaching throughout the school.

Resources required

You can download the resources required for this training session from the online resources. They include:

- PowerPoint presentation: 6 Creating a coaching culture for students
- 6A Scenarios sheet

Twilight session: overview plan

Timeline of session	Resources needed	Description of activity
Before you start	• Tables and chairs arranged in small groups • Projector and PowerPoint presentation • Large display board for feedback sticky notes	• Ask staff to bring with them examples (anonymised) of pastoral problems that they currently have with students, which they can use for the final task as an alternative to the worksheet. • Display first slide as participants enter the room, so as to clarify the questions that set the stage for the session.
5 mins	• Slides 1–2	**Introduction and objectives** • Establish the purpose of the session and reflect on the pastoral problems people have brought with them. Introduce session objectives.

Timeline of session	Resources needed	Description of activity
10 mins	• Slides 3–4 • Full version of the Bill Gates account of Mrs Caffiere can be accessed at https://www.gatesnotes.com/Education/A-Teacher-Who-Changed-My-Life	**The teacher who changed my life** • Introduce Bill Gates's story of Mrs Caffiere. • Ask participants to reflect on the adults in education who had a profound impact on them. Who was their best teacher, and why? • Participants share stories at with their table groups.
10 mins	• Slides 5–12	**Seeing coaching in action** • Ask participants to try and examine strategies used by Mrs Caffiere. How many can they spot? • Ask for feedback from individuals or table groups. • Go through the short section of Gates's account in detail and analyse the six key strategies.
10 mins	• Slides 13–14	**Current good practice** • Ask participants to share their own experiences of supporting students. • Discuss what made the difference for them when changing students' life chances. • They should, ideally, find some commonalities between their own current practice and what Mrs Caffiere did. • Introduce NFER research on the effects of coaching.
15 mins	• Slides 15–18 • Scenarios sheet	**GROW and STRIDE** • Introduce GROW and STRIDE models for staff. • Ask participants to 'coach the school' and try applying the models to scenarios (either those supplied, or those that they have brought to the session).
5 mins	• Slides 19–20 • Sticky notes in two colours (green and yellow)	**Where are we now?** • Use green and yellow sticky notes to reflect on current practice and ways to move forward.
5 mins	• Display board	**Reflection and feedback** • Time for questions and sharing of feedback on display board.

Twilight session: PowerPoint presentation

Introduction and objectives (Slides 1–2)

Display slide 1 when participants enter with the question 'How can coaching strategies help us to solve student problems?'; it will help to prepare them for the session. Then, discuss the session objectives to give participants an idea of the structure of the session.

Outline and objectives of session

- To share our current experiences of student support in this and other schools.
- To understand the GROW and STRIDE strategies for coaching.
- To explore how these coaching strategies could work in practice with students.
- To consider how we can most effectively begin to create a coaching culture.

The teacher who changed my life *(Slides 3–4)*

Use Bill Gate's story on slide 3 of the teacher who changed his life as a model and prompt for participants' own experiences of teachers. Next get participants to think about and share a story about a teacher who changed their life. This activity should encourage participants to share experiences and start to think positively about coaching-style experiences.

Seeing coaching in action *(Slides 5–12)*

This is what coaching means

1. Treating someone as an equal.
2. Finding out about where they are now.
3. Challenging them to go further.
4. Making time for them.
5. Using probing questions that deeply engage.
6. Sincerely listening to their ideas.

Ask participants to consider, in their groups, what strategies Bill Gates's teacher was using (see slides 5–11). Ask for feedback using a nominated person from each table, or take individual ideas from the floor. Then go through the underlined elements on the slide one by one, discussing each strategy in turn. Give participants the chance to reflect on the number of strategies used in such a short account. Emphasise how these are the key building blocks used for coaching.

Current good practice *(Slides 13–14)*

Ideally, the use of the Bill Gates example will have made participants consider their own experience in this light. They should by now be thinking about what they have done through the lens of coaching. This will make it much easier to

> ## What was the best way you ever supported a student?
>
> - The expression 'enhanced life chances' is a common one in educational evaluations. What have you done that you think enhanced a student's life chances?
>
> - Discuss in your group.
>
> - What makes this incident in particular stand out for you? What kind of strategies did you use?

persuade them to use more formal strategies. Take participants through the NFER research evidence on slide 14 about the benefits of coaching for the individual and institution (Part 1, Chapter 4, page 63). Ask if this reflects their own experience, and if not, why not.

GROW and STRIDE *(Slides 15–18)*

> ## GROW model
>
> - GOAL: set objectives, both for the session and longer-term. What are you trying to achieve?
> - REALITY: make sure you have a realistic appraisal of the current state of affairs. Honesty is key here.
> - OPTIONS: think of strategies and ideas to move things forward. What would different alternatives achieve? Think through the consequences.
> - WAY FORWARD: what do you have to do to get things moving and take action – today, tomorrow, next week, in the long term?

Take participants through the methodology of the GROW model of coaching. Point out how it echoes the 'commonsense' of what Mrs Caffiere did to help Bill Gates. Go through the STRIDE model in the same way. Again, make the connections with Mrs Caffiere. What are the differences with GROW, and why might one model be better in certain situations?

> ## STRIDE model
>
> - STRENGTHS: reflect on your strengths and current effectiveness – what is going well?
> - TARGETS: identify SMART targets, and reasons for setting them. Are you sure you are focused on what is most important?
> - REAL SITUATION: be realistic about where you are now – what are the opportunities, what are the barriers?
> - IDEAS: open out to ideas and suggestions – take time to explore a real range of possibilities – don't be afraid of lateral thinking.
> - DECISION: make a choice. You can't do everything, so you will need to select the best options going forward.
> - EVALUATION: review what you've done, and look at its impact.

Introduce the 'Let's coach the school' activity, and the idea that we are working to do better what we already do to some extent. What are the school's main problems in pastoral or academic terms? How can coaching help with these? Ask participants to be ready with their scenarios, if they have brought them. By asking participants to discuss the difference between GROW and STRIDE you are actually encouraging them to think about using one of these models – which one they choose does not ultimately matter (though STRIDE is more evaluative). Using real-life scenarios will increase uptake of strategies in the future. Use the scenarios worksheet (see online resources 6A Scenarios sheet).

Where are we now? *(Slides 19)*

Evaluate how participants are currently using coaching strategies – again, encouraging staff to believe that this is not utterly new, but an extension of existing good practice, will tend to give you better take-up. Make sure that you give people a chance to look at others' ideas and to discuss them – this can often be the most valuable part of the session for ensuring enthusiasm going forward.

Reflection and feedback *(Slide 20)*

Ask participants to share ideas, and read each other's post-its so as to get a sense of shared purpose. How well do they think the session has achieved its objectives? What do they feel they have discovered in the session? What did they enjoy most as an activity? What would they change?

4 Evaluating CPD

'Everything that can be counted does not necessarily count; everything that counts cannot necessarily be counted.' (Albert Einstein)

Current practice evaluation

Before you start trying to evaluate INSET, it is worth reflecting on your current practice with a quiz such as the one below. This will allow you, among other things, to see whether members of staff who should be leading and contributing to INSET, such as those on UPS, are being given appropriate opportunities to develop as leaders and presenters.

Current INSET evaluation quiz

Name	
Department	
Number of years in teaching	
Number of years at [this school]	
NQT Y/N	
UPS Y/N	
TLR responsibility Y/N	
Subject/Year leader Y/N	
Senior leader Y/N	

Please tick which forms of INSET you have used and led, for this year and previous years, and give a brief evaluation of their usefulness in the appropriate box:

INSET description	Attended in the past year	Attended previously	Led in the past year	Led previously	Usefulness in improving student outcomes 1–10 (where 10 is high)	Usefulness in terms of personal development 1–10 (where 10 is high)	Paid for by school? Y/N
INSET days							
Twilight INSET days							
CPD after school – in-house training							
CPD after school – professional provider							

INSET description	Attended in the past year	Attended previously	Led in the past year	Led previously	Usefulness in improving student outcomes 1–10 (where 10 is high)	Usefulness in terms of personal development 1–10 (where 10 is high)	Paid for by school? Y/N
Conferences outside school – professional providers							
Sessions by exam boards for e.g. new specifications							
Coaching trios or Professional Learning Communities							
Drip feeds or Good practice sessions							
Twilight sessions (series)							
Shared CPD with other schools							
Further study (e.g. MA)							
Talks or events by specialist interest organisations							
TeachMeet sessions							
Coaching or mentoring sessions							
What is the most effective piece of CPD you have ever experienced, and why?							
Further comments (if wished)							

Fig. 13 Evaluation quiz

Once you have taken in the quizzes, and looked through them, you should rapidly be able to see the distribution of the INSET training that you have funded, and the perceived effectiveness of this. It is especially interesting when members of staff select training in previous years as being more effective than that in the past year, and this is always worth investigating.

Moving forward, you will need to think about how best to evaluate your new CPD, and a simple enquiry about perceived effectiveness is unlikely to get you there.

Traditional methods of CPD evaluation: the research picture

There has been much research on how to evaluate the impact of all kinds of action taken in schools, and yet it is still the area where many practitioners struggle. It is not a new problem. Back in 1959, a researcher called D.L. Kirkpatrick developed an evaluation model for business CPD that became widely used and respected. The book he developed from his initial ideas *Evaluating Training Programs: The Four Levels* is still the basis of much CPD assessment. It consists of four main parts, or stages, which the evaluator moves through at a rate determined by time pressure or budget. Each level is more effective as a measure, but more demanding in terms of application. His four stages were:

- Reactions – the minimum level of evaluation. It asks how participants feel as a result of the training, and what are their first ideas about how relevant and helpful it is. This level of evaluation is still very common, and can be seen most typically in the training day evaluation questionnaires that ask you about the quality of refreshments or location, and are of limited usefulness as they are intensely subjective. Yes, it is good to know that your participants were happy with the training, but ultimately that does not tell you if the training was worthwhile – you might do as well taking them all out for tea.
- Learning – this more challenging evaluation is designed to check what has been learned as a result of the session. It might consist of a short test or quiz – perhaps multiple choice questions – at the end of training, or even a more formal exam. This kind of evaluation can be done online, and it is still common in safeguarding training, PREVENT training and fire safety training, where it is necessary to be able to say that participants have confirmed their level of awareness of certain rules or procedures. Ideally participants would be quizzed before and after the programme takes place, as otherwise you are not really evaluating real learning as a result of the session but simply checking competence.

- Behaviour – at this level, evaluation seeks to discover whether what has been learned is actually modifying the behaviour of the participants. In other words, do they have a more than notional understanding of the ways in which the skills can be applied in everyday practice? This is the kind of evaluation that can be difficult to do in school, as you might need to use observation evidence, for instance.
- Results – this evaluation depends on what the organisation is seeking to gain from the training. It is easy to see how this works in a business model, where you might be able to deal in simple terms with profit and loss in a particular area, but harder to quantify in education, where the measures used to evaluate schools and to evaluate teacher practice are themselves much debated. In one example, the progress levels of students or the Assessment 8 and Progress 8 scores, for instance, could be used, whereas in another it would be necessary to use student voice and observation.

The advantage of Kirkpatrick's model is that it is relatively simple to use, and fairly systematic. However, as a business-designed model it is not as useful for education as it could be, and in the final stages, in particular, it does not always offer useful models of assessment. T. R. Guskey (in *Evaluating professional development*) noted that Kirkpatrick's model was helpful in evaluating 'what' but less useful when it came to 'why', and suggested an adapted model, which Goodall et al. favour in their 2005 study *Evaluating the Impact of Continuing Professional Development*.

This model includes an extra level, between 'learning' and 'behaviour', to evaluate the extent to which the organisation supported the change that was undertaken as a result of the CPD. The value of this additional level is obvious when it comes to evaluating whole school CPD, as it ensures that organisational support is in place for change.

The main problem with this adapted model is that there is a necessary time lag between the three first levels and the two final ones, and this is not always clear. The danger is that evaluation will start with the participant responses and not get a lot further because of uncertainty as to how to evaluate.

Tailor-made CPD evaluation

A more effective way of evaluating is to think in a more holistic manner of the whole process. In any evaluation there should be six steps that you take, and at each step you need to bear in mind the other five.

Six-step CPD evaluation

Step 1: Identify your stakeholders

It is important to work out, before you start, who it is that you are aiming your evaluation at. Who are you ultimately evaluating for? Where is this information going? Why is it necessary? Are you thinking of reporting to governors, parents, teachers, students? Is your primary concern financial, results-oriented, qualitative or anecdotal? This process will allow you to decide on what will be the most effective elements to evaluate.

When you are considering this, you should think about it as carefully as you think about audience for a CPD session. It is not trivial to consider how differently governors and parents may regard staff training – it is common sense. I have produced a very effective evaluation of Year 7's first few weeks in secondary school which went back to their primary schools as postcards. It was unusual, but it served the purpose of reaching its intended audience with huge success.

In the same way, consider how the audience will understand or receive your data. An audience which understands a data-based reporting system, such as governors, will struggle with 'soft' data, and feel that it is inexact, while you may find sometimes that an audience of parents or students will actually be happier to get real comments and student voice, and be less concerned about overall data trends.

Step 2: Describe your process and desired results

This will be helpful for you when writing up your final evaluation, so it is well worth taking time on it now. When you are creating a programme for CPD, you need to think about what you are trying to achieve, and the ultimate end of your training. If you put some thought into it at this stage, you will be rewarded by a more useful set of results.

For instance, I designed a piece of training to prepare staff for OFSTED, working with an inspector. The results desired could easily have been tied to the judgement of a future report, with success in inspection evaluating the CPD. However, this seemed too far away and too uncertain a goal. Instead, I thought carefully about why I had actually commissioned the training, and worked out that it was in order to increase staff confidence and knowledge of the OFSTED process. This was something that it was much easier to evaluate with a very simple evaluation system, using sticky notes (see below).

Step 3: Design the evaluation

Again, don't feel that you have to be tied to traditional forms of evaluation of CPD, but be guided by what is most useful to you. As an example, here is a section of my OFSTED training evaluation.

Before the session, teachers were asked what their current feelings and thoughts were about OFSTED, and how they would feel about an imminent inspection. The comments ranged from fairly positive to extremely negative, with some neutral statements about the process, with the distribution as in the chart below.

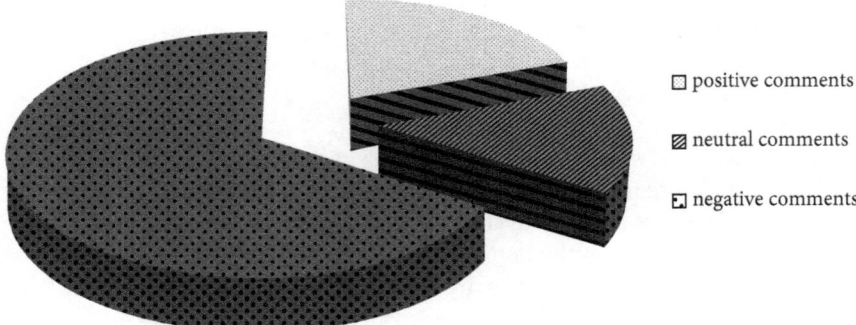

Fig. 14 Pie chart showing comments before training

Positive comments *included a recognition that OFSTED were established to 'strive for the greater good', 'wanting the best for school and students' and 'to help a school develop'. Some teachers saw the inspection as 'a learning process, an opportunity to improve', with others actively defending OFSTED as 'good people maligned in press and clearly needed by profession' commenting that they 'should be given more leeway in observations by teachers', and noting that 'these days OFSTED are in school to help... maybe that wasn't always the case', and 'they are on our side'.*

Neutral comments *did not express a strong opinion about the inspection process, but simply observed that OFSTED were 'interested in data' or 'here to check SLT judgement of the school, not to judge individual teachers', though some of these worried about certain aspects of data checking, as, for instance, 'how much of their decision is already fixed by the data they have already seen on the school'.*

Negative comments *formed a clear majority of the responses, and suggested that there was a lot of unfocused anxiety about the inspection process, with some teachers mentioning that they had not personally experienced an inspection yet, but that they saw it as an intimidating process. The language of the negative responses was generally quite strong, with inspections characterised as 'incredibly scary and oppressive', 'stressful for everyone', 'time-consuming, unreasonable', and characterised by 'lots of paperwork' 'ticking boxes' and 'lots of red tape'. The inspection team were seen as 'having an agenda', with inspectors themselves seen as 'judgemental', 'overwhelming', 'fussy', 'high pressure', 'picky', 'know it all', 'black suits looking for every* *fault', and even 'stony emotionless faces picking out a multitude of tiny details'! The perception of OFSTED as an institution was strikingly negative, with teachers seeing it as 'reacting to fads and whims of the government of the day' and 'not necessarily providing a realistic overview of what a school is like – because they don't know'. Teachers also commented that the process of school inspection was 'demanding', 'stressful and emotionally exhausting for staff' and 'unimportant to students'.*

Following the session, teachers were asked to write down their impressions of OFSTED following the input from the lead inspector, and how they would now feel about an imminent inspection. At this time the overwhelming majority of the comments were positive, with only one negative, as in the chart below:

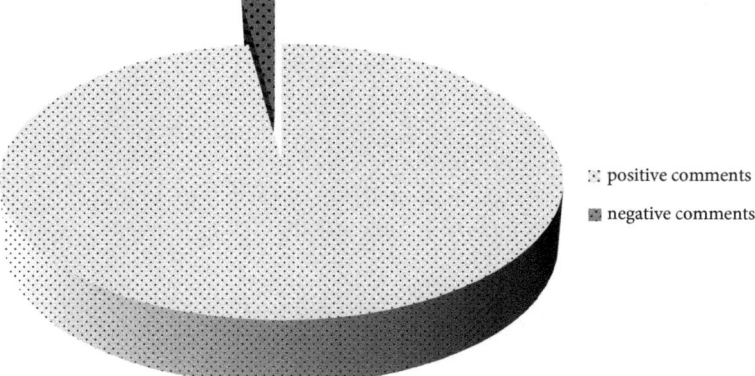

positive comments

negative comments

Fig. 15 Pie chart showing comments after training

The single negative comment *was relatively mild, suggesting a different format for the presentation 'would have been good to have had more examples of good practice (videos) followed by discussion in groups', and so was strikingly more engaged than the same member of staff's initial comment, which was dismissive of OFSTED as 'reacting to fads and whims of the government of the day'.*

Positive comments *following the session were extremely focused on teaching and learning. However, there were some overall comments which are worth noting in terms of the experience of teachers and their perceptions of the inspection process. Many seemed to feel a great deal more positive, reporting that they had learned 'OFSTED doesn't have to mean that they are trying to catch you out', 'Much more positive and helpful than I expected', 'OFSTED are a bit nicer than I originally thought!' and 'OFSTED are there for all pupils'. At times, this clearly had larger personal resonance; for instance, one teacher reported having felt 'devastated by OFSTED at a visit many years ago' and now feeling 'glad to hear there is a humane face to the process', and another commented how 'feedback is much better now it doesn't have a grade'.*

Many teachers commented that it was 'interesting to know about progress over time' and how lesson judgements were 'supplemented by data and progress to inform decisions'. They also commented that they 'really enjoyed hearing about handwriting and presentation' and were glad to have found out about the 'big focus on handwriting and feedback'.

You can easily see how the two charts, based on the sticky notes comments, produce an immediately clear piece of evaluative data about the effects of the session that was nonetheless easy and straightforward to create. Adding in specific comments make it clear to the audience how the distinction between 'positive', 'negative' and 'neutral' was arrived at. Here, the evaluation has been designed to clarify the issues that the CPD was designed to have an impact on. Further analysis of teacher comments provided useful input as to the detail of what had been learned.

4: Gather evidence

The evidence that you gather for CPD evaluation can be drawn from a wide range of sources. What is important is that you are careful to try and make some evaluation before the CPD occurs so that you can really measure the impact of each session, and hopefully distinguish it from other such evaluations.

Be careful that you gather evidence in a way that is staff-friendly – no one wants to have to fill in pages and pages of evaluations, no matter how useful they will ultimately be – and you can find that the simpler the evaluation, the better the uptake. There are several ways you can gather evidence. The following represent only a few, but may give you some ideas:

- **SurveyMonkey** (www.surveymonkey.co.uk)
  This is extremely useful in gathering data and helping to evaluate it. It consists of an online database, from which you can devise your own surveys, or use questions already thought up by others. The questions can take a variety of forms – from simple yes/no answers, through ranking choices, to commentary – and although it is free to sign up to the most basic package, you may find that the school already has a subscription which you can use to create more detailed ways to create analysis and feedback.
  The great advantage of SurveyMonkey is that it is easy to send a survey to people by e-mail – you can distribute a survey to a list of people, or only a select few with relative ease. You will find that often people are happier to confide in an anonymous weblink, and also happier to fill in something that does not have to be done on the spot. As a result, you may get more honest and reflective answers – but also more brutal ones!

- **Sticky notes**
  The simple sticky note is much underrated when it comes to evaluation, but it is quick, easy and effective. Almost no one minds filling in a sticky note to let you know what they thought of something – it is so quick that it is hardly resented. Asking people to place them on a display board as they enter or leave makes for minimal interruption, and a straightforward comparison between starting and finishing impressions. Sticky notes are also invaluable for getting feedback on good points about current practice, and can be used anonymously with great ease.

- **Tick lists**
  Like sticky notes, tick lists have the benefit of speed and brevity. They need to be quite carefully thought through to be useful. Make sure that you are really looking for a quantitative rather than a qualitative analysis if you use them, as most of your data will consist of counting ticks.

- **Ratings charts**
  These kind of charts that ask you to rate from 1–5 different aspects of CPD are frustrating, for different reasons, to both the evaluated and the evaluator. You will discover that a surprising number of people want to hesitate in the middle or sit on the fence when they evaluate something, and if you give an uneven number (such as satisfaction 1–5), you can guarantee that many will choose 3 for almost everything. Always choose even numbers, and be careful about statements such as 'slightly disagree' in your choices. Think about it. How are you going to evaluate that usefully?
  You might not want to be like a friend of mine who always puts the most positive spin possible on evaluations – participants almost have to choose between whether something was 'useful', 'very useful' or 'stupendously useful' and can find it hard to express negative opinions – but it is certainly tempting to ensure that your choices reflect what you would like to find out about. At the very least, if you are evaluating impact, at least use the word in the evaluation.

- **Marking drops and moderation**
  Looking at student work is one of the best ways of evaluating CPD, because sometimes you can see a visible shift as a technique or strategy becomes used by your staff. In addition, if members of staff know that they are going to have another marking drop (after your initial one to gauge current practice) then they will also be more focused on trying out the strategies.
  Inter-departmental moderation works in a similar way, and is a great way of sharing practice within departments. One excellent department I know of makes a habit of bringing a selection of books for a 'marking swap' to every department meeting, letting all staff get a taste of the strategies their colleagues are using.

- **Student voice**
  One interesting method of evaluation is to use pupil interviews (see Sarah Coskeran below). This certainly gives you a different perspective on CPD and

allows you to think about impact in the classroom. However, do be aware that you need to think about the questions you ask first. Being positive and precise in what you ask is necessary if this form of evaluation is not to become too anecdotal.

Great minds: Sarah Coskeran

Sarah Coskeran writes on ways of evaluating training effectively using pupil voice: 'Ensuring Your School's CPD is Effective' Headteacher Update (June 2015)
www.headteacher-update.com/best-practice-article/ensuring-your-schools-cpd-is-effective/86119/

5: Analyse results

When evaluating impact, don't be short-sighted. It is absolutely fine to say that something has not yet had a chance to embed, and that your CPD is ongoing, but it is not acceptable to leave your data and not analyse it because you are worried that you have not had a chance to make an impact. Remember that every piece of unfavourable data represents a chance for dramatic improvement in the future, and should be taken as an opportunity and not a failure.

When you analyse results, comparison is your friend. Compare to yourself, to other schools, to national averages... If you have a system in school such as 4Matrix, which will allow you to compare data within the school across subjects and also to national averages, then learn how to use it for maximum effectiveness. There is nothing more frustrating than just doing things without knowing if they make a difference.

If you are looking at impact on teaching and learning, then use observation data, but not just raw judgements (if you are even doing these any more). Note how often a strategy is used, look at the quality and quantity of marking in a marking drop for the same student – there are numerous ways of checking impact.

Don't be afraid of 'soft' data. Depending on how you analyse it, it can present you with really valuable insights, and can make a part of a larger impact study. For instance, through handwriting analysis I managed to compare before and after impressions of OFSTED in our pre-OFSTED training day and got the following table:

Comment at start of session: what I think about OFSTED	Comment at end of session: what I now think about OFSTED
1. 'A nerve-wracking experience. Worried that an area I am responsible for is highlighted as requiring improvement.'	1. 'I have really appreciated the insight into OFSTED's working. It has also been great to listen to an honest and human account of her work.'
2. '(Ab)used politically to drive through changes that are not properly derived from research based evidence. Not as useful as school advisers should be!'	2. 'Are you a typical lead inspector? If so, then this evening has been very reassuring.'
3. 'What are OFSTED like? Like waking up from an incredibly scary and oppressive dream to find that you are actually being observed.'	3. 'A very reassuring and illuminating presentation.'
4. 'Lesson plan for all lessons; observation at any time; pupil's behaviour can be seen as teacher's fault.'	4. 'No lesson observation sheets needed; OFSTED are looking for good practice.'
5. 'Stressful for everyone, evaluative, creating lots of paperwork, not necessarily providing a realistic evaluation of what a school is like – because they don't know.'	5. 'It was useful to know that a lot of planning and paperwork isn't necessary – identifying the context makes sense.'
6. 'What is OFSTED like? Scary, judgemental, panic, overwhelmed (with workload). Is silent working bad? What does an outstanding lesson look like?'	6. 'What have I discovered? Not to put on a show and to work to the pace of the students.'

You can see from this that although the data is 'soft', it is presented in a 'hard' manner in terms of impact. Presented in the right way, in the context of a report, it can be extremely effective and form the basis of further analysis.

6: Report findings

Having gone to all this trouble to evaluate your CPD, you are back at the beginning, thinking of the audience. Who are you going to report the findings to? Ideally, you should not only think of your primary audience – those who are going to evaluate your evaluation – but also your secondary audience; that is, the staff who actually took part in the CPD. It is very helpful for them to see how professionally you are taking their continued development, and you will often find that they are fascinated and interested to find out the overall impact of a particular study.

Sharing findings with students is also something valuable. It is good for students to see that those who teach them are working hard to improve their own learning. We shared the results of a literacy survey that had involved teacher CPD and student voice with students, and found them fascinated by the idea that teachers were actively working to improve practice so as to have a visible impact on their progress. It certainly helped them to be more engaged in the ongoing strategies, and curious about their continued effect.

John Hattie is clear but brutal: if something that you do in school doesn't have an impact on student progress, then it isn't working. Just like any other element of school, CPD needs to be monitored and evaluated so that we can track its effectiveness.

Assessing impact

One study which Hattie included in *Visible Learning* (2008) used effect sizes to ascertain which professional development activities had the greatest impact. This found that the activities that had the biggest effect on student achievement were ones where:

- the teacher's learning opportunities occurred over an extended time
- external experts were used when appropriate
- teachers were engaged in deep learning about ways to improve student outcomes
- teachers' assumptions were challenged
- the school leadership supported the professional development.

Looking at these features in detail is worthwhile when considering how to evaluate. Typically, schools in the UK spend much less on CPD than equivalent schools in other countries; one reason may be that they are unconvinced about the impact that it has, and wary, in a time of restricted school budgets, of spending money on something that does not have a measurable impact. Another reason may simply be that it is not seen as an important priority for schools. Making sure that your CPD has recordable impact will make it much easier for you to plan and budget effectively in the future. Making sure that it is meaningful will result in better participation from everyone involved.

A typical feature of outstanding schools is that the CPD is well thought through and integrated to the needs of each staff member.

Takeaway

Reflection

Look through the INSET evaluations that you have already done, and consider if there are any patterns. Does it seem as though different groups of staff have different needs and enjoy different things? How could you better accommodate them in the future?

Pass it on

Sharing with colleagues outside your school setting

Ask a local school if it would be prepared to share with you the outline evaluations of training that they have done. What was their most successful piece of training, and how did they decide on this? Have they considered joining with you for training? You could call out to other local schools through the hashtag #BloomsCPD.

Sharing with staff in your school

Use a staff meeting or briefing to raise the idea of how you evaluate the impact of CPD in school. Link this to performance management if you can, and explain how you want to make CPD something that has a direct impact on how children learn. In our school, we run 15 minute sessions before department or year group meetings to introduce an idea which we would then like people to try in the following meeting. Try doing the same, and ask staff to take time in the following meeting to focus on how what they have done in CPD has affected their day to day practice in department or year group teams.

Share and tweet

Ask 'What was your best piece of CPD and why?' on twitter, using the hashtag #BloomsCPD, and try and pick up ideas from others about effective CPD with real impact.

CPD book club recommendation

Realising the Power of Professional Learning by Helen Timperley.

Blogger's corner

The SecEd blog is a useful one for reading about other schools' efforts to evaluate CPD. See, for instance, Bridget Clay's post: http://www.sec-ed. co.uk/blog/how-should-we-evaluate-cpd/

TO DO LIST

- [ ] Create a SurveyMonkey survey for staff to see how effective existing CPD is in school. SurveyMonkey will allow you to analyse the results easily for discussion
- [ ] Contact a local school to ask about sharing your evaluations of training with each other
- [ ] Introduce a 15-minute 'dripfeed' session for staff about evaluating CPD before the next department or year-group meeting, and ask them to make discussion of CPD the first agenda item in their meeting
- [ ] Go to Twitter and search for 'Best CPD'. Choose one of the tweets that interests you and retweet it to start a conversation
- [ ] Read *Realising the Power of Professional Learning*
- [ ] Look at the SecEd blog for Bridget Clay's post on evaluating CPD

Bibliography and further reading

Adler, R., Rosenfeld, L. and Proctor, R. (2001), *Interplay: the process of interpersonal communication* (8th edition). Oxford: OUP.

Aguilar, E. (2013), *The Art of Coaching: Effective Strategies for School Transformation*. San Francisco: Jossey-Bass.

Allison, S. and Harbour, M. (2009), *The Coaching Toolkit: A Practical Guide For Your School*. London: Sage.

Beere, J. and Broughton, T. (2013), *The Perfect Teacher Coach*. Camarthen: Independent Thinking Press.

Bell, M. and Cordingley, P. (2014), 'Characteristics of High Performing Schools'. Coventry: Centre for the Use of Research and Evidence in Education (CUREE).

Bird, J. and Gornall, S. (2016), *The Art of Coaching: A Handbook of Tips and Tools*. Abingdon: Routledge.

Bliss, T., Down, R., Hollis, I. and Lythgoe, T. (2011), *Transition: A Peer Mentoring System*. Milton Keynes: Speechmark Publishing.

Bruce, M. and Bridgeland, J. (2014), *The Mentoring Effect: Young People's perspectives on the Outcomes and Availability of Mentoring*. Report for MENTOR, the National Mentoring Partnership. Boston, MA: MENTOR.

Bungay Stanier, M. (2011), 'Do More Great Work' – Talks at Google (www.youtube.com/watch?v=9PFYnDGDJqw).

Bungay Stanier, M. (2016), *The Coaching Habit: Say Less, Ask More & Change the Way You Lead Forever*. Toronto: Box of Crayons Press.

Bungay Stanier, M. 'The Coaching Habit Videos': www.boxofcrayons.biz/the-coaching-habit-videos.

Collier, P. J. (2015), *Developing Effective Student Peer Mentoring Programs: A Practitioner's Guide to Program Design, Delivery, Evaluation and Training*. Sterling: Stylus Publishing.

Cordingley, P. (2016), 'CPDL that works for pupils as well as teachers: evidence based tools for embedding high-quality coaching' http://www.curee.co.uk/files/publication/%5Bsite-timestamp%5D/CPDL_that_works_for_pupils_as_well_as_TDT_OUP.pdf.

Coskeran, S. (2015), 'Ensuring Your School's CPD is Effective'. Headteacher Update (www.headteacher-update.com/best-practice-article/ensuring-your-schools-cpd-is-effective/86119).

DfES (2011), *Teachers' Standards: Guidance for School Leaders, School Staff and Governing Bodies*. Crown copyright.

Didau, D. and Rose, N. (2016), *What Every Teacher Needs to Know About Psychology*. Woodbridge: John Catt Educational.

Gallwey, W. T. (1975), *The Inner Game of Tennis: The Ultimate Guide to the Mental Side of Peak Performance*. London: Pan.

Gates, B. (2016), 'A Teacher Who Changed My Life' (https://www.gatesnotes.com/Education/A-Teacher-Who-Changed-My-Life).

Goodall, J., Day, C., Lindsay, G., Muijs, D. and Harris, A. (2005), 'Evaluating the Impact of Continuing Professional Development (CPD)'. London: DfES RR 695.

Guskey, T. R. (2000), *Evaluating professional development*. CA: Corwin Press.

Hackel, K. (2012), 'How Joe Jonas is Using His Celeb Status for Good'. Seventeen (www.seventeen.com/celebrity/movies-tv/a18833/joe-jonas-acuvue).

Hattie, J. (2009), *Visible Learning: A Synthesis of Over 800 Meta-analyses Relating to Achievement*. Abingdon: Routledge.

Herrera, C., DuBois, D. L. and Grossman, J. B. (2013), *The Role of Risk: Mentoring Experiences and Outcomes for Youth with Varying Risk Profiles*. New York, NY: A Public/Private Ventures project distributed by MDRC.

Hook, P. (2006), *The Coaching and Reflecting Pocketbook*. Alresford: Teacher's Pocketbooks.

Houlston, C., Smith, P. K. and Jessel, J. (2009), Investigating the extent and use of peer support initiatives' in *English schools Educational Psychology* Vol 29, No 3, May 2009.

Kennelly, L. and Monrad, M. (2007), *Approaches to dropout prevention: Heeding early warning signs with appropriate interventions.* Washington: National High School Center, American Institutes for Research, U.S. Department of Education.

Kirby, J. (2013), 'What Makes Effective CPD?' (pragmaticreform.wordpress.com/2013/06/01/cpd).

Kirkpatrick, D. L. (1994), *Evaluating Training Programs: The Four Levels.* Oakland: Berrett-Koehler.

Lord, P., Atkinson, M. and Mitchell, H. (2008), 'Mentoring and Coaching for Professionals: A Study of the Research Evidence'. Slough: NFER.

www.mentoring.org/why-mentoring/mentoring-impact.

Mentoring and Befriending Foundation (2010), 'Peer Mentoring in Schools: A Review of the Evidence Base of the Benefits of Peer Mentoring in Schools Including Findings From the MBF Outcomes Measurement Programme'. Manchester: MBF.

Morrison McGill, R. (2012), 'Training Day Pitfalls: What to Avoid and How to Put it Right!' (www.teachertoolkit.me/2012/10/15/badcpd).

Myatt, M. (2016), *High Challenge, Low Threat: How the Best Leaders Find the Balance.* Woodbridge: John Catt Educational.

Nutt, P., (2002), *Why Decisions Fail: Avoiding the Blunders and Traps that Lead to Debacles.* Oakland: Berrett-Koehler.

Parsloe, E., (2009), *Coaching and Mentoring: Practical Conversations to Improve Learning.* London: Kogan Page.

Petty, G. (2012/13), 'The First and Only Commandment is "Know Thy Impact"'. *InTuition*, 11, 10–11 (set.et-foundation.co.uk/media/114212/iflwinter40.pdf).

Powell, M. A. (1997), *Peer Tutoring and Mentoring Services for Disadvantaged Secondary School Students.* Sacramento: California Research Bureau California State Library vol. 4 no. 2 May 19, 1997.

Sherrington, T. (2015), 'Developing Our In-house System for Improving Teaching.' (headguruteacher.com/2015/01/23/developing-our-in-house-system-for-improving-teaching).

Starr, J. (2011), *Brilliant Coaching: How to be a Brilliant Coach in Your Workplace.* (2nd Edition) Harlow: Pearson Education.

Starr, J. (2014), *The Mentoring Manual: Your Step by Step Guide to Being a Better Mentor.* Harlow: Pearson Education.

Starr, J. (2016), 'The Coaching Conversation' (www.youtube.com/watch?v=ydJsrxaW_q4).

Starr, J. (2016), *The Coaching Manual: The Definitive Guide to the Process, Principles and Skills of Personal Coaching.* (4th Edition) Harlow: Pearson Education.

Thoreau, H. D. (1865), *Letters to Various Persons.* Boston: Ticknor and Fields.

Thurlow, M. L., Sinclair, M. F. and Johnson, D. R. (2002), *Students with disabilities who drop out of school – Implications for policy and practice.* Minneapolis: University of Minnesota, Institute on Community Integration, National Center on Secondary Education and Transition.

Timperley, H. (2011), *Realising the Power of Professional Learning.* Oxford: OUP.

Tracy, B. (2002), *Eat That Frog! 21 Great Ways to Stop Procrastinating and Get More Done in Less Time.* Oakland: Berrett-Koehler Publishers.

Washington, D. (2015), 'The Mentors He'll Never Forget' Guideposts (www.guideposts.org/positive-living/the-mentors-hell-never-forget?).

Whitmore, J. (2009), *Coaching for Performance: GROWing Human Potential and Purpose – The Principles and Practice of Coaching and Leadership.* (4th edition) London: Nicholas Brealey Publishing.

Wiliam, D. and Black, P. (1990), *Inside the Black Box: Raising Standards through Classroom Assessment.* King's College: London.

Wiliam, D. (2016), *Leadership for Teacher Learning: Creating a Culture Where All Teachers Improve So That All Students Succeed.* Florida: Learning Sciences International.

Wilkinson, D. (2012), 'The GROW model in action' (www.youtube.com/watch?v=6f3X2PEsV-Q).

Index

diagnostic listening skills, active listening vs. 154–6
difficult conversations 67–8, 220–4
do-it disc 75
dress, and self-confidence 93
drip feeds (good practice sessions) 154, 168, 262

Eat That Frog! (Tracy) 67–8
80/20 rule 68, 84
Einstein, Albert 261
e-mails 13, 84, 85, 93, 104, 105, 167, 268
embedded practice 146–61
  active and diagnostic listening skills 154–6
  cultural change 153–4
  non-negotiables 148–53
    'amnesty'/'capability' proceedings 151
    lesson observations and discussions 150–1
    openness and honesty 151–2
    protected locations 150
    protected time 149
    working on skills between sessions 152–3
  'open' culture 153–4
  policy vs. practice (consistency and inconsistencies) 147–8
  student coaching strategies 156–8
  student-led project 156
  student mentoring strategies (peer-to-peer mentoring) 158–60
'Evaluating the impact of CPD' (Goodall et al.) 166, 264
Evaluating Training Programs: The Four Levels (Kirkpatrick) 263–4
exam boards, sessions by 168, 262
expert-novice support 64
external sessions, by specialist organisations 149, 168

Facebook 108, 159
FAQs 152
feedback 119–20, 174, 185, 189, 191, 194–6, 198, 200–2, 213, 220, 224, 234, 237, 239, 241, 242, 245, 249, 253, 259
feedback observations 150
frog-eating model 67–9
further study 168, 262

Gallwey, W. T. 10
Gates, Bill 256, 257, 258
'golden lessons' 151
Goodall, Janet 166, 264
Gornall, Sarah 73–5
GROW model
  goals 70
  options 71
  PowerPoint presentation 258
  reality 70, 92, 114
  'way forward'/'will' 71
Guskey, T. R. 264

habits, productive 69, 71–3, 92–3, 113
Hattie, John 165, 272
Historical Association, The 168
holistic coaching style 49, 264

icebreakers, ideas for 88–9, 95
informal conversation 76, 85, 95
in-house CPD
  vs. out-of-house CPD 173–4
  coaching sessions 226
  mentoring sessions 181
  NTEN's five steps for effective CPD 174–5
  planning and preparation 173–7
  planning checklist 175–7
Inner Game of Tennis, The (Gallwey) 10, 70
INSET days 167, 171, 261
INSET evaluation quiz 261–3
Inside the Black Box (Wiliam) 157